The Last Years of
the Brooklyn Dodgers

ALSO BY RUDY MARZANO

*The Brooklyn Dodgers in the 1940s:
How Robinson, MacPhail, Reiser
and Rickey Changed Baseball* (McFarland, 2005)

The Last Years of the Brooklyn Dodgers

A History, 1950–1957

RUDY MARZANO

McFarland & Company, Inc., Publishers
Jefferson, North Carolina, and London

LIBRARY OF CONGRESS CATALOGUING-IN-PUBLICATION DATA

Marzano, Rudy, 1927–
　　The last years of the Brooklyn Dodgers : a history, 1950–1957 / Rudy Marzano.
　　　　p.　cm.
　　Includes bibliographical references and index.

　　ISBN-13: 978-0-7864-3006-2
　　softcover : 50# alkaline paper ∞

　　1. Brooklyn Dodgers (Baseball team)—History—20th century. 2. Brooklyn Dodgers (Baseball team)—Influence.　I. Title.
GV875.B7M345　2008
796.357'640974723—dc22　　　　　　　　　　　　2007035649

British Library cataloguing data are available

©2008 Rudy Marzano. All rights reserved

No part of this book may be reproduced or transmitted in any form or by any means, electronic or mechanical, including photocopying or recording, or by any information storage and retrieval system, without permission in writing from the publisher.

On the cover: (top) The Yankees' Billy Martin and Dodger catcher Roy Campanella in a home plate collision during the 1953 World Series; (bottom) Demolition of Ebbets Field, spring of 1960

Manufactured in the United States of America

McFarland & Company, Inc., Publishers
　Box 611, Jefferson, North Carolina 28640
　　www.mcfarlandpub.com

For my two Elizabeths,
and to Barbara, James, Mary,
Ann, Ruth, Jane and Ellen

Acknowledgments

Thanks to my wife Betty for seeing me through another book.

Thanks to my old AT&T buddies, some among the best proofreaders in the world: Jim Bell, Bill Jamieson, Dwight Johnson, Dave Manahan and Dave Sullivan. Their constant encouragement saw me over some rough spots, like my first problem ever with writer's block.

And thanks to the New Jersey newspaper people whose kind attention to my first book helped give me the incentive to write this sequel: Joe Adelizzi of the *Asbury Park Press*, Sid Dorfman and Pat Turner of the *Newark Star-Ledger*, Carolynne Van Houten of the *Ocean County Observer*, Jeff Cummins of the *Maplewood South Orange News-Record* and Brian McGinn of the *Ocean County Star*. Also to those who praised my book in unsigned articles.

To Dave Anderson of the *New York Times*, my thanks for his help in bringing back memories of Brooklyn and the Dodgers from those days he covered them for the *Brooklyn Eagle* and then the *Journal American*.

And thanks to my departed friends on the sports staff of the *Newark Evening News* who, through years of workdays and nights on Market Street, and lunches and drinks in Newark's Arnold's Bar and The Press Club, imparted to me many of the insights I have recounted in this book. We spoke many an hour of games they covered and ballplayers they knew and wrote about over the years they traveled with the Dodgers, Giants and Yankees. I treasure my memories of Len Elliot, Hy Goldberg, Paul Horowitz, Ed Friel, Joe McLaughlin, Bill Dougherty and Bill Quinn especially, on a sports staff that New Jersey will never see the likes of again.

And to the staffs at the Beaverdam Public Library in Point Pleasant, the Point Pleasant Beach Public Library, the Toms River Public Library and the Ocean County College Library, also in Toms River. All in my beloved New Jersey.

In addition to Dave Anderson, I thank others who have given me their insights into the game, including Bobby Bragan, Carl Erskine, Gene Hermanski, Stan Isaacs, Clem Labine, Eddie Miksis, Johnny Rutherford, Howie Schultz, Sal Yvars, and Bobby Morgan.

And, not last in my appreciation, a special thanks to the folks at the Society for American Baseball Research in Cleveland for putting the entire *New York Times* and *Los Angeles Times* archive, among others, on their website, a move that has saved me countless hours in travel time to various libraries around the New Jersey/New York area.

Rudy Marzano
Point Pleasant, New Jersey

Table of Contents

Acknowledgments vii

Introduction 1

ONE ◆ 1950: The Struggle for Power 9
TWO ◆ 1951: The Shot Heard All Over Flatbush 44
THREE ◆ 1952: Dressen Survives His Mistakes 76
FOUR ◆ 1953: Race Was Always a Problem 97
FIVE ◆ 1954: Behind the Giants Again 118
SIX ◆ 1955: Finally, the Year of Jubilee 135
SEVEN ◆ 1956: Inching Their Way Westward 155
EIGHT ◆ 1957: Over the Sierras to La-La Land 177

Aftermath 189
Chapter Notes 195
Bibliography 201
Index 205

Introduction

This book covers the final years in the life of the Brooklyn Dodgers Baseball Club. My previous book, *The Brooklyn Dodgers in the 1940s*, also published by McFarland, took them from 1939 to 1949, momentous years during which much of the modern game was shaped at Ebbets Field by Larry MacPhail, Branch Rickey, Jackie Robinson and Pete Reiser.

We say goodbye here to the old ballpark and, since I feel everyone and everything should go out with dignity, there are misconceptions about the players and the team that should be corrected. Many were started and perpetuated by the Manhattan press, men from New York papers who looked on Brooklyn with disdain and condescension, and felt Ebbets Field was too far a subway ride from their midtown city rooms and drinking establishments.

In a 1990 book about the Dodgers the author refers at once to Brooklynese, where people who live along "Toity-toid Street" say "dese," "dose," and "dem."[1] This has been the style of so many writers down through the years. This writer has apparently never lived in Brooklyn or watched the Dodgers in Ebbets Field. He is from New York City, across the river where condescending to Brooklyn and the Dodgers had always been a press box priority. He quotes Hollywood Brooklyn as spoken by marvelous character actors such as Ed Brophy, Allan Jenkins and, during the war, William Bendix, a Dodger fan in the movie *Guadalcanal Diary*.

Brooklyn's attractions would be known all over the country if it had been founded in just about any other state, where a city of three million would be dominant. But there was always Manhattan looking down and denigrating. Prospect Park, for example, was every bit the equal of Central Park. I haven't seen it in years but in my youth it had more open space, seemed more country-like than Central Park. But it's in Brooklyn, not "the city" as we called Manhattan during my time.

I was taken to my first game at Ebbets Field in 1934 and during the next 23 years I attended 200 or so games there (many on a *Newark Evening News* press pass). I never once heard Wait 'Til Next Year, Dem Bums, Oisk, the

People's Choice, Tolty-Told Street, or any of the other "colorful" distortions hatched in the press boxes or featured in the routines of comedians like the late Phil Foster.

It was all make believe, all Hollywood, all press-driven. Take "Dem Bums," a phrase repeated almost everywhere except in Brooklyn. The Bum, we are asked to believe, was born one day in the early 1930s during a dismal Dodger season. The *New York Times* reported that Willard Mullin, sports cartoonist for the *New York World-Telegram*, was leaving Ebbets Field for his office when he hailed a cab whose driver asked: "What did our bums do today?"

Mullin, it was said, then had a vision. The Brooklyn Bum would represent the Dodgers: battered hat, untidy beard, a cigar stub in his ugly face, and raggedy clothes. Mullin died some 50 years later at age 76, world famous for that one cartoon, which the *Times* ran along with his obituary.[2]

In my youth the cartoon was despised in Brooklyn, but the *World-Telegram* was a New York City paper and, again, it seemed always to be open season on the Dodgers and their fans. The Yankees and the Giants were never given such treatment. It was Babe Ruth and Lou Gehrig, with the Stadium "The House That Ruth Built." Over at Coogan's Bluff it was John McGraw and Christie Mathewson and Mel Ott in the historic Polo Grounds.

All of that to me explains the intense loyalty of Dodger fans to this day. You never hear nostalgic moaning over the departure of the Giants. Their fans, seeing the disintegration of the area surrounding the Polo Grounds, knew the team had to move. Therefore, there isn't, and never was, the hatred for Horace Stoneham that there still is for Walter O'Malley. Another factor is that New York City was not stripped of its only ball club, as Brooklyn was. The Yankees stayed and remain powerful.

To the people of Brooklyn the Dodgers were like the son who is always picked on and bullied, a son to rally around and stick up for. Thus, the affection for the team, in good times and bad, and the deep sadness when it was taken away. Where else would fans give an ovation to Gil Hodges after he made his 21st consecutive out in a World Series? Compare: In 1951, as the Giants were closing in on the Dodgers, they won 16 straight games. Before a home crowd they lost the next game and were *booed*. That could not have happened in Brooklyn.

Finally, where else could the invention of the batting helmet, a development that has virtually eliminated serious head injuries, be ignored and then credited to another team and another man, the Pittsburgh Pirates' Branch Rickey?

The *Brooklyn Eagle* was incensed at all this, the derision and neglect, to the point that not once in the history of that newspaper did the Bum cartoon appear, nor any of the other disparagements. But there is a 1993 publication by Historical Briefs Incorporated, some 175 pages of Dodger history as reprinted from the first pages of the *Eagle*'s sports sections from 1901 to 1956—55 years of Dodgers baseball as seen by the *Brooklyn Eagle* and, as with

Oisk, Cherce and the rest, the Bum never appears, not once. Yet what did the Briefs people call the book? They titled it *Them Wonderful Bums*. How do you counter this kind of thinking?

The people of Brooklyn, and Dodger fans in particular, never tried to, knowing it was hopeless. So they just ignored it all, as did the *Eagle* and its staff, remaining loyal to the team all through the dismal 1920s and 1930s, two decades during which the New York writers came up with another team nickname that was not only false, but degrading: A whole generation, and more, of Brooklyn Dodgers were called "The Daffiness Boys."

They weren't daffy at all. They were a succession of losing teams without the verve and color that go with winners. So the New York writers invented the verve and the color—they had to write about something. Losers don't make good copy but invented goofy stories do.

Their poster boy for those years was Floyd Caves "Babe" Herman, an excellent ballplayer maligned again and again in the New York papers. This was a man who hit .381 and .393 in 1929 and 1930 and left the game with a .324 lifetime batting average. This was a man who played right field, the place where a strong arm and good judgment are both givens. Ruth, Kaline, Furillo, Bauer, Walker, Slaughter and the like played right field. Unless he was down to the dregs, a manager would be crazy to put a clown out there.

If you read Tot Holmes' *Brooklyn's Babe* you'll see that Herman never tripled into a triple play, never got hit in the head by a fly ball, never put a lighted cigar into his pocket, or did any of the inanities he's famous, or infamous, for. The main reason he was a target was that he didn't really care what was written about him. He knew his own worth and didn't bother to correct anyone who didn't.

At times when told some of the zany stories he would smile and say: "I don't care what they write about me. They have to make a living too."[3] Sportswriters feast on players with that kind of attitude. One of them, Tom Meany, used to say that Babe always had to pay the price for being a legend,[4] an easygoing legend.

There was, however, always an innate shrewdness in the man, a quality overshadowed during his playing days. But after he went home to Glendale, California, Babe became a very wealthy man through real estate dealings and his poultry farm.[5] Daffy indeed. I suspect sportswriters didn't see the shrewdness because they didn't want to. The other Babe made better copy.

He was traded to Cincinnati in 1932 but there remained the likes of Hack Wilson and Van Lingle Mungo, a pair whose antics would have cast a weird pall over any team. There are stories and stories now about both men, mainly centered on their "daffiness," the press box synonym for drunkenness.

There is the Wilson "worms" story, at least two versions that I know of. One takes place in the Dodger clubhouse where manager Max Carey, a graduate of Concordia College, decided to teach Hack a lesson about liquor during a team meeting. Max stood at a table, the story goes, on which he placed two glasses, one filled with water, the other with gin, Hack's favorite drink. On a dish were two worms, one of which Carey dropped into the water, the other into the gin. The water worm wriggled around as the gin worm died. "That mean anything to you, Wilson?" Carey asked. "Sure, skipper," Wilson answered. "It proves if you drink gin you'll never have no worms."[6]

Now we switch to the Chicago Cub clubhouse where Joe McCarthy, then Cub manager, supposedly put a couple of worms in a glass of alcohol as a lesson to—the very same Hack Wilson. After the alcohol killed both worms Joe asked Wilson if he learned anything from their deaths. "Sure," Wilson replied, "if I keep drinking likker I'll never have no worms."[7]

The first story is from Harold Parrott, Dodger Road Secretary and former sportswriter for the *Eagle*. The other is from Yankee announcer Mel Allen with sportswriter Ed Fitzgerald. Like old soldiers, this type of baseball yarn never dies. The characters change but the fairy tales live on as those who write baseball's lore feed on one another from generation to generation.

There are too many such spurious stories in too many books to go into more than a few so I'll just cite one more to prove the point, a story supposedly related by Pete Reiser years after he retired.

Reiser was talking about how he was beaned in 1941 by Ike Pearson, a side-arming righthander with the Philadelphia Phillies. Pete said he spent the night in Brooklyn's Peck Memorial Hospital with what the doctors called a "serious head injury." From here on the story gets very dramatic.

Pete tells how he had walked the floor most of the night, so he was able to move around his room the next morning as doctors watched and finally released him on a promise that he wouldn't play ball for a week. Pete goes to the ballpark and sits behind Durocher, who persuades him to suit up for morale purposes.

The bases are loaded, the score tied, and as Ike Pearson comes on in relief, Durocher tells Pete to grab a bat. He is about to hit against the pitcher who beaned him just the day before, we are told. Is he gun-shy about being hit, this man with a "serious" injury? No sir. The story has it that Pete hits a pinch-hit grand slam to win the game 8–4.[8]

This has Bill Stern written all over it but nobody ever checked it out. It appeared in many a column on Pete's death, including Red Smith's in the *Times*. I didn't believe it so I checked it out in the New York papers. Pete did get beaned by Ike Pearson and was taken to Peck Memorial on April 23, but was out of action on the injured list for a time. So he couldn't have faced Pearson the next day. In fact, he didn't face him until May 25, when he did beat him with an inside-the-park grand slam.[9] That's more than a month, not overnight as the fable goes. That story, untrue as it is, went unchallenged for some 25 years and will probably survive this debunking. The why is simple: a man getting out of a hospital bed to hit a grand slam is dramatic. The truth, the real grand slam a month later, is mundane. So the fable will live on.

So will lots of others, including that the "Brooklyn Bum" was beloved, that for years the Dodgers were daffy and that Babe Herman was a clown. Babe finally got away from it all when he was traded, but Wilson and Mungo carried on the bogus tradition of "daffiness."

Wilson was with the Dodgers only two years, coming from the Cubs where he hit 56 homers and drove in 190 runs in 1930. That one year—a single year—got him into the Hall of Fame, voted in by the Veterans Committee in 1979. Twelve years, 244 home runs and a .307 batting average and he's in the Hall. *Ave* Gil Hodges. Hack was out of the game at 34 and died in Baltimore at 48. Neither in Chicago or Brooklyn was he ever "daffy."

As for Mungo, he on occasion did things like wreck a hotel room and put his fist through a train window. But the writers in those days in most cases ignored what went on off the field. It was all right to say a player was daffy but the word *drunk* was forbidden in the press box.

To give him his due, Mungo at times bordered on greatness, winning 120 against 115 losses for mostly bad teams. Today he lives on in a wonderfully nostalgic song that has a string of old baseball names as its lyrics. The title: *Van Lingle Mungo.* And no wonder.

Came the 1940s and a new generation of Dodgers, as Larry MacPhail brought the team to the top of the National League, where it stayed for most years until the move. The Manhattan press had to let up somewhat because the ballclubs MacPhail put together had the respect of both leagues.

But Dixie Walker became The People's Cherce, Carl Erskine became Oisk, Whitlow Wyatt became Whitelaw and the dese, dems, and doses were still recognized as Brooklynspeak. Nor did The Bum change at all. It was the unofficial symbol of the Brooklyn Dodgers—except in most of Brooklyn and its daily newspaper.

So the press box condescension continued, unchanged by the fact that Brooklyn had become one of baseball's elite teams. It got to the point where the players noticed that the "big" writers were wary of riding all the way to Ebbets Field where, in their minds, "The Bums" played.

"A lot of the big writers never wanted to come to Brooklyn to see us play," Duke Snider told Roger Kahn years later. "They'd only catch us when they had to in the World Series. Then they'd tell us what we were doing wrong. We resented it, Pee Wee, Jackie and all the rest of us. We didn't say it out loud. You don't want to fight the whole New York press. But we resented it."

When pressed by Kahn, Snider singled out Red Smith, the leader of the pack. "He didn't go to Dodger games. You were there. He wasn't with you."[10] Kahn wrote later that Smith went to his grave thinking of Brooklyn as a "provincial outpost." Smith from Wisconsin, the sophisticate from Green Bay.[11]

And Red was consistent in his condescension, for back in the 1930s Harold Parrott, then the *Brooklyn Eagle*'s sports editor, offered him a job while he was working in Philadelphia. Smith sniffed that Brooklyn was farther away from Broadway than Philadelphia was.[12]

The irony in all of this is that Ebbets Field was by far the most historic of the three New York ballparks in its influence on the modern game. It was there that Larry MacPhail arranged with NBC for the first major league telecast, and then had the first team batting helmets developed, for which he is seldom credited. It was there that Jackie Robinson broke the color line, making baseball not only interracial, but eventually international. It was there that Branch Rickey, in a vain attempt to save the career of Pete Reiser, led the way in padding the outfield walls and laying down a warning track around the perimeter, thus saving many an outfielder's career and possibly life. And it was there that baseball statistics came to life after Rickey hired Alan Roth away from the National Hockey League and installed him at Ebbets Field as the first team statistician in baseball history.

How many people know about all this? Take the padded walls and warning tracks, for examples. When you think of it, those were among the most important baseball developments of the 20th century, two moves by Branch Rickey that changed the way the outfield is played by making the walls much less dangerous. Outfielders today make catches that would have been suicidal without the padding. Pete Reiser, potentially the best center fielder of his generation, is proof of that.

Both were virtually ignored by the metropolitan press. Only the *Eagle* had enough editorial judgment to realize the importance of what was going on. Since it was Brooklyn's hometown paper the fans didn't care what the others covered or ignored. They were loyal to both the *Eagle* and the Dodgers through the lean and the good years. And whether the team was good or bad there was always a sense of community about the ballpark, always a sense that even when there was booing the crowd was basically good-natured with a taste for the comical.

I saw this during my first visit to Ebbets Field, way back in 1934 when my brother took me to see a Friday afternoon Giant-Dodger game (the first of many since it was the Depression and his work was sporadic). I saved the box score in my scrapbook until years later when it disappeared during a move. Hal Schumacher beat Ray Benge, but that didn't matter to me at the time.

What got my attention was the pitcher coming on in relief of Benge. As the new man came out of the bullpen the crowd started chanting "boom, boom, boom, boom" in time with his footsteps. I turned to my brother and asked: "Fran, why are they yelling boom boom?"

"That's Boom Boom Beck," he answered. "When he's pitching they kid him by saying boom off the bat, boom off the wall. Boom Boom Beck." As a seven-year-old I was delighted, and from that moment on I was a Dodger fan and whenever I played stickball during that year-plus we lived in Brooklyn I was "Boom Boom" Beck.

It was all in fun and Boom Boom enjoyed it, knowing the fans were really on his side because they knew he wasn't that bad a pitcher. He proved that by lasting 12 years in the big leagues, mostly for second division teams.

Those days were long gone when I took up the Dodger story in my first book carrying them from 1939 to 1949. They were years of great teams, but of victory matched by frustration: the Owen passed ball (spitball) in 1941, second place with 104 wins in '42, losing the playoff in '46 and losing the Series in '47 and '49. That string of disappointments year after year.

Surely, as we entered the 1950s we felt our luck would change. The law of averages would have to catch up with this star-crossed team, this collection of some of the finest ballplayers ever assembled in one city. But it was not to be.

As bad as some of the 1940s had been there was worse to come: another series of losses, two in the closing days of the season; more World Series disappointments wrapped around that one shining 1955 moment, and then the worst fate of all: Extinction, as toward the end of the decade the Brooklyn Dodgers Baseball Club, the most profitable team in the game, disappeared forever, the victim, as the *Daily News'* Dick Young would write, of an acute case of Walter O'Malley's greed followed by severe political complications.

New York baseball was losing a team that, in its cohesiveness, was unique in the annals of the game. Anyone involved, even on the periphery, with that group of ballplayers was soon drawn into its close-knit friendliness, the result of men who played together for years and whose wives and children all were part of the family-like environment.

This was a problem for many newspapermen: their being sucked into the team atmosphere and becoming partisan. Roger Kahn is a case in point. His *Herald-Tribune* editor, the renowned Stanley Woodward, had to keep shifting his writers, including Kahn, off the Brooklyn coverage.

"Baseball writers always develop a great attachment for the Brooklyn ballclub if long exposed to it," he once said. "We found it advisable to shift Brooklyn writers frequently. If we hadn't we would have found that we had on our hands a member of the Brooklyn ballclub rather than a newspaper reporter. You watch a Brooklyn writer for symptoms, and before they become virulent, you must shift him to the Yankees, or to tennis and golf."[13] Thus, even the writers became fans of that unforgettable team.

As we follow the Brooklyn Dodgers to their bitter end, there are stops along the way for other baseball scenes, other players and other teams. For this is about baseball, and those who read it are, like me, interested in all the personalities—zany or otherwise—and sometimes the drama and occasional scandals that strike all teams, making this game like no other.

Baseball, timeless. Once America's game, now the world's.

◆ ONE ◆

1950

The Struggle for Power

It was now the middle of the 20th century and the face of sports in America was taking on a universal look that started in 1945 at the close of World War II. Other sports than baseball had begun their roads to national popularity, and by 1950 baseball was not the only game in town. It was still America's game, but others were crowding in as the Lords of Baseball looked on unconcerned.

Television was taking hold and no game was better on TV than basketball and, to a lesser extent, football. The cameras could follow the ball and show more action than baseball's then standard view, a camera behind home plate. As a result, salaries were going up and many of the nation's athletes made other choices than their fathers had open to them.

The New York Knickerbockers' 1950 lineup shows the change as well as any other: Ernie Vandewehge, Vince Boryla, Dick McGuire, Harry Gallatin, Sweetwater Clifton and Connie Simmons. Soon other superb athletes like Carl Braun and Bob Cousy would come along, joined a bit later by Wilt Chamberlain and Bill Russell. The National Basketball Association had come of age and was filled with men who 10 years earlier would have no had choice but baseball, if anything.

The same went for golf, as the modern pro tour had formed, led by supergolfers Byron Nelson, Sammy Snead and Ben Hogan. This new breed of pro golfers would soon be making big money, with the days of the touring pros having to eat in the country club kitchens far behind them.

Professional football was starting to inch up on the college game, and already was old enough to have its first fix scandal. Frank Filchock and Merle Hapes of the New York Giants were in trouble for not reporting a $2,500 bribe they were offered to see to it the Giants lost by more than 10 points against the Chicago Bears in the NFL's 1946 championship game, won by Chicago, 24–14 at the Polo Grounds.

Although neither was charged with accepting the money, it was enough that they hadn't reported it early enough. Filchock, the team's quarterback, retired but played one more game, with the Baltimore Colts in 1950. Fullback Hapes never played again.

Yet the game in those days was never the feverish, hyped showboat and constantly sold out spectacle that it has become over the years. By 1958 it had attained great popularity, but for a Giant playoff game against Cleveland that year Yankee Stadium was not sold out. Six of us left Glen Ridge, New Jersey, that morning, drove to the Stadium and bought tickets for good seats at the gate and watched the Giants win 10–0.*

As baseball's 1950 spring training season was beginning we as a nation proved again that we could fight a war with our left hand while the home front, as in World Wars I and II, went on with its usual concerns about things like sports, the stock market and a fascination with Hollywood sluts and their male counterparts.

As Chinese troops were crossing the Yalu River, leading to a longer and more bitterly fought war in Korea, baseball went on as usual with its All-Star game and World Series, and we were more worried about the Academy Awards than the rise of Joe McCarthy, or the strength of the Chicoms, as we started to call them.

In those days in our fascination with Hollywood we at least knew that the stars and the studios were staunch allies as we went to war, making picture after picture praising our military and selling millions of war bonds to help finance the fighting. Today there's a different breed out there on the Coast, with the 2006 Academy Awards a case in point. As Jonathan Stewart and the likes of George Clooney droned on through the telecast, there was not one mention of the war on terror, Iraq, or Afghanistan. This on an evening when thousands of our troops were fighting and dying thousand of miles away. No other nation in history has been able, as we are in our might, to mix such frivolity with the fierceness of war.

As the casualties were mounting in Korea, it was springtime, with the ball teams gathered in Florida to get in shape for the coming season. Most of the ballplayers arrived on time, for the Korean War draft wasn't nearly as encompassing as in World War II. Unlike then, it was hardly noticeable, except when stars like Ted Williams and Jerry Coleman were drafted back into the Marines.

The Dodgers were reporting in at Vero Beach, Florida, that spring, the team morale surprisingly high, seemingly unaffected by the loss of the previous autumn and the classic power struggle going on in the team's executive offices at 15 Montague Street, some four-plus miles from Ebbets Field.

Walter O'Malley had been plotting for years to get rid of Dodger President

---

That was the game kick-returner and end Don Maynard was cut after dropping, without damage, two punt returns. Giants coach Jim Lee Howell said he had "bad hands." With the Jets, Maynard became one of the great pass catchers in NFL history and is now in the Football Hall of Fame.

Branch Rickey, and with the players gathering at their Vero Beach training camp, his day of triumph was approaching, as he got the others on the Board of Directors to back him. All Dodger executives knew that Rickey's time as club president would end that coming October, the month his contract would run out, when he would sell his 25 percent share of the team.

Branch was now 69 years old, with a lifetime of accomplishments behind him. That was one of his problems with O'Malley, who had made lots of money as a lawyer but hadn't distinguished himself in anything of real note. His dislike of Rickey was based in large part on envy of his illustrious accomplishments: major league catcher, inventor of the farm system, signing Jackie Robinson, father of the padded walls and warning tracks, college professor and his reputation as the shrewdest trader in the game.

At this time the Brooklyn Dodgers Baseball Club had but seven years to live, and there has always been the possibility that Rickey's dismissal was O'Malley's first move toward the West Coast. Walter knew that Rickey would fight any move to take the team out of Brooklyn so, among other reasons, he had to go.

That seems outright speculation, of course, but not so outright when certain things come to mind: Why was O'Malley panicked into giving in to Rickey's financial bluff when he threatened to sell his 25 percent interest to realtor William Zeckendorf?[1] The stakes in those negotiations were approximately $700,000 Rickey would gain by using Zeckendorf as a stalking horse, yet O'Malley gritted his teeth and gave in, no doubt because buying Rickey's 25 percent would make him half owner of the Dodgers.

In mid–1953, while rumors of the team's moving to Los Angeles were floating around New York, why was California's Governor Earl Warren a guest in O'Malley's box during a night game at Ebbets Field?[2] Two days before that O'Malley was quoted by Roscoe McGowen, the Dodger beat man for the *Times*, as saying he had been approached with a proposition to move the Dodgers to the Pacific Coast. O'Malley added that the move was not being considered. Certainly not!

And why has Walter's son, Peter, refused down through the years to make public his father's correspondence regarding the Dodgers, Ebbets Field, and the move to California?[3] To this day, long after the Los Angeles franchise has been sold by the O'Malleys, those papers are still a secret.

The answers are obvious: Zeckendorf, one of the most powerful real estate brokers in New York, would have been a formidable force toward keeping the team in Brooklyn, or at least in the metropolitan area

What would Governor Warren be doing at Ebbets Field with O'Malley other than to discuss moving the Dodgers to Los Angeles? They weren't friends and had never even met before. And as far as can be discovered, Warren was the first California governor to visit Ebbets Field since it was built 40 years before, in 1913. Of course they were discussing the move to California.

That spring Rickey knew he was a lame duck but continued his everyday operations, with O'Malley looking over his shoulder. The spring training camp seemed a happy one, no holdouts, and Robinson, internationally known by now, was content with the $35,000 Rickey signed him for.

Many wondered at the time why Robinson signed for so little, especially given his combative nature. On the same day, Joe DiMaggio was signing another $100,000 contract. Of course DiMaggio was an international icon, but because of the heel spur he had played in only 79 games in 1949, while Robinson was the batting champion at .342 and voted Most Valuable Player. Both men were drawing cards, with DiMaggio the biggest draw in baseball, one reason the Yankees paid him so well.

A case in point: as the Yankees got back to New York after spring training in 1947 they came to Newark for their annual exhibition game against the Bears. Even though we all knew Joe would not play the entire game, Ruppert Stadium was so packed that an area in center field, between the stands as in the Polo Grounds, was roped off for extra standing room. Anything in there would be a ground-rule double.*

Joe played for his usual three innings and even when he struck out his first time up he got a standing ovation. Unknown to a lot of New Yorkers, Newark was his town for privacy, relaxation or whatever, a word that covers a lot of ground in this instance.

But, even granted DiMaggio's spectacular comeback against the Red Sox, when he practically destroyed them up in Fenway, and his status as one of the all-time greats,[†] the salary spread there seems unreasonable. But Robinson was satisfied, and a contented Robinson augured well for the season—falsely, as it proved.

It seems strange that the team as a whole was so upbeat, given the club's history of losing the big ones during the 1940s. Players who were not even with the team during those years knew all about 1941 and Casey's spitball to Owen, the team that lost in 1942 while winning 104 games, the 1946 playoff loss to the Cardinals, and the 1947 and 1949 World Series losses to the Yankees and Joe Page.

The professionals knew that whole '40s business wasn't as bad as the losses made it seem. In '41 the team was simply outplayed by the Yankees.

---

*I had my first experience with catching a ball during that DiMaggio game. I was about three back from the rope holding us in center field between the stands. A ground rule double came and I caught it on the bounce. Then it was like being in a madhouse. People were grabbing at me and one dislodged the ball, which disappeared. Not to disparage Newark of that time. I've seen the same frenzy whenever a ball goes into the stands, in any stadium, in any city. Thankfully, no one was hurt.

†Lou Boudreau, asked why he chose DiMaggio for the '49 All Star Game when he was not even on the fan's ballot, replied: "Joe DiMaggio is Joe DiMaggio." Sporting News.com '49 All Star game.

Pete Reiser blamed himself for the 1942 loss, admitting that for stretches at a time he shouldn't have been playing. Still, there's no shame in finishing second when you win 104 games. In '46 Durocher did a great job getting them into the playoff, but his pitching staff fell apart at the wrong time. In '47 and '49, despite all the Yankee stars, Brooklyn probably would have won both of those Series except for Joe Page, then at his peak. Naturally, the players felt those losses deeply because of the money involved.

For Brooklyn fans it was different, though, a difference the beat writers never seemed to understand. We were from Brooklyn, of course, but also from Newark and New Jersey suburbs like East Orange and Montclair, and from Long Island, from lower Connecticut, and occasionally from all over the country.* We fans were disappointed at the losses but there was always the excitement of being in the hunt, of all those dramatic last weeks of September, of winning or losing by a hair. Even 1948, a lost year by Ebbets Field standards, the team finished in third place, 7½ games out. There was never the utter hopelessness that fans of the St. Louis Browns or Philadelphia Phillies and Athletics suffered through year after year.

In other words, there is the losing when your team is 24 games out by mid–August or the losing when Bobby Thomson hits the most famous home run in baseball history. It can be heartbreaking, but the excitement is always there. Ebbets Field was always throbbing.

As the team came together at Vero Beach, O'Malley was continuing his by then relentless criticism of Rickey by constant complaints: Rickey was making too much money from the sale of players, he was using the company's plane too often, the Florida training camp was too expensive, and on and on. O'Malley hadn't objected when the team transferred from Havana to Vero Beach, for example, but two years later any kind of bitching was good enough.

By this time Walter had convinced himself that he was not just a lawyer but also a baseball man, that he had learned enough to go on his own without Rickey. Not true at all, of course. In fact, Rickey's career as a major league catcher—four seasons until his arm went—was one of the major reasons for O'Malley's jealousy of him. The envy led Walter to make up a playing background for himself, since it galled him that Branch had the respect among major leaguers that he could never have, that Rickey could talk to his men as one player to another.

He once told Roger Kahn about his exploits at the University of Pennsylvania. "I played a little ball and pretty darn well until at Penn a ground ball intersected with my nose and I thought better of participation on the field." Not a word of it true.[4]

His weak grasp of the game showed when he rehired Chuck Dressen for

---

*As examples: Ella Raines, Audie Murphy and Mona Freeman would visit Ebbets Field on trips east.

the 1952 season. All of Brooklyn knew that Dressen's not using Labine in September cost the team the '51 pennant, and that the playoff game had been lost in large part because he ordered Hodges to hold first base unnecessarily in that ninth inning. But not Walter. Had Rickey been in charge the pennant would not have been lost, for his infallible baseball antenna would have told him within hours that Labine, the team's hottest pitcher, was being kept on the bench, punishment for disobeying an order.

The year before, Labine had been one of the young pitchers brought to Vero Beach after a great year at Brooklyn's St. Paul farm team. He pitched in only one game, however, before being sent back to St. Paul for more experience, a move that helped him develop into one of the great relief pitchers of his era and, on occasion, a front-line starter.

The Dodger team of that spring must have been something special, either that or the old clichés about rookies being scorned and treated as job threats were going out of fashion, for Labine told me during a telephone interview that all the Dodger rookies in that camp were treated well. "We didn't have lockers or anything like that," he said. "We hung our clothes on a nail, but the players were friendly, even offered advice to guys who might take their jobs. You could tell the morale was very high."

Labine isn't alone in speaking of their friendliness to rookies. A few years later Don Drysdale spoke of the treatment he got when he arrived at his first spring training camp. "On some clubs in those days there was a war between the veterans and the rooks. Every rookie was threatening to the veterans. But with the old Brooklyn Dodgers, hey, suddenly I had a bunch of brand-new uncles."[5] Don was 19 at the time.

Labine, during his brief stay that season, sensed from players' comments that the team thought salary treatment might be better under O'Malley, since Rickey was one of baseball's hard bargainers, in a class with Hank Greenberg and Ed Barrow.

"Again, team morale was very high," he said, "but the friction between Rickey and O'Malley was very visible. It had to be. Rickey was a good general manager, one of the very best. He knew baseball as well as anyone, and more than most. Walter did not have his knowledge. The writers didn't have much effect on us. Maybe once in a while. As to the 'Bum' cartoon, I liked Willard Mullin. He was an okay guy. In fact, I got along with all the writers except Dick Young."[6] Young, as we shall see, was very aggressive, to the point where many players felt as Labine did.

As camp started, the Tommy Brown experiment was still going on: could you take a kid of 16, sign him for wartime ball, and make a major leaguer of him without ever sending him to the minors. Sometimes it works—a Mel Ott or an Al Kaline—but most times not. If Brown, at 6 feet 1, could have hit big league pitchers the way he hit middle-aged photographers he might have become a star, but it never happened. He was a batting practice slugger, though, the kind they called "two o'clock hitters" in the old days.

For one of the few times in his career Rickey's judgment failed him. He hung on to that kid for six years, waiting and waiting for that powerful batting practice swing to appear during games. Finally, with Rickey gone, O'Malley traded the then 23-year-old to Philadelphia. His Brooklyn legacy: 15 homers in six seasons, and a nasty disposition.

Bobby Morgan was different. He showed up in camp at 23 with all the credentials for a super career: the 1949 Most Valuable Player for Montreal in the International League, a .337 batting average and 112 runs batted in. But, since he could play several positions, he became a utility man, backup for Cox and Reese.

The Dodgers held on to him for three seasons waiting for that International League potential to

Clem Labine became one of the game's great relief pitchers during his years at Ebbets Field. With one of the best curve balls of his time, he proved on occasion he could have been a top starter, notably by his shutouts of the Giants in the 1951 playoffs and Yankees in the 1956 World Series. He was 59–35 with Brooklyn and led the league in saves twice.

flower, but it never did. He hit .240 during his Brooklyn years and lacked the speed that kept some other low average hitters, an Eddie Miksis for example, as starters for years.* What hurt Bobby, aside from his .240 average, was his negative attitude toward black players. This was the early 1950s, not '47 or '48 when racial remarks were far more common.

When he was traded to the Phillies in 1954 it's unlikely that many of the Dodgers were sorry to see him go, for not only had he become a fringe player, but one who could upset his teammates at times.

Example: Writer Roger Kahn tells of the time George Shuba made a wobbly catch in left and then a great catch in left center. In between innings

---

*Miksis hit but .236 but, unlike Morgan, he could play infield or outfield and was one of the fastest men of his time and a good clutch hitter, all of which added up to a 14-year career. The Times obituary editor, ignoring the Dodger mystique and Miksis' role in Bevens almost World Series no-hitter, wrote to me that he was a journeyman, unworthy of an obit. Ave Eddie, Spider Jorgensen, all you Brooklyn Dodger "journeymen."

Morgan was heard to say loudly: "Hey, I think they're going for our weak spot."

He was talking about a major league outfielder, with a personality that made him popular with his teammates and fans. Plus George was a much better hitter than Morgan, even with a bad knee that he nursed through seven years at Ebbets Field before it ended his career at age 31.*

"What he should have said," Shuba told Kahn, "was 'nice catch.'"[7] True. Such a remark would have been bad enough from a Furillo, a Hodges or a Pafko, but from a guy playing utility it bordered on the unforgivable. It is a tribute to Shuba's good nature that he didn't disrupt the clubhouse over it. With his strength and physique he could have.

Robinson, happy with his new contract, reported to camp on March 6th, and to Burt Shotton's relief came in at a reasonable 215 pounds, reasonable in that his goal of playing at 200 or so was within reach. This wasn't always so with Jackie, who once was put on waivers as a disciplinary measure when he reported in at between 230 and 235.

That was Jackie's second year, when he ballooned after an off season during which every black organization in the metropolitan area wanted him as an after-dinner speaker. The dinners added up, to Rickey's dismay. But Branch, as always, knew what he was doing.

He warned both Pete Reiser and Jackie about being overweight. Pete listened, Jackie didn't. Rickey knew that, there in the late '40s with Jackie the only black player in the majors, few, if any, other teams that would accept a black man on their roster. But, just in case, he took him off waivers before anyone could claim him.

The disciplinary measure eventually worked, but as Rickey once said, "[T]he source of greatest apprehension on this club is Jackie Robinson's weight." For a man not quite 6 feet tall, reporting in at 215 could be seen as a bit excessive, especially since Jackie was now in his 30s, when a ballplayer's weight starts to become a problem.

The team's pitching down in Vero seemed set, with Shotton counting on Don Newcombe, Preacher Roe, Ralph Branca and Rex Barney as his starters with Labine in the bullpen. But Branca by this time was having arm trouble and was heading into a 7 and 9 season when he pitched but 142 innings. Ralph was only 24 but even so had seen his best days. He had a few indifferent seasons left before retiring in 1956, thus ending a disappointing career, given his size, youth and physical gifts.

The team was saddened at what was happening to Rex Barney. A big, likeable man, only 26 years old, he had just about had it. After two seasons during which he seemed to be learning control—including a no-hitter against the Giants in 1948—he fell completely apart, and neither he nor anyone else could figure out why.

His 1948 no-hitter was at the Polo Grounds, on September 9th, an unseasonably cold and rainy night. Classes had just started at Rutgers and the rest of New Jersey's colleges, so for many of us a weekday night game was out of the question. So we listened to Red Barber, thinking that another great Dodger pitcher had arrived.

But this was another year, and in an exhibition game in Mobile, Rex blew a six-run lead by walking seven men in one inning, leaving Rickey wondering what he could do with a man who couldn't control one of the great fastballs in baseball history.

He decided to send him back to Vero Beach for what proved to be a hopeless attempt to bring his control back. Rickey had tried everything, including psychiatry, but nothing had worked. Still trying, Branch said: "We [still] hope to do something for him and his wildness. We've tried everything. I can think of nothing else to help the boy."[8]

Arthur Daley wrote on April 11th that Rex's problem was "upstairs," that he was perhaps too intelligent, "a mite too imaginative," a pitcher who worried too much. But the team would not quit on him, Daley wrote, because "he has shown such breath-taking flashes of greatness that no team would dare quit on him."

But during the season even Rickey decided Rex would never repeat his 1948 and 1949 seasons, that he would never overcome his psychological problems. After going 2 and 1, 33⅓ innings pitched and a 6.42 ERA, Rex was released and not picked up by any other team. All of baseball knew that one of the potentially great pitchers in the game was through. One thing was certain about Rex: fear on the mound was not one of his problems. He was part of a tank crew with Patton's Third Army as they were driving across Europe before being ordered to halt so that the Russians could take Berlin.

As the Dodgers traveled north from Mobile, they stopped for an exhibition game in Atlanta that showed the extraordinary drawing power of Jackie Robinson in the South. Race was certainly a factor in drawing more than 6,000 blacks to the game, but there were some 12,000 whites also, all jammed into a minor league park, with the blacks overflowing the restraining ropes keeping them on the hill in center and four terraced tiers in right field.

For the first time in the park's history, management announced that black spectators would be allowed to occupy the right field bleachers. Joe King of the *New York World-Telegram* described the wild charge from center and right fields, as black fans scrambled to sit in the previously forbidden territory.[9] King speculated that the turnout of blacks posed the question to officials of the Texas League and Southern Association: how long could they hold out against signing Negro players?

The Brooks opened their season in Philadelphia on April 18 with Newcombe, Erskine, Pat McGlothin, Barney and Labine belted around in a 9 to 1 loss to Robin Roberts, one of the few times Roberts could handle the Dodgers.

The game was somewhat special in that it marked the return of first baseman Eddie Waitkus, who the previous June 15 was shot by Ruth Steinhagen, a deranged woman who lured him to her Chicago hotel room to shoot him with a .22 caliber rifle. Police said she had never met him, but had fixated on him for several years and finally decided to kill him, after which she intended suicide, but lost her nerve. "He reminded me of my father and I wanted the thrill of murdering him," she told police in a rambling statement. "He entered the room and sat down in a chair and I said I have a surprise for you. I got the gun and told him to move toward the window where I shot him." As Eddie slumped to the floor she called the front desk to report that she had just shot a man.

Eddie, 30 and a bachelor at the time, was severely wounded as the bullet lodged near his heart. It took four operations to treat the wound and it wasn't until July 11 that he was allowed to get up and take walks in his hospital room. He went home a month later but was unable to play for the rest of the season.

Miss Steinhagen, a 19-year-old, six-foot typist, said in another rambling statement that she saw Waitkus play every chance she got but that for two years she had planned to kill him "to relieve my tension."[10] She was eventually committed to a mental hospital where she remained until 1955.

Despite the shooting, Eddie played six more years in the majors and ended his 11-year career with a .285 lifetime average. He became best known, however, as the model for Bernard Malamud's lead character in his best-selling 1952 novel *The Natural*. The story has the hero, ballplayer Roy Hobbs, lured to a Chicago hotel room and shot by a young woman he had never met before. Then in 1984, 12 years after Eddie died of cancer, Robert Redford starred in the movie based on the book, assuring that Waitkus would be remembered for the book and movie far more than for the fine career he had.

The Brooks had a joyous home opener as Preacher Roe went all nine for an 8–1 win over the Giants. Sal Maglie appeared for the first time since he jumped the Giants in 1946 for a brief fling at Mexican ball. He gave up three hits and two walks in three innings, no hint here that as the season progressed he would become one of the better pitchers in the game, going 18 and 4 to lead to league with an .818 percentage.

The following week the brief and undistinguished Dodger career of knuckleballer Willard Ramsdell ended after the Brooks dropped two of three to St. Louis on their first road trip west. Joe Hatten had a three-hit shutout going into the ninth but was relieved by Ramsdell. Willie then gave up the tying run on a single and then Red Schoendienst scored the winner on a Ramsdell wild-pitch knuckler that got away from Bruce Edwards.

After a Dodger win the next day Ramsdell was called into the getaway game in the 13th, loaded the bases and gave up the winning runs on a single by Joe Garagiola. He was soon traded to the Cincinnati Reds for "something over the waiver price," according to Bob Cooke of the *New York Herald-Tribune*.

Larry McPhail and Branch Rickey, the men who built the Brooklyn Dodger dynasty, sit heads-together in an Ebbets Field box. In their tenures they also changed the way the game is played: McPhail by developing the batting helmet in 1940 and Rickey by padding the walls and laying a warning track on the outfield perimeter in Ebbets Field. Rickey, known as "The Master Trader," got Roe and Cox for almost nothing in 1947.

In his column Cooke asked the question that many had been asking for years. He specifically mentioned Cincinnati but it could have applied to several other National League clubs: when will the other team owners stop letting "the Mahatma* sandbag them again and again." Ramsdell, he pointed out, was top drawer in Triple A but had "little or no big league value."

Cooke cut it off there, not going into why Rickey was a master trader who got value year after year for players of questionable ability. Just one trade proves the point: December 8, 1947, Preacher Roe, Billy Cox and Gene Mauch from the Pirates for Dixie Walker, Hal Gregg and Vic Lombardi.

That was the best trade in the history of the Brooklyn Dodgers, maybe the greatest ever for any team. Walker, nearing the end, Lombardi 12 and 11,

---

*Sportswriter Tom Meany, reading John Gunther's description of Ghandi as a combination of "God, Tammany Hall and my father," thought this of Rickey, and the name stuck.

and Gregg 4 and 5 during the season, for soon-to-be one of the great pitchers and great third basemen in baseball history. The league owners never seemed to wise up to Rickey's sales talks as he waved his big cigars in their faces. Perhaps it was the smoke.

In mid–May the Cardinals came to town for a three-game series, which the Dodgers swept, putting them in first place over the Phillies. The third game was a stunner as Brooklyn, down 8 to 0, scored four runs in the eighth inning and five in the ninth to win 9–8.

Cards third baseman Tommy Glaviano handed Brooklyn the victory by making three errors in the ninth inning, tying a dubious major league record for third base errors in one inning held by: Phil Giering, Braves, 1904; Lew Riggs, Dodgers, 1942; and Billy Cox, Dodgers, 1949. Yes, Billy Cox.

Cincinnati came in and Johnny Schmitz opened the series beating the Brooks 5–4. Schmitz, like Frank Lary against the Yankees, was a Dodger killer. At that point he was 17 and 15 against them, remarkable since he worked mostly for clubs in last place or close to it. Only Max Lanier, pitching for the powerful Cardinals, had a better record against Brooklyn.

After Johnny beat them again they traded for him in the Gene Hermanski/Eddie Miksis deal with the Cubs, but he was never effective for Brooklyn and soon drifted to the Yankees with no better results. The Dodger killer had one effective season left, 11 and 8 with the Senators in 1954.

Brooklyn got some unexpected pitching help when Dan Bankhead got hot with four straight wins. Since he was the first black pitcher in major league history, there were millions rooting for him, and against him. Dan may have come up too late—his "baseball age" was 27—or he might have been just another minor league flash, in his case the Negro Leagues. In any event, he seemed an old-looking 27.

In any event, 1950 was his only decent year, but even with his 9 and 4 record his ERA was a lofty 5.50. He drifted away in '51 after being 0 and 1 with a 15.43 ERA. He seemed to have good stuff, leading many Dodger fans to suspect that if he had spent a good solid season or two in Triple A, as did Robinson, Monte Irvin, Hank Thompson and others, he might have been a winner. The Negro Leagues were not the major leagues, no matter how politically correctly we discuss them today.* As it is, a hundred years from now Dan will be the answer to the trivia question: who was the first black major league pitcher?

As Bankhead got hot, Dick Wakefield did not, and as a result the Yankees, who had hoped he'd make a comeback with them, sold his contract to Oakland of the Pacific Coast League. Dick was the original "bonus baby," a

---

Larry Doby, for example, was hitting .414 against Negro League pitching when Cleveland signed him. His lifetime American League average was .283, good enough in his case to get him elected to the Hall of Fame.

20-year-old the Detroit Tigers signed for $51,000 off the campus of the University of Michigan.

Wakefield, like Bankhead and many others, suffered from being brought up too soon, of having to play on the major league level without any minor league experience. A few make it, but most, like Tommy Brown, Ron Swoboda and Clint Hartung, never really did. Some may think Swoboda misplaced on that list since he lasted nine years. He, too, was thought to have great potential when signed but was just a .242 career hitter with 73 home runs. On-the-job training doesn't work very often on the major league level.

Wakefield was temperamental and mercurial, sometimes the best guy in the world, but often snarly and quick to take offense. His problem was not only the adulation given big-time campus athletes, but that he was spoiled by the war years. In 1943 he hit .316 and then .355 in '44, before he went into the Navy in 1945.

When he got back he never seemed to realize that he had been hitting against kids and wartime retreads. He was so full of himself that in spring training he made a friendly bet with Ted Williams that he would outhit him in '46 — Ted Williams, no less. Williams hit .342, Wakefield .268.

When Detroit finally gave up on him and traded him to the Yankees in December of 1949 he had the grace to write an open letter to the Tigers and Detroit fans apologizing for his lack of cooperation with the press and his relatively poor performance as a Tiger. In thanking everyone for their support he wrote that of his "many mistakes" his most grievous was in accepting the $51,000 bonus and therefore not having the advantage of minor league experience.[11]

This bonus business cost Dodger fans many a headache in the mid–1950s. Sandy Koufax was a Brooklyn bonus baby in 1955 at a time when such players had to remain with the parent club for at least two seasons. During 1955 through 1957 he pitched 203-plus innings, went 9 and 10 with 108 walks. During many of his no-decision games he was knocked out early, prompting fans to predict: well, Koufax'll give up four or five runs the first two innings and then we'll catch up. Of course, fans didn't know, as we shall see later, that many of Sandy's problems were caused by Alston's lack of faith in him at the time. A pitcher whose manager has no confidence in him is lost. As we know, he blossomed into one of the greats of all time in Los Angeles. Los Angeles, of course, the city of Hollywood degenerates and Walter O'Malley and O.J. Simpson.

Brooklyn closed out the month of May with a 6–1 win over the Phillies that put them back in first place, just ahead of the Cardinals. The game highlights were three homers by their moody slugger, Duke Snider, a remarkable ballplayer. People who have never been in Ebbets Field and seen the confines Dodger outfielders had to work in for half the season can't credit Snider with being the superb centerfielder he was, certainly one of the all-time greats. It's always Willy Mays, Willy Mays and that catch he made in the '54 World Series. The catch, however, was in the Polo Grounds and would have been made by any number of speedy centerfielders—Mantle, Snider, Jackie Brandt, Paul Blair, Bobby Del Greco* and the like. Mays simply outran the ball way out there in right center, never having to worry about crashing into the wall.

Joe DiMaggio felt the Gionfriddo catch of his deep drive in the '47 Series was better. "Mays' catch was a great one," he said, "but he had plenty of room. Running back, all he had to worry about was the ball. On my drive Gionfriddo had to worry about the ball and those iron gates. He had to worry about running out of room, about getting hurt."[12] With two on, the ball was hit so hard and far that DiMaggio was certain he had tied up that sixth game and, for one of the few times in his career, showed his frustration by kicking the dirt as he approached second base after Gionfriddo caught the ball and then banged into the iron gate.

The Mays catch was remarkable in the quick turn and arm Willie showed as he whirled and threw to the infield to hold the two runners on base. In later years Willie bristled when it was said that the play was "instinctive." That was anticipation and intelligence, he would say. And many others agreed.

Snider's problem was himself, as we shall see. When something went wrong it was always somebody else's fault—the fans, the umpires, occasionally the writers. But through the years he was also a superb hitter until, like the Dodger fans that rooted for him, he was done in by that ridiculous Coliseum with its center and right field distances. The lack of concern O'Malley and the other owners had for the purity of baseball was shown as they defiled the game by allowing major league games to be played in that hideous football stadium.

In mid–June the Dodgers were rolling along in first place when the club owners of both leagues, "The Lords of Baseball" as Dick Young termed them, were said to have bribed Danny Gardella to drop his anti-trust suit against organized baseball.

Gardella was suing the game because he wasn't allowed back in when he returned, disillusioned and penitent, after jumping to the Mexican League in 1946. He was one of the first to skip south of the border because he knew that baseball executives regarded him as no better than a wartime replacement. In 1944 and '45 he hit a combined .267 in 168 games as a 4-F Giant outfielder against wartime pitching staffs, kids and castoffs as they were called then.

The suit had been dismissed once, leaving the owners confident that their cozy reserve clause was unassailable. Under it a player signed with a team for

---

Relatively unremembered, Bobby Del Greco was a wondrous center fielder, fast and sure-handed. But he just couldn't hit major league pitching. Six major league teams over a nine-year period hoped his hitting would come around, but it never did, his lifetime average but .229.

Danny Gardella, little known and unremembered by most, was in retrospect one of the most important men ever to play major league baseball. He filed the first major suit against the reserve clause, claiming it was in violation of antitrust laws. He was bought off but the memory remained, leading eventually to the cancellation of the reserve clause.

life. If he didn't play for that team he didn't play, period. The clause had been created as a result of an Oliver Wendell Holmes 1922 Supreme Court ruling that baseball was "not trade or commerce" but a sport, and thus immune from the antitrust laws.[13] Gardella's lawyers had challenged this concept, claiming the reserve clause was "monopolistic" and a violation of both the Sherman and Clayton anti-trust laws in that it was clearly in restraint of trade.

On February 9, 1949, they succeeded in their move for reinstatement when the United States Court of Appeals overruled the lower court, saying the suit should not have been dismissed and that, in Judge Learned Hand's written opinion, the reserve clause would have to go if baseball is declared a monopoly.[14]

It was then the owners realized the danger, that their lifetime hold on players was in jeopardy. So, as a group of gangsters would do, they bribed Danny with, in his words, $300,000.[15] The Commissioner was silent and of all the owners, only Fred Saigh of the St. Louis Cardinals denied the bribery. But Gardella had been in such a strong position that Saigh wasn't believed. The feeling generally was that in the face of Judge Hand's opinion, there would be no challenge, since there was so much at stake.

The reserve clause is long gone now, with the players organized years ago into a union so strong that, in an age of weak commissioners, they now virtually rule the game. Free agency has been the result, with salaries escalated to the point where Alexander Rodriguez of the Yankees makes more per at bat than players like Pee Wee Reese and Carl Furillo made in an entire season—that's per at bat. Take Robinson, for example. Jackie's top salary in his 10 years was $42,500. Rodriguez, who does not perform nearly as well as Robinson in big games, earns $25.5 million a season because of the owner down in Texas who signed him for that amount. Divide that by a standard of, say, 600 at bats and you get some $41,000 for Alex every time he goes up to the plate. Whether he hits a homer, walks or strikes out, it's still $41,000. No player in history was ever, or is ever, worth that kind of money.

Furillo's life after he retired illustrates the difference between baseball generations—today when .240 hitters make $3 million a year and are set for life, and yesterday when, for many, life was a hardscrabble existence after their playing days were over. Furillo worked for a while on construction of the World Trade Center; occasionally he would be seen in one of the New York newspapers wearing a hardhat while installing elevator doors at the center.

But later he was battling chronic leukemia, working all the while as a night watchman. "Some of the tests [for the disease] are bad," he told the writer Roger Kahn, "but you know I never made real money while playing ball. So what can I do? I always worked. I got to work."[16] That from one of the finest right fielders in the game's history, a man who, if Rodriguez makes $25 million a season, would be worth at least $15 million a year today, probably more.

Kahn had interviewed Furillo for his book *The Boys of Summer*, one of the best baseball books ever written. Roger covered the Dodgers in the golden days of the early 1950s, after working his way up from copy boy to sports writer, at age 25, on the *Herald-Tribune*. He was Brooklyn-born and Dodger-bred, having grown up near Ebbets Field and filled with Dodger lore by his father, Gordon, a high school teacher and the originator of the then-popular radio show, *Information Please*. Roger wasn't a "homer," but a lot of us Dodger fans could read between his lines and know that he was a clandestine rooter. The Brooklyn team was no doubt aware of his secret loyalty and this, plus his skills, gave him special entrée to the player's private lives after baseball.

Gardella's suit was the first successful attack on the owners' position, and even though he was bought off, it revealed the owners' vulnerability: the reserve clause could be had. Somewhere today's players should erect a statue to Danny Gardella. This wartime major leaguer, at the time a hospital attendant in Mount Vernon, New York, took the first step that eventually led to free agency, to the Marvin Millers and the rest who eventually made Rodriguez' ridiculous salary possible.

Three days after the Gardella announcement the Pirates came into Ebbets Field where Ralph Kiner, leading the way in a 16–11 Pittsburgh win, put on one of the greatest displays of batting power ever. In his first five at bats Ralph hit a homer, struck out looking, followed by a single, a double and a triple. Then, as though hitting for the cycle wasn't enough, he hit another home run, thereby going 5 for 6 and driving in eight runs. His first homer was hit so hard it broke one slat of a seat in the upper deck, center field. Intact since 1913, it could be seen on television, broken while fans nearby scrambled for the ball.

Brooklyn used seven pitchers during the game, a sure sign the staff was getting ragged. Joe Hatten's last year would be a negligible 2 and 2, Branca would be 7 and 9, and Podbielan and Erskine so-so. Shotton's three dependable pitchers were Newcombe, Roe and Erv Palica. The team's hitting, however, kept them near the top all season.

That same week Joe DiMaggio got his 2,000th hit, a clean single to center in Cleveland. Arthur Daley in the *Times* pointed out that Joe would never have a chance at 3,000 because of the three years he spent in the Army during the war. Regrettable, but not unfair, since there were hundreds of major leaguers who went to war, many of them deprived of a chance at some record or other. DiMaggio at least made the Hall of Fame. That great shortstop, Cecil Travis, with his frozen feet suffered during the Battle of the Bulge, didn't. Travis, you may remember, was the finest hitting shortstop of his era, .327 lifetime before going into the Army. In 1941 he hit .359 and led the league in hits with 218. Williams, however, took the batting crown with his magnificent .406. As Shirley Povitch of the *Washington Post* wrote of Travis on his return, doctors saved his feet but he never regained the spring and speed needed for a comeback in the majors.

What hurts today among baseball purists is the cheering by fans and sportswriters for Rodriguez' breaking DiMaggio's record of 46 homers by a right-handed Yankee batter in a season. All fail to point out that when the Stadium was remodeled most of the outfield fences were brought in some 50 feet, a considerable distance when comparing home run totals. Mel Allen, who saw Joe during most of his career, estimated that because of that deep left and left-center canyon he was deprived of 200 or so home runs during the 13 years he played.

Leo Mazzone, a pitching coach almost in a class with Johnny Sain, discussed the shrinking of today's stadiums with Roger Kahn for Kahn's book *The Head Game*. "Look at today's parks," he said, "they're smaller than the ones they replaced. You know what's happened there." Kahn cited Yankee Stadium to him: dead center was 461, now 410, and the left center power alley was 457 and is now 411. "Then there's the actual baseball," Mazzone said. "I know it's juiced. You know it's juiced. So does everyone who pays attention, and I don't care who denies it."

He also pointed out other batter-friendly developments: lower mounds, a smaller strike zone and the "armor" most hitters now wear to the plate.[17] All good solid reasons why DiMaggio's record gave way to Rodriguez and why every other week somebody seems to hitting his 500th home run. (Mazzone didn't mention steroids.)

A week after DiMaggio's historic hit, his long-time manager, Joe McCarthy, retired. It was strange seeing McCarthy in that Boston uniform after 16 years and nine pennants with the Yankees. Joe had managed the Chicago Cubs for five years before coming to New York, his teams finishing in the first division every year, including winning the pennant in 1929 and second place in 1930. Joe was therefore highly skilled, not just the "pushbutton" manager the writers called him. Yes, the Yankees always had that rich farm system with Newark, for example, just miles away, but Joe was a good judge of talent and always knew who was available. Certainly he proved that with the Cubs, a team that didn't have nearly the resources the mighty New York Yankees have always had.

Just the year before, the Red Sox suffered through one of the most painful losses the game has ever seen as McCarthy's luck, phenomenal with the Yankees, ran out.* A blooper of the cheapest variety cost him the pennant. Ted Williams remembered as he painfully recalled it forty years later.

Jerry Coleman up, bases loaded in the last of the eighth. Jerry is fooled by an outside pitch from Tex Hughson and bloops it over first just out of Billy Goodman's reach for three runs and the ball game, 5 to 3. As one result, Joe McCarthy does not go out a winner when he retired in mid-season the following year.

---

*Few pennants are won without some, or a lot, of luck. Example: Gene Bearden had one great year in him. Lou Boudreau was lucky enough to be Cleveland manager at the time, and Bearden helped win the pennant for him.

Williams, speaking to writer David Halberstam for *Summer of '49*, was still swearing about Coleman's blooper in 1989. "Oh God, that cheap hit," he said, "that cheap Goddamn hit. It's like yesterday. Coleman up, Tex makes a good pitch. A damn good pitch. Then Bobby [Doerr] is going out and Zeke [Zarilla] is coming in. Oh Jesus, I can still see it with my eyes closed. Zeke is diving for it and then I see it squirting toward the foul line. In the locker room McCarthy was graceful. He left for the Yankee locker room to congratulate them. Me, I couldn't talk. I felt as if someone had died."

When Joe retired, Arthur Daley countered the pushbutton charge with a baseball axiom: Merely having good ballplayers isn't enough; the manager has to know what to do with them. Daley also quoted Yankee President Ed Barrow in calling McCarthy baseball's greatest manager and adding: "In developing young ballplayers McCarthy never had an equal."

The Dodgers closed out June in first place but on a scary note as Furillo was hospitalized after being hit by a Sheldon Jones fastball. It was in the eighth inning of what became a 5–3 win over the Giants at Ebbets Field. Carl had hit a two-run homer in the fourth inning and when he came up four innings later he was struck behind the left ear while trying to avoid a Jones pitch that came in high and inside. There were the usual charges that it was deliberate, but Jones said the ball sailed on him and that Furillo seemed to fall back into the pitch.

Carl was hospitalized overnight as a precaution and discharged the next day after X-rays were negative. Although he was not seriously hurt, the beaning had serious consequences several years later, for Carl was convinced as he was carried off the field that the pitch had been deliberate, ordered by Durocher. Carl at the time was hitting .325 and had been on a hot streak for several weeks. Because of this, and the homer he had hit, a number of the Dodgers openly and angrily agreed that the pitch was a beanball.[18] These people knew Durocher.

From that day on Furillo hated Durocher and wasn't hesitant to say it. Their verbal feud lasted for three years until in 1953, as we shall see later, it erupted into one of the most frightening on-field brawls in the annals of New York baseball. Furillo was a quiet man and didn't socialize much, possibly, according to Clem Labine, because of his limited eighth-grade education. "He may have felt some of the other players were aloof because they were better educated," Clem said. "He just wouldn't socialize."[19] But he was tough and fearless and never forgot an injury or slight done to him. On the other hand, he never looked for trouble but, again, confronted it when it came.

Two days later, uninjured and ready to play, Carl served notice on all National League pitchers that he was through being a target, no matter the situation. "The next guy who throws at me is going to get this bat right across the knuckles of the hand he pitches with. I'm through being a good guy."

At this time the *Herald-Tribune* ran a story that, for one of the few times in his career, showed that Rickey, the consummate horse trader, had misjudged his quarry. The man who had gotten Roe and Cox for almost nothing, bluffed once too often and suffered for it, costing the Dodgers one of the best pitchers in the game.

Rickey, Harold Rosenthal wrote, had a chance during spring training to trade Ralph Branca and Erv Palica straight up for Larry Jansen, something Branch would have jumped at if he hadn't outsmarted himself by underrating Giant owner Horace Stoneham. After all, Jansen was one of the league's premier pitchers with a 54–33 record over the period 1947–1949, including 21 wins in '47.

Branca was headed into a 7 and 9 season and even though he had gone 13 and 5 the year before, his ERA had been 4.39 and his arm questionable. All that promise, all that talent and he had just one somewhat decent year left in him, '51 when he was 13 and 12. Palica was just 22 and showed great promise, but had yet to produce by mid–1950.

Rickey wanted more in the trade and no doubt thought Stoneham would be just another patsy in this deal, as there were rumors that the owner was distracted by personal problems. Leo Durocher contended that Stoneham drank, saying that, when he did, he became unmanageable. And, he added, "To say that Horace can drink is to say that Sinatra can sing."[20]

This time Stoneham or one of his front office executives, possibly one that had been burned by Rickey before, turned the deal down. One can see Rickey staring out of the window of his Montague Street office, chomping on his cigar, thinking, like the legendary fisherman, of the one that got away.

As July began there was another hullabaloo about the number of home runs being hit in both leagues: as of June 25 there had been 888 total homers, a figure that established eight new major league records. As could be expected, A.G. Spaulding, the company that made all the balls for both leagues, denied that there was anything different in the composition or manufacture of the balls that would make them more resilient and thus travel farther. Luther Coleman, Spaulding's vice president, said many factors could be involved in the home run spree but "a change in the manufacture and ingredients and official resiliency of the ball is not one of them." He said one factor could be that the pitchers were not as good as in the past.[21]

Many in the game disagreed, despite bounce tests that invariably proved the balls the same down through the years. Hank Greenberg felt that bounce tests were invalid, that testing one ball meant nothing, that there are differences between balls when they are manufactured by the thousands.

Yankee president George Weiss and Ty Cobb denied that the pitching was substandard, and were emphatic in stating that in the best interests of the game the ball should be standardized, made according to past materials and measurements. It hasn't and never will happen for the simple reason that many, if not most, fans love home runs. You can be sure if Barry Bonds ever gets to the at bat where he is trying for home run number 756 to break Hank Aaron's record there will be millions rooting for him, no matter his personality and questions about his training habits.

It would be interesting if someone like Alan Roth, baseball's first team statistician, could have come up with a method of standardizing the home run itself. There are so many variables: park size, number of at bats, corking, illegal substances and the like, that it has become hard to gauge the meaning of home run totals, especially in the past few years.

Should park size be a factor? Bill Skowron once said that one of the factors keeping Gil Hodges out of the Hall of Fame was the size of Ebbets Field. Certainly the slugging of right-handed hitters like Hodges and Campanella was aided by the closeness of those left field stands. (Heresy, but true, from a Dodger fan of the 1934–1957 era.)

No right-minded fan can deny that at bats are crucial to many records. Take Aaron and Ruth: Aaron, 12,364 at bats; Ruth, 8,399. That's a difference of 3,965 at bats—6½ seasons at 600 at bats per. On the other hand, you can't take anything away from Hank Aaron. He lasted 23 years and got those at bats because he took care of himself, unlike Mantle and many others. And in those 23 years not one breathe of scandal, not one untoward incident with fans, police or anyone else. Still, 3,965 at bats are a lot of extra at bats.

Total hits are also out of balance. Pete Rose had 14,053 at bats, the most in history, in his relentless pursuit of Ty Cobb. He was 37 years old and had been in decline for years, with word around the league that the only manager in baseball who would play him in his final seasons was himself. When he got that final 4,256th hit had 2,624 at bats more than Cobb. That's roughly four-and-a-half seasons, a lot of extra at bats.

The variables such as how a man takes care of himself, whether he cheats or not, whether his legs hold up, or how many pitches he has in his arm, will always be with us. But the least baseball could have done over the years was to make some attempt to standardize the parks as new ones have been added.

On July 4th one of the most unusual tragedies in baseball history took place at the Polo Grounds before the start of a doubleheader between the Giants and Dodgers. As fans filed into the upper deck, a man talking to a young boy next to him was seen to slump over with blood gushing from his head.

His death instantaneous, he was identified as Bernard Doyle, a 58-year-old former fight manager and resident of Fairview, New Jersey, who was at the game with the teenage son of a friend. Eighty detectives worked on the theory that the shot had come over the Polo Grounds roof, probably fired from a nearby house. After several days during which more than 1,200 people were questioned, a 14-year-old boy, Robert Mario Peebles, confessed to the shooting. The boy said he fired a .45-caliber pistol at a 45-degree angle randomly, not intending to aim at the Polo Grounds.[22]

At All-Star time the Dodgers dominated the National League as usual. This time seven made the team: Newcombe, Roe, Reese, Snider, Robinson,

Hodges and Campanella. What became the start of a trend that ended years of American League domination, the Nationals won on home runs by Ralph Kinder, who tied it in the ninth, and Red Schoendienst, who won it in the 14th.

In the game's first inning the Red Sox' pennant hopes were jolted when Ted Williams, in hauling in a drive by Kiner, ran into Fenway Park's famed "Green Monster" and suffered a fractured elbow. This act of selflessness confounded Boston writers like Dave Egan, of the *Boston Globe*, who were constantly taunting him for "not hustling" and other faults, some true, but most not.

The Sox announced the following day that Clyde Vollmer, a journeyman lifetime .251 hitter would replace Williams who, while being operated on, had seven bone chips removed from his elbow. That legendary Yankee luck cut in again as the injury to Williams limited him to 89 games, virtually assuring them of the pennant.

Mid–July saw the blossoming of Erv Palica into a major league pitcher as he got his first win, 1 to 0 over the Cubs at Wrigley Field. For the rest of 1950 Palica was one of the mainstays of the Brooklyn staff. Handled right he might have become a consistent winner, but, as we shall see later, he was ruined by Chuck Dressen.

Erv finished at 13 and 8, which in itself would have been more than expected of a 22-year-old. But down the stretch he was the best pitcher on the staff. As Brooklyn was chasing the Phillies and almost caught them, Palica was 7 and 0. He was 6 and 8 when his streak started and won those seven when every game counted as Brooklyn was closing in on first place. But, as Palica would learn, along with Clem Labine, Dressen ego often took over from his brain.

On July 21 the *Herald-Tribune* carried an Associated Press story on the rapid collapsing of minor leagues throughout the country. The story said some teams were going under outright, and others were being taken over by their leagues or by townspeople determined to keep them going.

However, nothing worked for long, and most of the leagues were gone within a few years. The news story attributed the troubles to a number of causes but the major reason beyond doubt was the spreading influence of television. Why, one could ask, would people watch a Three-I-League team when the Cardinals or the Browns were beamed into their homes for nothing?

The situation was getting desperate in the New York area where minor league teams like the Newark Bears and Jersey City Giants of the International League and the Newark Eagles of the Negro National League had flourished for years. But with the fan base of all three teams living within the broadcast range of the New York TV stations, the Yankees, Giants, and Dodgers were seriously cutting into their attendance.

But television was not all. Black fans had been a significant factor on the

New Jersey minor league scene for years, not only for the Newark Eagles, but for the Jersey Giants and Newark Bears as well. Now the Dodgers had Robinson, Campanella, Newcombe and Bankhead while Monte Irvin and Hank Thompson were playing at the Polo Grounds. They were soon siphoning off black fans from New Jersey by the thousands for good reason: why would a black fan not want to see Robinson and the others in the flesh?

Attendance was so down in 1949 that the Newark Bears, once one of the great minor league franchises, were abandoned by their parent Yankees because of declining attendance. To add to that misfortune, on June 25th the *Newark Star-Ledger* announced that it would no longer list Newark in the International League standings because "they obviously do not belong in Triple A competition, being 18½ games out of first." They'd be restored, the paper stated, when "they again become a Triple A club." It never happened. The Chicago Cubs bought the team in January of 1950, saying it would move the franchise to Springfield, Massachusetts.

The Bears are a perfect example to gauge the decline. This had been a booming franchise, even after the war for a while. Just miles from Yankee Stadium, it was always stocked with future Yanks like Jerry Coleman, Yogi Berra, Johnny Lindell, and many others. Not too many years before, there were the 1937 Bears, acknowledged as the finest minor league team in history, a team that could have competed in the major leagues: Joe Gordon, Charlie Keller, Tommy Henrich (briefly), Joe Beggs, Willard Hershberger,* Spud Chandler, Marius Russo, Atley Donald, Babe Dahlgren, George McQuinn, Buddy Rosar and Nolen Richardson were its stars. But just a decade or so later the Bears, like the others, couldn't survive the onslaughts of television.

Attendance at Ruppert Stadium, both for the Bears and the Eagles, was at its height in the mid and late 1930s when future Yankees Charlie Keller and Joe Gordon led the team. There were times when as many as 16,000, counting a roped-off center field, were in attendance when the nearby Jersey City Giants came to town.

The decline began in 1947 when Robinson joined the Dodgers and Larry Doby signed with the Indians. Then it steepened with the spread of television. By 1949 the Newark Eagles were out of business, as their owner, Mrs. Effa Manley, announced she was going bankrupt in Newark and was therefore moving the team to Houston. Three reasons for her economic plunge were that during the previous two years she had lost Don Newcombe and Roy Campanella to the Dodgers and Larry Doby to Cleveland. Then in 1949 she lost Monte Irvin to the Giants. A baseball axiom: fans follow stars.

It wasn't long before the Negro Leagues all but vanished as the trickle that had been the '47 signings of Robinson and Doby became a flood in the

---

*The only major leaguer to ever commit suicide during the season. Willard suffered from depression and, in addition, suicide ran in his family.

1950s after Doby became a star and Jackie became one of the best players in baseball with his 1949 MVP and Batting Championship. Black baseball could not survive this, and within a few years an entire way of life vanished. The Homestead Grays, the Kansas City Monarchs, the Baltimore Elite Giants—all teams that like the Newark Eagles had years of tradition behind them—gradually faded away, and the rest followed.

Just a decade before, none of us believed this could ever happen. My neighborhood, like most in Newark, was filled with Bear fans. Every year we would be part of the Knot Hole Gang for grade school students, 10 games for 50 cents (as I recall). It seems an impossible price, but that Newark Bear management knew how to market a product. We Knot Holers went to many other games and were loyal to that team for years, until the Yankees pulled out. The big leagues should be that smart, but they won't wake up until it's too late.

One problem for us was that it was 1939 and 50 cents could buy a lot of things besides Knot Hole tickets. My mother, old-line Scotch-Irish as she was, would give me money for a book or sheet music, but 50 cents for baseball games? Never. So, ten of us usually chipped in a dime apiece and shared.

I was as loyal as anyone until one Saturday in 1939 when I learned that all of our ballplayers weren't the heroes we school kids made of them. After the game that day I waited outside the players' entrance getting autographs. It was my greatest day. I got Ed Levy, Mickey Witig, Tommy Holmes, George Scharein, Tommy Padden, Walt Judnick, Buddy Blair, and the ones that made all my friends jealous, Johnny Neun, the manager, and Earl Harper, the announcer.

Neun later became a Yankee manager, but Harper was a god in Newark for years before he went on to the big leagues, or wherever he went. He was very intense, telling us to walk around our chair if the Bears were in trouble. For huge trouble he'd tell us to walk around the block. I'd be walking up Central Avenue and see friends walking, all to Harper's orders.

As Harper was going to his car, Alex Kampouris came out, and as I approached him he yelled: "Get away from me, kid. Leave me the hell alone." I was hurt and angry and followed him to his cab. He got in and I said: "Yeah, you're the home run king, but you're the strikeout king, too." Before the cab started up he leaned out the window and threw a punch at me, saying: "You little son of a bitch." I ducked the punch, but started to tear up as he sped away. I was only 12 years old and had just seen behind the heroic façade. How was I to know the frustration a man like Kampouris felt after being demoted from the big leagues? At that age I thought the Newark Bears were really big time.

On August 12th with his Giants 10 games behind the league-leading Phillies, Eddie Stanky reached a new low in childishness as he stood behind second base waving his arms to distract Phillies hitters. There was nothing in the rules against this, for it had never been done before. However, it touched off a full-fledged brawl with both teams overflowing onto the field, and Stanky, Bill Rigney and Andy Seminick thumbed out of the game.

The next day league president Ford Frick banned any practice intended to annoy and distract the batter, specifically citing Stanky and his waving incidents. Frick should have fined and suspended the little troublemaker. They called him "The Brat" in the press box because that's exactly what he was, a 34-year-old bad little boy.

Later that week, for the first time in his career, Joe DiMaggio was benched for not hitting. It didn't last long, for Joe ended the year at .301, but it was a shocker all the same. Arthur Daley, in a thoughtful, moving *Times* column, wrote that DiMaggio might have reached the end of his career. Daley pointed out what never seemed obvious at the time, that DiMaggio never brought his skills back from the war, that the three Army years and the ulcers that wracked him had taken more out of him than many realized. Joe, Daley wrote, was no longer the superlative hitter and baserunner and graceful outfielder he had been back in 1942.[23]

The figures back him up. Before going into the service Joe was a .339 hitter—1349 hits in 3978 at bats. From 1946 on he hit .304—865 hits in 2873 at bats. As for fielding, the story has it that DiMaggio's arm had gone but it had been so feared for so many years that it took opponents more than a season to find it out. It's understandable. For people who never saw him play, the DiMaggio aura might seem a myth. But for my generation it was always there, so much so that most, we Dodger fans included, never realized he was in decline.

We should have but it's understandable that we didn't. The man transcended race, religion, ethnicity or even baseball loyalties. He was THE ballplayer of our generation. Plus, we were blinded by his feats. The 51-game hitting streak was always in our minds, and then came 1949, just the year before.

As June was ending, Joe had missed 65 games with a bone spur on his heel that suddenly disappeared. He came back against the Red Sox in Fenway, the enemy's stronghold, and in three games just about destroyed the Sox. Four home runs and nine RBI in 11 times at bat. Performances like that tend to dull analytical perception.

There was an evening back in 1968 when I, along with some other people, spent several hours with DiMaggio. I wrote of it in my first book, but it's worth repeating here. It was an open secret among Newark sportswriters that Newark was DiMaggio's place for relaxation, the place where the mob along Bloomfield Avenue would do anything for him. To the New York tabloids he was a Toots Shor guy, drinking with Jimmy Cannon or some other hotshot columnist, and squiring the Broadway showgirls.

That wasn't DiMaggio's world at all, except for publicity purposes. Joe was a very private man and sought his real pleasures outside of the limelight, where Newark surely was most of the time. The mob was his benefactor and guardian of his privacy. If Joe was eating at his favorite restaurant, the Victoria Castle off Bloomfield Avenue, the word was: If Mr. DiMaggio speaks to you, fine. If not, leave him alone. And that included women. It was seen to that Joe never lacked for feminine companionship.

None of this ever appeared in the *Newark Evening News* or *Newark Star-Ledger*. I always thought there was a secret pride among us that Newark was Joe's favorite city on the Eastern seaboard and that we should let well enough alone. I don't recall even one picture of Joe in Newark in either paper.

I got a call this day from the head of a bank on Bloomfield Avenue, asking me if I'd like to meet Joe DiMaggio. The occasion was the opening of a restaurant owned by the grandson of one of Joe's Newark friends, with him there as a favor. We entered the place, on northern Roseville Avenue, and saw DiMaggio seated at the head of a rectangular table, with three elderly Italian gentlemen on each side.

My friend and I sat at the opposite end, facing DiMaggio, who at 54 was tall, handsome and impeccably dressed. And he was at ease, among people he knew would not bring up awkward subjects, such as Marilyn. The old guys around him, however, were tense and quiet, actually frightened to be in the presence of the great DiMaggio.

No one spoke for what seemed like minutes. Finally my instincts as a newspaperman took over and I asked: "Joe, how's Dom?" The old gentlemen looked at me like I was crazy. *Talking to Joe D and calling him Joe.* "Oh, he's fine," DiMaggio said, "he owns half of Boston."

"How about Vince?" I asked. "Vince is fine too," Joe replied. "He owns half of Pittsburgh. I'm the only bum in the family. I'm the only one without a job." The place broke up, the ice was broken and general conversation started. I went up to the bar later and apologized to DiMaggio for calling him Joe.

"Don't worry about it," he said. "I knew exactly what you were doing and it worked. Everybody relaxed. Besides, most people call me Joe." I then posed a question I had always wanted to ask a great major leaguer: who is or was the greatest ballplayer who ever lived? Without hesitation he said: "Babe Ruth, without doubt. Cobb's number two, but first comes the Babe. Most people don't know that he was the best lefthander of his time. He would have made the Hall as a pitcher if he wasn't such a great hitter." I shook his hand and left, feeling good about the great DiMag agreeing with me, or vice versa.

On August 17th the *Brooklyn Eagle* called any hopes the Dodgers had for the pennant gone, with the pitching staff almost swept away by the Giants in a 16 to 7 disaster. The Giants scored nine runs in the first inning off Erskine, Hatten and Chris Van Cuyk. Writer Harold Burr didn't write "the Dodgers is dead" but he came close. Like many sportswriters he had little faith when the going was bad, with the Dodgers 7½ games out.

Rickey told Shotton the next day that he could expect no pitching help from the farm teams, that he'd have to go with what he had. Well, Mr. Burr was wrong. Led by Newcombe, Roe and Palica, the staff might well have won the pennant if it were not for an error in judgment by Shotton on the last day of the season.

As if on signal after Rickey's pitching announcement, the team went on a six-game winning streak, with the sixth win over the Pirates being one to remember, a 17-inning night game, tied up by a Kiner homer in the eighth and then, three innings after both teams scored in the 14th, Hermanski homered to win it. The winning streak extended to 10 games, leading Shotton to think that if they could stay within seven or eight games of the Phillies they still had a chance for a final drive. And they did, falling just short on the final day.

August closed on an historic note for Gil Hodges as he became only the second man in the modern era to hit four home runs in a nine-inning game. The Dodgers won 19–3 with Gil batting in nine runs. His first was off Warren Spahn, then off Normie Roy and Bob Hall and in the eighth inning off Johnny Antonelli. In 1932 Gehrig had been the first to hit four in the 20th century. Previously it was done by Bobby Lowe of the Boston Nationals and Ed Delahanty of the Phils in the 1890s.

On September 6th Don Newcombe tried to sweep a night double-header at Shibe Park all by himself. And he almost did. Big Don took on the first-place Phillies in the first game and shut them out on a 2 to 0 three-hitter. Shotton, a bit sheepishly, asked him if he could go the second game if he were "given the next day off to go fishing." The pitching situation must have been desperate that week for Shotton to risk one of his big winners. But Don was willing and gave up two runs before being lifted for a pinch hitter in the eighth, behind 3–2. The Dodgers, up against their principal opponents, rallied for three runs in ninth to win and cut the Phillies' lead to 5½ games.

Two days later the Dodgers suffered a loss that probably cost

It is August 31, 1950, as Gil Hodges poses with four bats, symbolic of the four home runs he has just hit against the Milwaukee Braves at Ebbetts Field. He thus became the second man in the 20th Century, following Lou Gehrig, to hit four homers in a nine-inning game.

them the pennant when Jackie Robinson, in knocking down a line drive over second by Jack Mayo of the Phillies, suffered a torn ligament in his left thumb. After doctors put his hand in a cast they predicted he'd be out for three weeks. They didn't know Jackie, had no idea of his competitive drive.

According to the box scores, he was out just 10 days before he pinch hit against the Cubs on the 18th and then the next day he was back full time, going 2 for 2. But those 10 days without him hurt the team as Bobby Morgan filled in.

The following week, on September 23rd as the team was closing in on the Phillies, the Branch Rickey era was ending. He still had a month or so to go on his contract, but on that September afternoon it was announced on page one of the *Eagle* that he had sold his 25 percent of the club to real estate power William Zeckendorf. But the announcement was actually a ploy by which Rickey snookered Walter O'Malley out of some $700,000.

Rickey knew for years that O'Malley was plotting against him, first in private and then, in the matter of the Studebaker awards, in public. O'Malley disliked Rickey from the start, jealous not only of his accomplishments and national renown in baseball, but of his knowledge of the classics and of history from his days as a professor at Allegheny College, where he taught English, German, Greek and Shakespearean drama.[24]

In private among his cronies he would call Rickey a "psalm-singing fake," of "slovenly appearance," and a man drawing an exorbitant salary while mishandling his players. O'Malley never said a word in public, for at that time he still wasn't that confident of his baseball knowledge and depended on Rickey. But then, to O'Malley's dismay, came the Studebakers.

Near the end of the 1946 season Rickey had decided that each World Series–eligible Dodger should get a new Studebaker because of the gallant fight they had put up against a superior St. Louis team, with its premier pitching staff, led by Pollet, Brecheen, and Dickson. He announced that the cars would be on their home field Saturday afternoon, September 28th, for the players or their wives to make their choices. As those of us old enough remember, any new car just after the war was a really big deal.

This got to O'Malley such that he revealed his feelings publicly for the first time as he appealed to the Dodger Board of Directors to quash the deal. This after the announcement was made public, the cars were displayed on the field and the players made their choices. A number of writers wrote years later that the cars were never given, that O'Malley had convinced the Dodger Board to rescind the offer.

The beat reporters got the story right. The *Eagle's* Harold Burr wrote on October 9 that the deal went through, making the entire team grateful to Rickey and somewhat leery of a man who would try to deny a promise after it had been made and published in all the newspapers.

Howie Schultz, Brooklyn's tall first baseman—too tall for military service—said in an interview that every player eligible got a car. "We got our cars," he said. "I got mine and all the rest of the guys got theirs. We heard nothing of the deal being cancelled." When asked his opinion of O'Malley he said, "I didn't know him. He never had much to do with the club at that time."* Those were the years O'Malley was on the Board of Directors and owned 25 per cent of the team but stayed in the background, watching and learning from Rickey.

As to Brooklyn fans at the time, Shultz found the demeaning jokes about them overstated in the press. "We were much closer to the fans than the players are today," he recalled. "It was a different age. Most of us took the subway home along with many of the fans and we always got to talking with them. It was a time when men came to the park in suits and wearing hats. The people I met in my four years with the Dodgers were generally well spoken. I never heard dese and dems around Ebbets Field."

When asked his opinion of Rickey, Howie remembered Rickey the hard bargainer. "I thought he took very unfair advantage of his rookies in salaries," he said. "I don't know what the others guys got, but Hal Gregg, Rex Barney, and I and Hermanski, Luis Olmo—I don't think any of us made over $500 a month."[25]

George Shuba can attest to Rickey and his staff's bargaining methods, deceit and trickery allegedly included. He recalled the year a rookie went to Buzzy Bavasi's office to ask for a raise. But before the discussion began Buzzy was called to another office for a phone call. "Buzzy positioned the kid's chair so that while he was gone the boy would notice a contract signed by Jackie Robinson for a certain amount [$21,000]," Shuba told me in a telephone interview. "The kid thought to himself that he couldn't ask for a raise if Robinson was making just that amount." He later found out the contract was a phony, one of the front office ploys at negotiation times.[26]

After O'Malley's failed Studebaker struggle the mutual animosity between him and Rickey became public, and by 1950 neither man could always control himself. Red Barber tells of a scene in the Dodger club box of them screaming and swearing at each other while he was trying to call the game.

"It was hard to broadcast," Red recalled, "because of Rickey and O'Malley screaming and yelling at each other, two strong men using strong language. I thought they would come to blows. I never heard anything like it. I kept very close to the mike so nothing they said would be picked up. There was blood on the moon."[27]

Both men had one important trait in common: short arms and low pockets, as the joke goes. Rickey's shrewdness when it came to money surfaced when, as his contract was expiring, O'Malley offered him $320,000 for his share of the team, the same amount he had paid years before. O'Malley had been used to dealing with patsies, underlings and politicians on the make for

---

*Schultz was with the Dodgers from 1943 until traded to the Phillies in May of 1947 for $50,000.

years and discounted Rickey's brains and innate cunning, as some other owners did through the years.

Occasionally O'Malley, probably the most hated man in Brooklyn history, had a soft side, usually when it came to his family. In 1931 he was engaged to Kay Hanson, who before the wedding was operated on for cancer of the larynx, an operation that left her voiceless, completely unable to speak. Walter's father suggested he call off the wedding but O'Malley refused. "No," he said, "she's the same girl I fell in love with."[28]

That's a far cry from the man who many young children growing up after the Dodgers left might have thought his first name was Son-of-a-Bitch, because in many areas of Brooklyn, and places like Newark, it was never O'Malley or Walter O'Malley, but always "that Son-of-a-Bitch O'Malley," such was and is the hatred.

The O'Malley who was now obviously in charge of the Dodgers was used to having his own way, never having to worry about money. Born to an affluent father, Edwin, City Markets Commissioner under Mayor John Hylan, Walter went to the best of schools: Culver Academy, the University of Pennsylvania and Fordham Law School. Raised in the Bronx, he grew up a Giants fan, which might explain his later callousness in his disregard for Dodger tradition and his treatment of the fans.

Walter had risen to prominence on the coattails of George McLaughlin, a power in New York: City Police Commissioner, vice chairman of the Triborough Bridge and Tunnel Authority and president of the Brooklyn Trust Company. McLaughlin was a heavy drinker and Walter attached himself to him by doing legal chores and seeing to it that he was there to drive McLaughlin home on the nights he had too much to drink. His reward: entry into baseball's elite when McLaughlin used his influence to have him named to the Dodgers' board of directors in 1932, and later team lawyer.*

Later McLaughlin, as president of the bank holding a Dodger mortgage, arranged for O'Malley and Rickey each to buy 25 per cent of the team.[29] With Rickey as president and O'Malley an owner, the behind-the-scenes power struggle was inevitable. The two didn't like each other from the start.

Walter, with his $320,000 offer, knew that Branch was not wealthy and could never raise so substantial a sum by himself. Rickey, in fact, was selling to pay some pressing debts, and because he knew he was outnumbered on the Board and didn't want to be a minority stockholder in an organization that paid no dividends. But he had an out and he was canny enough to use it.

Red Barber, one of the ultimate Brooklyn insiders, has written that in the

---

It has been written, erroneously, that when Walter became Dodger counsel he replaced Wendell Willkie. In none of Willkie's biographies are the Dodgers mentioned. Of many obits only the Times *mistakenly mentions the team connection. More likely, Willkie's firm represented Brooklyn Bank & Trust, then Dodger mortgage holder, but not Willkie himself. What would an Indiana lawyer be doing representing the Dodgers?*

original agreement among the owners, if one was selling, the other owners had the right of first refusal but had to meet whatever price was being offered from the outside.

Rickey went to an old friend and fraternity brother, John Galbraith, owner of the Pittsburgh Pirates, for help. Galbraith put him in touch with real estate power Zeckendorf, who talked it over with Branch and then made a public offer to him of $1,000,050 for his shares. This, of course, enraged O'Malley, partly because of the money it was going to cost in meeting the Zeckendorf price, but also because he hated to be outmaneuvered.

The Zeckendorf offer was obviously a setup to squeeze O'Malley, for when it was over, that $50,000 tacked on to the one million was the $50,000 Rickey paid to Zeckendorf for his part of the deal.[30] It wasn't illegal and even if it was O'Malley couldn't prove it. So he fumed and bit hard on one of the 12 or more expensive cigars he smoked a day as he saw that extra $700,000 or so go to his former rival.

For once, in his longing to stay in Brooklyn, Branch's common sense deserted him. After all he went through with O'Malley over the years and after the Zeckendorf deal was announced, he stated at a September 25th press conference that he "would certainly consider" remaining as Dodger general manager. O'Malley took the occasion to have Rickey deny that there had ever been any friction or unpleasantness between him and the Board of Directors. "My years here have been most pleasant and I have full authority to operate," Rickey said with a straight face. As he stood there he must have been delusional that day to even think that O'Malley would retain him. His departure had been O'Malley's goal for four years or more.

Duke Snider was the one Dodger to come out publicly as glad to see Rickey go. Snider told *The Sporting News* that the team no longer had the "Rickey jitters," which he defined as the fear of being sold. "A lot of us feel more secure now that Rickey's gone," he said. "We're not afraid of being sold now." It must have escaped Snider that the men of real major league ability—among them Furillo, Reese, Hodges, Robinson, Campanella, Cox, Snider himself and the team's many quality pitchers—were not sold, that Rickey never even thought of selling them.

As Rickey was preparing to leave Brooklyn, Red Smith, not one of his admirers, was even-handed in his appraisal of the man. "He is responsible for the unfavorable press he has had," Smith wrote. "Because he is wordy and loves to make speeches and frequently combines his eloquence with a pomposity of manner, many have marked him down as a rush of wind in an empty corridor."

Years later after Branch's death he wrote: "To say that Branch Rickey had the finest mind ever brought to baseball is to damn with faint praise, like describing Isaac Stern as a fiddler. He changed the face of organized baseball more completely than Babe Ruth changed the strategy of play." He was referring, of course, to the farm system, Robinson, padded walls and warning tracks, and statistician Allan Roth.

While this front-office turmoil was going on the Dodgers put on one of the most remarkable stretch drives in memory, forgotten now because on the last day of the season they fell short, thanks in great part to their manager's carelessness in not looking over his bench for speed, in letting Cal Abrams remain on base while Eddie Miksis, fast as they come, fidgeted, sitting frustrated in the dugout.

On September 19 they were nine full games behind the league-leading Phillies. During the next twelve days they cut the lead to one — an amazing eight-game reduction in fewer than two weeks. Their record: 12 and 3, but the key was that they beat the first-place Phillies four out of five.

Those remarkable games, with Hodges on a home run spree, are worth citing briefly. On October 20–22 they took four from the Pirates behind Newcombe, Palica, Erskine and Palica again in relief, with Hodges hitting three home runs, one a grand slam, Snider hitting two, and single homers by Miksis and Brown. The next series they beat the Phils twice behind Newcombe, 3–2, in the first game, with Hodges hitting one with two on for all the Dodger runs. In the other Palica not only shut out the Phils, but hit a grand slam.

They took two of three from the Giants, Roe winning his 19th and Branca the other, backed by another three-run homer by Hodges. Then a split with the Braves in four games, cutting the lead to four as the Phillies lost. Hodges won the first game for Bankhead with a three-run homer, his 33rd, that broke a 6 to 6 tie.

Needing four straight to tie the Phillies, they took another double-header from the Braves, coming from behind both games, the second on a two-run homer by Robinson in the seventh inning for a 7–6 victory. At the *Times* they were now the "astonishing Dodgers."

A memorable scene from the second game of that double-header: Sam Jethroe was in center field as storm clouds were gathering in mid-game. Someone hit a fly ball to fairly short center and, as Jethroe was coming in for the ball, what looked like a deluge was almost upon him. The camera was right on him as he caught the ball just as the rain, heavy enough now to stop the game, hit him. As it was, the camera caught one of the most dramatic shots ever seen on televised baseball. There was Jethroe in broad daylight one second and engulfed the next in a storm gray as nightfall.

As Sam was about to make the catch the Boston bench was jumping up and shouting for him to drop the ball, for had Sam not made it, the game, called because of the rainstorm, would not have been official, vitally important in so tight a race. Jethroe, by the way, was a heady ballplayer. The storm came on so suddenly he obviously was unaware, else he would have dropped the ball, negating the game.

The next day Palica beat the Phils again, 7 to 3, for his 13th win, mainly on homers by Snider and Campanella against Jim Konstanty. Palica was pitching under the most intense pressure of the year, since a loss would end the season with the Phils on top. This was the pitcher Chuck "I'll Think of Something" Dressen called gutless in mid–1951.

The final game of the season was at Ebbets Field against the Phillies on October 1st. The excitement was intense from the first pitch, since all knew that if Brooklyn won they would tie Philadelphia, resulting in the second playoff in National League history.

It was Robin Roberts against Don Newcombe, both still in there as the game went into the 10th inning tied 1 to 1. Roberts had been in charge, so effective that he had six assists and Waitkus had 17 putouts at first base, but Newcombe was belted around, saved by great fielding.

Both early runs came in the sixth inning. With Dick Sisler, George's son, on third, Willie "Puddin' Head" Jones rifled a single between third and short, Sisler scoring. With Brooklyn up Reese hit one with the bases empty to break Roberts' shutout. Brooklyn should have won the game in the ninth inning were it not for Shotton not thinking at a crucial moment, and Cal Abrams' careless baserunning.

The inning opened with Abrams walking and then Reese lining a clean single to left center, with Abrams, a notoriously slow runner, stopping at second. Here was Shotton's grievous mistake. He had Eddie Miksis on the bench, one of the fastest men in baseball, and he chose to stay with Abrams, even though he was held close to second as Philadelphia set its infield for the sacrifice.

Miksis was furious as he sat watching helplessly as Abrams clung to second. His looks toward Shotton were useless as Shotton never even glanced his way. The Phils were in close, looking for the sacrifice bunt, but Snider crossed them up with a clean single to center, which should have won the game. Abrams' wide turn at third, ignored in most game writeups, drove Miksis and the others off the bench. "Abrams practically went into the dugout and got a drink of water [before heading to the plate]," Eddie told me years later. "And that dumb son of a bitch Shotton. I'm the fastest man on the ballclub. He forgot I was on the bench and let Abrams run."

He was right. Even on television it seemed to be the widest turn ever seen by a man rounding for home. And Abrams was slow. Shotton had been in the game since 1909, eight years as a major leaguer, and certainly knew the value of speed on the bases. What could he have been thinking?

When I reminded Eddie that Richie Asburn was perfectly positioned and seemed to make an almost perfect throw, Eddie said: "I don't care where he was playing or what kind of throw he made. He never would have thrown me out. Abrams was really slow."[31]

So the teams went into the 10th tied one-all. The inning started terribly for the Brooks as Roberts, a .167 hitter, singled through the middle, followed by a Waitkus pop-fly single into short center. After Ashburn bunted into a force at third, Sisler came up. He already had three hits for the day and, on a 2–2 count, hit the pennant-winning home run into the left field stands, 342 feet away as the *Times* pointed out, adding that it was the biggest and probably the shortest home run in Sisler's career.

A highlight of that dramatic homer was Sisler's shout to the Dodger bench as he rounded third. Dick had a stuttering problem, sometimes severe, and since childhood was often kidded about it, including some bench jockeying.[32] The Dodgers no doubt had done their share of riding him and he remembered it, as all stutterers always remember being made fun of.*

The park, of course, was silent except for the Phillie bench as the ball disappeared into the stands. Sisler, knowing it was the highlight of his career, was joyously running the bases. As he touched third and headed for home he shouted to the Dodger dugout, as heard all over the infield: "Take that, you Dodgers," in a clear, distinct voice without a sign of a stutter.[33] Could ever a stutterer's revenge be so sweet? This nice young man, a dangerous hitter at times, but always overshadowed by his Hall-of-Fame father, conquered his demon at the supreme moment of his life. Dick could never measure up to his famous father, of course, but George, for all his .340 average and Hall of Fame honors, never experienced such a moment and, with the weak teams he played on, never got into a World Series.

Thus ended a remarkable season, one lost by a manager's lapse and Abrams' senseless baserunning. The Phillies, known then as the Whiz Kids, were swept in four by the Yankees. This was a very young team that seemed intimidated by the New Yorkers. It may have been that they were simply dazed, worn out by the pressure of the last two weeks of the season. The Dodgers, after all, had come out of nowhere, just days after 30,000 Phillie fans greeted their team as pennant winners. It wasn't a high-scoring Series, starting with a 1 to 0 Yankee win against Konstanty, a surprise starter. The Yankees scored only 11 runs but the Phils just five as they hit an anemic .216 for the four games.

A disgraceful sidelight of the Series was Grover Cleveland Alexander among the standees in the mezzazine of Shibe Park, surrounded by people who had no idea who he was. The *Times'* Louis Effrat wrote that he had been flown in from his St. Paul, Nebraska, home (Effrat didn't say by whom) and given a standee ticket by the Phillies.

Old Pete, as he was called, had been standing for three innings and his 63-year-old legs were feeling it, when a veteran baseball writer, old enough to know the Hall of Famer, spotted him and reacted immediately. He arranged for a seat to be set up in the press box, which Pete gratefully accepted. In

---

*I speak from experience. I was a desperate stutterer in grammar school, a lot better in high school and got over it in the Navy. The only fights I had in those bad days were with boys who made fun of my stutter. Stutterers the world over would have cheered for Sisler had they known of his revenge on the Dodgers.

return Pete regaled the writers with his memories, such as how much trouble he had pitching to Rogers Hornsby but none at all to Babe Ruth.[34]

How could the Phillies management be so callous? Here was a man who pitched seven years for the team, compiling a 190-88 record on his way to 373 career wins and the Hall of Fame, shunted aside by a team he won almost 200 games for. With all the media hungry for features, that couldn't happen today. Imagine Tom Seaver being ignored in his old age?

The Rickey era ended on October 27 during a press conference at Brooklyn's Bossert Hotel. He gave a short, emotional speech saying how much he had enjoyed his Brooklyn years and then sat down with tears in his eyes. O'Malley got up and said he was "terribly sorry and hurt personally that we now have to face this resignation." The days of Fresco Thompson and E.J. "Buzzy" Bavasi under O'Malley had begun as Pittsburgh owner John Galbraith was about to hire, as Red Smith said, "the finest brain baseball has ever seen."

The man's greatest contribution to baseball, outside of Robinson, is constantly overlooked or worse, unknown to most baseball historians, fans and writers in general: in trying to save Pete Reiser's career he padded the walls and laid down a warning track at Ebbets Field, changing how outfielders play the game, the catches they make, knowing that they'll bounce off the foam rubber safely.

For example, and there are many, one fine historian wrote, "The most important of Rickey's innovations was the St. Louis farm system."[35] No sir. The farm system was important in its day, but it's long gone now, killed mostly by television. The walls and tracks will be here as long as the game is played and, it cannot be said too often, have through the years prevented many injuries, and probably even saved lives.

The day after Rickey left, signs went up in the Brooklyn executive offices saying: "From this day forward anyone in the Brooklyn Dodger offices who mentions the name of Branch Rickey will be fined a dollar on the spot." They were ordered by O'Malley, who "was terribly sorry" to have to take Rickey's resignation.[36]

◆ Two ◆

1951
The Shot Heard All Over Flatbush

The year 1951 started on a dismal note for the Brooklyn Dodgers, although none of us fans at the time knew it. The hiring of Chuck Dressen took a while to sink in, for some an entire season or more. In place of Burt Shotton, into the clubhouse came a 5-foot-5 former second baseman, a man with an ego so huge that many of the writers—and players—agreed that the title of his autobiography would be "I." The players even had a little joke about him among themselves. If one of them pointed to his eye, the others knew he was talking about Charlie. The man was so self-centered, so taken up with his self-proclaimed baseball genius, that on more than one occasion with his team behind, he would say: "Hang in there, fellas. I'll think of something."

"I never heard him say it," Clem Labine said, "but it happened. I heard from the players that those were his very words."[1] Late in the season in his handling of Labine that kind of ego and the stubbornness that usually goes with it cost the team the pennant.

Even in the area of sign stealing, where he was supposedly expert, he proved to be ineffective, although to many of us sign stealing by third-base coaches is not a lost art, it's a never-was art. But Charlie bragged about it and was believed by many. At times, however, he could be dangerous, as Joe DiMaggio once related.

Dressen, when he was a coach for the Yankees, once claimed to have found a flaw in the delivery of Fred Hutchinson, fastballer for the Tigers. He told DiMaggio that Hutch "cocks his glove" when he's going to throw a curveball. "I can tip ya," he told Joe. "We gotta wait for the right spot but at the right time with men on base I'll pick it up. Then I'll whistle good and loud. That means curve."

At the "right time" with men on base Charlie whistled to DiMaggio. "That's how the little son of a bitch almost got me killed," Joe said afterwards. "I heard the whistle. The pitch started toward my head. I hung in, waiting for it to break. It never broke an inch. I barely got my head out of the way. I told Dressen no more help. I intend to stay alive."[2]

Another of Dressen's "expert" sign stealings had far more serious consequences, resulting in the near ruin of one of baseball's best hitters. One week after the Dodgers bought Joe Medwick from the Cardinals back in June of 1940 he was beaned by Cardinal pitcher Bob Bowman. This has been written up a number of times by known writers, all of whom got the story wrong because they didn't check it out thoroughly enough.

Most accounts have Joe being hit by Bowman because there was bad blood between them when they were teammates on the Cardinals. Also there is the reported scene between Bowman and Durocher in a hotel elevator that morning, with Bowman vowing revenge on the Dodgers. Bowman said he had words with Durocher but denied saying anything about revenge, stressing that he and Medwick had always been friends as teammates.[3]

There is another version of the beaning, from Max Lanier, Dodger-killing Cardinal pitcher, a teammate of Bowman's, who was there. Dressen, Lanier said, was in the Dodger third-base coaching box as Medwick approached the plate and, as usual, had signals that would tip Joe as to what pitch was coming. Lanier said Charlie thought he had Bowman figured out, but that when he signaled Joe that a curve was coming Bowman threw a fastball that Joe stepped right into as ball bashed into the side of his head.[4] When he recovered enough to carry on a rational conversation, Joe backed up Lanier's account, saying that there were no hard feelings between him and Bowman.

Injured more than was first thought, Joe spent a week in the hospital with a concussion and then, as Larry MacPhail said, insisted on coming back too soon. In any event, Medwick was never the same again. According to the National League beat writers, like Tommy Holmes of the *Eagle*, he was somewhat gun-shy for the rest of his career. The figures tend to prove this: in the seven years as a Cardinal he was a .338 hitter, .374 in 1937, his Triple Crown year. For the next nine seasons he hit .305, retiring at .324. Strange to say, but the beaning, thanks to Charlie, turned a great hitter into a merely good one.

There is an historic plus side to the story, however, one that changed baseball forever. Larry MacPhail, then Dodger president, decided to do something about beanings. Medwick, after all, had cost the Dodgers $125,000 plus four second line players. Larry got in touch with brain specialists at Johns Hopkins who designed for him plastic inserts that would fit into the batter's cap. Thus was born the first batting helmet, grandfather of today's full helmets. Though a good many people have forgotten it, or never knew it, it was a MacPhail invention, one of the most important baseball innovations of the 20th century.

By the next March the caps were ready, called plastic protectors by Roscoe McGowen in his story out of the Dodgers training camp in Havana. He quotes MacPhail as saying: "Every player in the Brooklyn organization will wear this protector and I predict that within a year every player in the major leagues will be wearing it."[5]

Again, today most people are unaware of this helmet development. During an interview with a Dodger pitcher, who was with the team for eight years before the move to Los Angeles, he was surprised at the MacPhail connection. "I thought Branch Rickey invented the batting helmet," he said. Eddie Miksis before he died called it "Mr. Rickey's helmet" in relating a beaning incident. Those two played for years at Ebbets Field, yet they never knew that Rickey and others refined the helmet. The idea was MacPhail's all along. Worse, in book after book about the Dodgers and Ebbets Field, some by distinguished historians, there is no mention at all of the helmets, again, one of the most important developments in baseball history.

According to Bobby Bragan, a player who used a helmet as soon as MacPhail issued them, they not only protected the batter, but gave both him and the pitcher a psychological lift, a feeling that a catastrophe like the death of Ray Chapman at the Polo Grounds in 1920 from a Carl Mays fastball had become more unlikely.

"From the start, as primitive as those first helmets seem now, they gave us all a feeling of security from the fastball," he said. "Even the pitchers got a lift, knowing that a sailing fastball would probably not cause serious injury. We didn't have them long before in my opinion one saved Pete Reiser's life. The ball hit the plastic insert so hard it could be heard all over Ebbets Field. When Pete slumped to the ground I thought he'd been killed."[6]

Sadly, in many areas they didn't catch on for years. A clip in the *Times* as late as June of 1951–11 years after the introduction of the batting helmet — records the death of yet another young ballplayer dying of a fractured skull because he was up at the plate unprotected.

Down in Class D on the Donathan Browns in Alabama, where veteran managers should have been advising young ballplayers, Otis Johnson, a star outfielder in that lower league, died of a fractured skull when hit by a pitched ball. He lost consciousness on the field and died the next morning, a high school teacher in the off season who left a widow and one child. As late as two years later Don Zimmer, a future Dodger, almost died, hit also when he neglected to wear a helmet. Out of 28 days in the hospital he was in a coma for 13.[7] Today things like that can't happen, since players are now required to wear the helmets.

In addition to his supposed signal stealing, Dressen's handing of pitchers was always faulty, as we shall see with the underworked Labine, the ruined Erv Palica and a Newcombe sadly overworked as he went up against the Giants in October. Clyde King, at times a most effective reliever, thought Charlie likeable and super confident, but a manager who was not good at handling a pitching staff.

"I think that Dressen did overuse and overwork his pitchers. My best year,

1951, I couldn't pitch the last three weeks," King told his baseball biographer. "I was a reliever back then and warmed up a lot without getting into the game, and this was hard on my arm,"[8] an opinion later expressed by Johnny Rutherford, a promising right-hander, probably ruined by a "nervous" Dressen.

Charlie also had some nutty ideas for pitchers. For example, in 1949 when he was still with the Yankees he decided that Allie Reynolds was too tense on the mound. The remedy: a shot of whiskey as he warmed up, another when the game started and then another in the third inning. Reynolds, not a drinker, had to leave the game after the third drink, barely able to stand up.[9]

Jackie Robinson got along well with Dressen, but early on in spring training he knew he would have trouble with O'Malley. His buffers, Rickey and Shotton, were gone and eventually everyone else who had been loyal to Rickey would join them. Shotton, after winning a pennant and losing one on the last day, knew beforehand he would be leaving. "I wasn't fired because of my record," he said while leaving Ebbets Field. "It's just that O'Malley wanted an organization without any Rickey men in it. The deal I got this time made me a little sour."[10]

"As soon as O'Malley took over the presidency of the club he made it clear that he was anti–Rickey," Jackie writes in his autobiography. "In 1950 he became furious whenever he heard his name. He knew I felt very deeply about Mr. Rickey and so I became the target of his insecurity. O'Malley's attitude toward me was viciously antagonistic. I learned later that he used to call me Mr. Rickey's prima donna."

At one meeting with Jackie and his wife, Walter called him a prima donna and crybaby to his face because he was out with a sore leg. Rachel exploded in resentment. "I've seen him play with sore legs, a sore back, sore arms without the team even knowing about them," she said in a rage. "Doing it not for praise, but because he was thinking about his team. You know, Mr. O'Malley, bringing Jack into organized baseball wasn't the greatest thing Mr. Rickey did for him. It was this: he stuck by him to the very end."

Before he left, Jack turned and said he could complain about a lot of things, including the "crummy" hotel he had to stay in. "It doesn't strike me as fair to have people sitting in comfort in an air-conditioned hotel lecture me about not complaining." Jackie may have realized then that spring training was just the start of his troubles with Walter. Later he said: "I knew what O'Malley's problem was. To put it bluntly, I was one of those 'uppity niggers' in Walter's book."[11]

The first month of the season saw the arrival on the national scene of Frank Saucier, property of the St. Louis Browns. After a season with the San Antonio Missions of the Texas League, Frank seemingly had it all: 23, 6-foot-1, 180, a graduate engineer and the "Minor League Player of the Year" for 1949. As *The Sporting News* recounted, the Browns could have gotten a fortune for him on the baseball market. Before he was brought up he hit .357 and .446 in the low minors. Plus, he was a long-ball-hitting catcher.

He was a total bust with the Browns and when they released him there were no takers. He played in only 18 games, but he may live forever in trivia games, since he was the man Eddie Gaedel, Bill Veeck's midget, pinch hit for against Bob Cain of the Detroit Tigers, who walked him.

Frank thus joined the many—thousands actually—of minor league stars who didn't make it, men who had plenty of seasoning before being brought up. In my youth there were Newark Bears Frankie Kelleher, George Washburn, Johnny Lindell (a star pitcher the Yankees made an outfielder), Joe Buzas and Bud Metheny during the war, Ed (Whitner) Levy, Buddy Blair and Don Savage, who might have been a star were it not for his severe diabetes. Those are Newark memories but there were plenty of others like Bobby Morgan, who dominated the International League, Joe Charboneau for Cleveland, and Chuck Connors, a killer in the minors. The majors are just too tough and competitive for many young men who were star athletes all their lives until they hit the big leagues. The leagues are so tough it even happens to veteran players. Read of Steve Blass' career.

I got a slight taste of the toughness once and it has lasted me all my life. I was managing editor of *Western Electric* magazine in 1968 and was doing a story on a kid named Gary Jestadt, son of one of our engineers, who was trying out for the Chicago Cubs.* Gary, a very likeable 21, was a third baseman trying to make a team with Ron Santo at third. He was eventually traded to Montreal.

I was lucky my first day at Scottsdale when introduced to Durocher. He gave me a welcoming smile and handshake when he found out I was with Western Electric, since he knew it as a subsidiary of AT&T, which, he said, "helped make me rich." Leo, very charming when he wanted to be, was in an expansive mood and gave me the run of the field with just one admonition: "Never turn your back on home plate." He then assigned coach Harry Bright to show me around.

Harry and I became friends and talked a lot of baseball. At one point I said I always wondered how it would be to face major league pitching and he agreed to let me find out without Durocher ever knowing. We got together with a tall young lefthander (Rich Nye, I think), picked because, being a right-handed hitter, I wouldn't have to face a frightening right-handed curve ball. "For Christ's sake, Rudy, don't swing," Harry said. "I'm not wearing a mask."

Don't swing! I couldn't have swung if I had wanted to. Even the curve from a lefty was frightening. And the fast balls were terrifying. It was probably my imagination, but to this day I think I heard the fast ones buzzing. From a guy who played sandlot ball in Newark and intramurals at Rutgers this major

---

Since Western employed almost 200,000 people, I thought there would be many sons of our families playing major league sports. There were, and it turned out to be an interesting series of stories.

league pitching was baseball from another planet. When it was over, Harry just smiled.* "You see how it is up here," he asked. I just nodded.

As spring training was starting, Albert B. Chandler was fired. This was the man who had the guts to approve the signing of Jackie Robinson and to suspend Leo Durocher. The vote by the club owners was nine to seven, leaving him three shy of the necessary 12 for reelection.

Chandler was too outspoken and too much his own man to be retained. Owners, who had gone through the many years of the autocratic rule of Judge Landis, were obviously tired of being dictated to. His place was taken by National League President Ford Frick, who was exactly what the owners wanted, a man who could be "handled."

Chandler, who planned on going back into politics, was understandably bitter. "When the clubs pushed me out they had a vacancy and decided to keep it. So they named Ford Frick."[12] The players liked Chandler as a man who would stand up to the owners. Fred Hutchison, American League player representative, said he did things like push through the pension plan despite opposition from virtually every team owner in both leagues.

The Dodgers opened the season losing to Robin Roberts and trying again to solve their perennial left field problem. Year after year, one left fielder after another. Hermanski solved the problem for a few years, despite his so-so fielding, but he went in the Pafko trade that coming June, and for some reason Andy was later let go in a trade still a mystery.

This time Don Thompson, a former Brave, filled in until Pafko arrived but was let go two years later for lack of hitting. Andy was sent to Milwaukee in '53, a career .287 hitter hardly given a chance even though he hit .287, with 19 homers and 85 RBIs, in his only full year. Chances are the dead hand of Walter O'Malley, in many ways the George Steinbrenner of his day, was involved in this.

The Brooks opened the season at home with a three-game sweep of the Giants, sweet at any time. Ralph Branca, winner in relief in the first game, was now being used by Dressen both as a starter and reliever, and he gave Charlie his last decent year: 13 and 12 and a 3.26 ERA in 204 innings pitched. They won the second on a single by Reese in the ninth for a 4 to 3 win and the third on a home run in the tenth by Carl Furillo off Sal Maglie. Newcombe won in relief, his second win of the series. Charlie occasionally mixed all of his starters and relievers, even though Labine had arrived and Clyde King was having his great year at 14 and 7 until his arm gave out in September.

The next day Furillo again drove in the winning run, this time off War-

---

*One mistake I made at Scottsdale: standing in the outfield one afternoon I turned to my left and there was Pete Reiser, my boyhood hero, about 20 feet away. He was looking at me quizzically, probably wondering what a guy in civvies was doing out there. (He'd been with the B team when I arrived so he didn't know who I was.) Why I didn't go over to introduce myself and shake his hand I'll never know.

ren Spahn in the 16th inning of what became a 2 to 1 Dodger victory. Spahn went all the way, before losing on an unearned run on as Gene Mauch erred on an easy grounder, allowing Billy Cox to third before he scored. Spahn, like Robin Roberts, lost a lot of games that way, their teams responsible on many occasions for their being tied at 245 losses.

As April was closing, the Giants lost their eleventh straight, falling into last place, as the Brooks routed Larry Jansen in the sixth inning, mainly on a two-run homer by Hodges. They snapped the streak the next day, 8 to 5, in a game in which fans saw the hatred between Robinson and Durocher flare up again, as intense as it had ever been since Durocher left Brooklyn.

Again it involved Maglie's constant dusting of Robinson, this time Jackie bunting up along the first base line to draw Sal over so he could knock him down. Maglie covered the bag and as Robinson came down the line he bumped the pitcher with his shoulder. They almost came to blows before the umpires stepped in. This was the first such bunt try by Robinson. The next, as we shall see, virtually ended the career of Giant second baseman Davey Williams.

Durocher called the bunt a "bush play" and Robinson replied that it had been taught to him by a "bush manager," taunts that had been getting nastier during the recent months, involving deeply personal insults that sometimes even included their wives, especially movie star Laraine Day, then married to Durocher.

These two truly hated one another, a strange situation in that Durocher was manager of the Dodgers when Robinson joined the team, and was one of his strongest supporters. It started when Leo went over to the Giants, and escalated when the bench jockeying got out of hand. It is odd that after all the years of snapping and snarling at one another, Robinson barely mentions Durocher in his autobiography.

"The Giants throw at you all the time," Robby told the press. "Maglie does it all the time. It's part of his equipment, throw at the hitter and then curve him outside. Jansen throws at you too but only when he doesn't have his good stuff. I learned that bunt play from Durocher who told us if they throw at you, bunt along the line and run right up their backs."[13]

That kind of feud, not at all uncommon back in those days, might at times seem a bit childish today, but you must remember these were two teams in the most highly competitive city in the world. As the song goes, if you can make it in New York you can make it anywhere. Not only was the city itself competitive, but there were television, radio and eight newspapers, all hungry for news and constantly trying to stir things up. Plus the stadiums were only miles apart, lending proximity to the mix of bitching and screaming.

For years the owners and media have tried to stir up a rivalry between the descendants, but the Los Angeles Dodgers and the San Francisco Giants and their fans just don't have the volatility that New York City generates.

Besides, those Coast fans were laid back to the extent that they preferred

Orlando Cepeda over Willie Mays, an egregious choice for the Hall of Fame over possibly the best man who ever played the game. Cededa is in the Hall despite being a convicted felon, having served time in a federal prison for attempting to smuggle 165 pounds of marijuana into Puerto Rico. If Cededa why not Pete Rose?

Surprisingly, for those too young too remember, a lot of players, black players included, were not on Robinson's side in this current feud, even though Durocher was almost universally disliked. One star Dodger, who asked to be unnamed even at this late date, said Jackie was becoming "a strict pain in the ass, always mouthing off, always finding something to stir things up." The sentiment among many black players was not much different.

It started with envy back in 1946 when Jackie was signed for Montreal by Rickey. Monte Irvin said many years later that the black players' feelings were never expressed publicly but that there was some jealousy throughout the Negro Leagues, partially because it was felt that there were better players such as Josh Gibson, Roy Campanella and Satchell Paige who should have been given the honor of being signed first.

"I was delighted," Irvin said years later. "I knew it would give all of us a chance to make it but there was a certain amount of jealousy. But they said Rickey wanted a man with a college education, able to express himself with the press. Jackie was perfect for this. We were truly for him one hundred per cent, but still there was some jealousy."

An aging Jackie Robinson takes a break at Vero Beach. His final years with the Dodgers were marked by clashes with manager Walter Alston over playing time. Until retirement Jackie never realized his body was older than his years. He had played so hard and so tough for almost a decade that by age 36 he was worn out. Surprisingly, many fellow Negro ballplayers resented his constant feuding with umpires and rival managers.

And, Monte added, there were those (of us) who did not appreciate his outspoken views. "Most players thought Jackie was interjecting himself into situations where he shouldn't have been. He was not a spokesman for anyone, but was assuming that role. Some thought: don't think for me and tell me what I should do. Most of the black players thought he was setting himself up as a spokesman for the entire Negro race."[14]

Certainly Jackie had a right to speak out given what he had gone through in his first two years. That was before the 1949 season when Rickey released him from his vow of silence and turning the other cheek. But as Irvin pointed out, by 1950 it just got to be too much; Robinson seeming to be getting out of hand.

National League president Ford Frick felt he could no longer stay out of the Durocher/Robinson feuding, blaming this latest incident on Robinson. Frick warned the Dodgers of "unsportsmanlike conduct" and said of Robinson: "I'm getting tired of hearing about his pop offs. What's going on with him over there?" The next day, saying he had received no reports of "dusting off" from the umpires, he added: "It's got to stop. I have warned the Brooklyn club that if they don't control him I will."

That same day O'Malley and Dressen came to Jackie's defense. "I have no reason to be dissatisfied with Robinson's conduct on or off the field," O'Malley said. Dressen meanwhile was telling reporters: "I've been trying to calm Jackie down," but "Stanky can kick dirt all over the place and gets away with it. But Robinson is watched like a sitting duck."

Just two days before that brouhaha, Lou Brissie, arguably the most remarkable pitcher in baseball history, was the principal in a three-team trade involving the Indians, White Sox and Athletics. Brissie wound up with Cleveland, Minnie Minoso with Chicago and Gus Zernial with Philadelphia.

Brissie's left leg had been so shattered by German artillery during the Italian campaign that, after he persuaded doctors not to amputate, it took 29 operations before he could walk properly, and even then the leg was wired in places. But playing with a brace he lasted seven years with a 44–48 record. One important bit of luck he had through those interminable operations was that he was left-handed, and thus able to pitch for all those years. Had he been right-handed it would have been impossible, for then his injured leg would have been his push off, or power, leg. Before the osteomyelitis that ended his career set in, he had years of 14 and 10, 16 and 11, and then in 1950, with Philadelphia in last place, he was 7 and 19, pitching 246 innings. There should have been a book and a movie about this guy but by now it will never happen.*

The Sporting News carried a story May 9 on the end of the brief major league career of Chuck Connors, the future television "Rifleman." Big Chuck

---

*In 2001 I wanted to write Brissie's biography but after speaking to him he referred me to another family member as his spokesman. He put so many restrictions on me—money, clearance, writing credit, etc.—that I gave it up. As far as I know it's never been done.

was born near Ebbets Field, where he played just one game for the Dodgers. He was released by the Cubs to the Pacific Coast League's Los Angeles Angels, where he tore up the peapatch, as Red Barber would say: 10 homers, 34 RBI and a .372 batting average in just a few weeks. An All American out of Seton Hall, he was 6-feet-5 and very good-looking. With those figures he might have gotten back to the majors, but after being approached by filmmakers with all that Hollywood gold he obviously figured: why bother? He no longer needed baseball.

On the 20th, as the Dodgers were taking over first place by beating the Reds twice, the Cincinnati police informed the FBI that three letters had been received threatening Jackie Robinson's life. All were signed "The Three Travelers," saying "the Negro Robinson" would be shot, one adding that it would be done "from a window."

Some 70 policemen patrolled the stands at Crosley Field while buildings with views of the ballpark were checked out. It proved a false alarm but there was some humor in the Dodger clubhouse, provided, as on many occasions, by Gene Hermanski.

Snider tells in his book *The Duke of Flatbush* that in a discussion on how to protect Robinson, Hermanski suggested giving everybody the number 42 so the shooter wouldn't be able to tell which one was Jackie. In an interview Hermanski elaborated: "It was a Sunday afternoon and Shotton came into the clubhouse to tell us of the death threats. After Shotton spoke there was a lull and I came up with this idea about Jackie's number. That broke up the room, relieved the tension. We all relaxed a bit."[15]

On the 25th Willie Mays, in from Minneapolis, reported to the Giants at Shibe Park. The 20-year-old had hit .477 in 35 games for the Millers and became an important part of that incredible Giant comeback later in the year. For a rookie he had a great year: 20 home runs, 59 RBI and a .274 batting average. Tommy Heath, the Minneapolis manager, advised Durocher to play him in center field, a Polo Grounds area that was "made for him."

May ended with the famous confrontation between Russ Meyer, then with the Phillies, and Robinson, and this time Jackie was blameless. The aptly-named Mad Monk exploded after Robinson eluded a rundown between home and third and scored. Dressen had put on the squeeze but Furillo missed on his bunt attempt. During the rundown Meyer dropped the ball as Jackie went past him.

Meyer approached Jackie and angrily jostled him. A fight was prevented when Campanella grabbed Jackie's arms and Eddie Sawyer got Meyer away. Russ, thinking that Robby had knocked the ball out of his hands, challenged him to a fight under the stands. Both men disappeared down the clubhouse runways with both teams pursuing fast enough to prevent punches thrown.

After the game, as his own teammates convinced him that he dropped the ball, he went into the Dodger clubhouse and apologized to Robinson. As they shook hands Robinson said: "I was as much to blame as he was."

Later that month Andy Pafko arrived at Ebbets field as Gene Hermanski, Eddie Miksis, Bruce Edwards and Joe Hatten left for Chicago, Andy's former team. Brooklyn fans rejoiced, thinking that the constant Dodger problem with left field was solved. Pafko, described in the *Times* as a star outfielder, was also a .295 hitter with power in his eight years at Wrigley Field. It was thought such an important move for the Dodgers, giving them one of the best outfields of all time, that it made page one of the *Times*.

But Stan Baumgartner of *The Sporting News* wasn't so sure. He made the mistake of comparing them to outfielders of the 1920s, specifically the Yankees' 1927 outfield of Babe Ruth at .356, Bob Meusel at .337 and Earle Combs at .356, averages not all that unusual for the 1920s. Baumgartner was a fine sportswriter for the *Philadelphia Bulletin*, especially good on baseball, since he had pitched six seasons with the Phillies. But he was wrong on this one. You cannot compare ballplayers of the '50s, or any era for that matter, with players of the 1920s.

Look back at the '20s records. Everybody was hitting in the .300s or even occasionally in the .400s. It was the era of the hitter after Babe Ruth switched from the mound to the outfield with the Yankees in 1919. It took the pitchers, historically used to the "hit 'em where they ain't" styles of the Wee Willie Keelers, years to adjust. (The hitters went wild as late as 1930. Look it up.)

Pafko was understandably delighted with the trade, going from seventh-place Chicago to league-leading Brooklyn. As he came into the Dodger clubhouse for the first time he was quoted as saying "it was like someone just handed me $5,000." Hermanski, when he heard of the remark said, "Yeah, my $5,000."

As is often the case, the day after Brooklyn made the trade Bruce Edwards beat them by batting in four runs in Chicago's 6 to 4 win at Wrigley Field. The Brooks made up for it somewhat the next night in St. Louis when Hodges hit a two-run homer in the ninth to win it 2 to 1 for Erskine. But, as Arthur Daley wrote, the "moaning and groaning," keening as the Irish would call it, went on and on all over the National League about the Pafko trade. He was seen by all as such a significant acquisition that the pennant was all but ceded to Brooklyn.

On the 22nd, Commissioner Chandler formally submitted his resignation, with July 15 as the date he would leave office. In a subsequent news conference he warned that those trying to sell baseball as a big business are mistaken. "If baseball were a big business," he added, "the Department of Commerce would take over and then you wouldn't need a commissioner." It was like when Eisenhower warned us to beware of the military-industrial complex some years later.

Before he left, Chandler said his decision in the Dick Wakefield case, where he had ruled against the Yankees in a salary dispute, cost him his job. If not for that, he said, the Yankees wouldn't have turned against him. "The

Yankees went out to get my job and I guess they did." He forgot that fighting the owners in winning pensions for the players must have played a part. And lest we forget in this more liberal age, most of baseball was against his approval of the Robinson signing.

In a parting shot, during his final appearance before Congress on baseball and antitrust matters, Chandler said: "Some of the owners are new, very new. Some are rich, very rich. And some don't know where first base is."[16] And he was so right. Down through the years they have listened to no one and have had rubber-stamp commissioners ever since Chandler. Two who were their own men didn't last. Fay Vincent was not renewed and Bart Giametti died in office.

As a result, the World Series is now played in late October, sometimes into November. (Those pitchers constantly blowing on their hands aren't spitballers. They're cold.) We have baseball coast-to-coast instead of three leagues, thus players are in jets at 35,000 feet half their lives, and God help the financial future of the game, with an Alexander Rodriguez making $25 million a year—for six months' work.

And worst of all, the game is losing our young. With even World Series games starting too late for school children to stay up and watch, never mind night game after night game during the season, where will the future fans come from, with children all over the country playing soccer instead of baseball? Little League is not the answer. Sandlot baseball is.

Against this sad background we now have players like Jason Giambi, Rafael Palmiero and others with their multi-million-dollar contracts. How long can teams like Kansas City, Pittsburgh and others hold out losing year after year because they can't pay those kinds of salaries, can't compete financially with New York or Chicago or Boston with their big fan bases and TV and radio money?

The All-Star picks were announced on July 3 and as usual Brooklyn was well represented: Newcombe, Roe, Hodges, Robinson, Reese, Snider and Campanella. A heart-warming choice for Brooklyn fans was the selection of Chicago's Bruce Edwards, a six-year Dodger before the Pafko trade. Bruce was an Ebbets Field favorite from the start when he hit .295 in 1947 and was a catcher who could throw.

He was benched a lot after Campanella arrived in 1948 but not just because of Campy's skills. Roy became a Hall of Famer, but in '48 few thought he would replace Edwards unless something went wrong, and it did. Bruce's arm went and by the time he nursed it back Campy was established. It was good to see Bruce on the All-Star list and to realize today that he lasted until 1956.

On July 6 Tommy Holmes, the *Brooklyn Eagle*'s one-armed sportswriter, wrote a column headlined "The Sad Passing of an Old Friend." Hugh Casey, former Dodger All-Star reliever, had killed himself with a rifle in an Atlanta hotel room, victim of depression, debts, a deteriorating marriage and a paternity suit. He was just 38.

Holmes relates how Hugh sat in the room, rifle aimed at his head, telling his wife on the phone that he'd kill himself as she desperately tried to talk him out of it. Casey was apparently most worried about the paternity suit filed by a Brooklyn woman who named him as the father of her son. "I begged him not to do it," his wife Kathleen told police, "but he said he was ready to die, his time had come." His last words, his wife said, were: "I am innocent of those charges." Then the shotgun blast, killing him instantly.[17]

The following week the ruination of Erv Palica, Brooklyn's best clutch pitcher in the closing weeks of 1950, was begun. After a bad stretch by the 23-year-old, manager Dressen called him "a gutless kid who doesn't belong in the majors."

Yet it was Palica who had kept the Dodgers in the race to catch the Phillies the year before, the kid who beat the Phils four times under intense pennant pressure while winning seven from August on. "I do the best I can," Palica said. "I know I'm not throwing as hard as I can. I try but for some reason the ball won't go. I've pitched some good ball but whenever I have a bad day Dressen jumps on me." Palica had problems Dressen ignored: his blood pressure had the team doctor worried, his wife was sick and he was concerned about his upcoming Army service.

Dressen had treated Billy Martin similarly once at Oakland. Martin called Dan Daniel, writing for *The Sporting News*, after reading of what Dressen did to Palica. After a play Dressen didn't like, Dressen lit into the second baseman in front of his teammates. Martin, who backed down from no one, called back, "You're a second-guessing manager."

"That'll cost you a hundred," Dressen yelled. "You're still a second-guesser," Martin shouted back. "Two hundred," Dressen came back. "Make it $300," Martin again shouted back. Dressen did but, said Martin: "The club never took the money from me." Palica showed many times that he had guts, but he never had Martin's chutzpah. He was in the Army the next year, and when he came out he was never the same, never recovered his 1950 form. But managers kept hoping until he retired in 1956, only 30 years old.

Dressen wasn't alone in such treatment of pitchers. Casey Stengel, when he didn't have those Yankee horses, wasn't always New York's resident genius. Both Warren Spahn and Johnny Sain tell of him when he managed them in the minors. Casey once called Spahn "gutless," Warren recalled for Roger Kahn in *The Head Game*. "I knew Casey both before and after he was a genius," Spahn added. Sain remembers Casey telling him: "You can only go five innings. You'll be a relief pitcher. You'll never be a big league starting pitcher."[18] Johnny Sain: 11 years, 139–116. Spahn: 21 years, the winningest left-hander in history with a 363–245 legacy.

Kahn could have put more stress on the psychological head game involving managers. Certainly his title applies to the constant battle involving the pitcher, catcher and batter. But there is another, perhaps more important game, the one between manager and pitcher, the one Dressen failed miserably with Palica.

Sain, thought by many to be the best pitching coach in the game's history, gave the following as the basis of his coaching style: "Pitchers, even big strong pitchers who can throw fastballs through the Washington Monument, are at their core delicate flowers. They need to be nurtured, supported, encouraged, admired."[19]

Most managers agree with Sain, to a point: that you cannot treat a pitcher the way you'd treat a first baseman or an outfielder. Pitchers are different: they're the center of attention during a game and they can never let down, never relax. Especially in modern times with the baseball so lively and parks, like Camden Yards, getting smaller. The stress factor, therefore, must be considered. You can't rip up a pitcher in front of his team and then expect a shutout. Most managers, like Joe Torre, would never do it. They're wise enough to be considerate. But remember, Charlie Dressen was a baseball genius. All anyone had to do was ask him.

In late July the New York musicians' union decided to attack the Dodger Sym-Phony as anti-labor because all they got for their tootling was free admission to Ebbets Field. "They don't get peanuts for their work," said the secretary for Local 802, American Federation of Musicians, adding that they should get at least $100 for their work, a sum that the members of the Sym-Phony did not ask for or want. In protest, the band members called on Kings County Judge Samuel Leibowitz to find a solution so that the Sym-Phony could go on tormenting our ears at every ball game.

In the face of this outrageous nonsense, the kind of union selfishness that today is sending our industries scurrying overseas, O'Malley decided on a Music Appreciation Day, telling fans that bringing a musical instrument to the game would get them in free, provided they play without pay.

Nothing like it was ever heard before at any game anywhere: fiddles, cymbals, saxophones, ocarinas, trumpets, you name it, were deafening during parts of the game. The Braves lost to the Dodgers, but those of us who were there agreed that the big loser was music. Judge Leibowitz, a man who loved music, soon saw to it that all parties reached an agreement, terms not disclosed.

On Sunday, August 12th, the Dodgers were 13 games ahead of the second-place Giants. The Brooks were 70 and 36 while the Giants were a lackluster 59 and 51. A check of the official standings at the end of each day shows that the Dodgers were never really 13½ games ahead, as has been printed countless times. The day before they had won the first game of a double-header, putting them for a couple of hours at that figure, but they lost the second game and were 13 up at day's end. That lead seemed insurmountable, as leads like that so late in the season always were in the past. Brooklyn was supremely confident, and why not?

The very next day the Giants chipped one-half game away as they beat the Phillies twice while Brooklyn took one from Boston. Two days later it was down to 11½ when George Spencer six-hit the Dodgers 4 to 2 at the Polo Grounds, breaking a string of six Brooklyn victories over the Giants. *The Times'* Joseph Sheehan, like the rest of us, thought the win "not of unusual significance." Nothing to worry about. Only a small leak just below the waterline.

Then in just four days—four days—the lead was nine. The greatest stretch drive in baseball history was starting to roll, and still, no one took it seriously. Why should we have? A nine-game lead on August 18 was no cause to worry.

After the Spencer win the Giants took two more to sweep the series, the first led by Wes Westrum, Willie Mays and Jim Hearn, 3 to 1, and then Maglie with a four-hitter, 2 to 1—brilliant pitching on both sides. In that second game Westrum hit two of his 99 career homers and rookie Mays made the first of his many spectacular throws to get Billy Cox at the plate, virtually clinching the game. That was the throw Dressen was quoted on as saying, "I'd like to see him do that again." The next day Maglie beat Newcombe, with the winning run coming in on a wild pitch.

The following day at Boston, Brooklyn split a double-header with the Braves, Erskine winning his 14th by a 3 to 1 score, and then Johnny Sain evening the day with his fifth win against 13 losses. It was one of Johnny's few off seasons, and not long after this win Billy Southworth traded him to the Yankees, where in a second career as a starter and reliever, he went 33 and 20 over three-plus seasons. Meanwhile the Giants got by the Phillies, lowering the Dodger lead to nine, a loss of four full games in just five days.

The Dodgers looked calm as they posed for their pennant photo after coming in from Boston the next day. Of the 33 in the picture only coaches Cookie Lavagetto and Jake Pitler looked unhappy, Jake sad and Cookie with a deep scowl. The photo was tempting fate, but not a player in the game would yet pick the Giants. Everyone thought their hot streak would end, as they always do.

That same day a picture appeared on the front page of the *Herald-Tribune* showing a 26-year-old midget pinch-hitting in a big league game, Bill Veeck at it again. The day before, he had 3-foot-7 Eddie Gaedel go to bat against Bob Cain in Detroit. Eddie, hitting for minor league sensation Frank Saucier, was told it would be worth his life if he swung, so he walked on four pitches, as those in the stadium and TV viewers watched in astonishment. Umpire Ed Hurley had questioned Eddie's eligibility but gave way after seeing his signed contract for $100. Jim Delsing ran for him and the game got back to normal.

None of Veeck's many stunts had ever seemed to threaten the game's integrity before. There were tongue-in-cheek dire predictions: why, a team of midgets might literally "walk away" with a pennant! Far-fetched, but good barroom conversation. It all ended the next day when American League president Will Harridge banned Eddie "in the best interests of baseball." The little guy died a decade later in a Chicago hotel under what police described as "suspicious circumstances." When Veeck died at age 71 many of his obituaries led off with the fact that he "once sent a midget up to bat." Thus, in a way Eddie never really left him.

To Dodger fans the next week seemed like a blur as the impossible Giants rolled to their 16th straight win when they took a double-header from the Cubs behind Larry Jansen and Al Corwin. *Al Corwin*? The Giants were so hot that even rookies were coming through, especially Corwin, who went 5 and 1 for them, a forgotten factor in that fabulous drive.

Everything was going for the Giants before and during that streak. One of the most crushing losses of the time was a weekend game, date forgotten, but it was a Saturday or Sunday because we were listening over a portable radio on the beach at Belmar. The Giants were up by one in mid-game when the Dodgers loaded the bases with one out. Reese lined a single through the box for two sure runs and the lead. But, and a big but, the ball hit second base and then right to Stanky. Eddie to Dark covering second to Lockman for the double play. Another Giant win.

The streak finally ended on the 28th when Howie Pollett, now with the Pirates, pitched a 2 to 0 shutout at the Polo Grounds. Pollett was past his glory days with the Cardinals but pitched decently for the next six years, mostly with the Cubs and Pirates, both usually deep in the second division.

As a result of the streak's end, *The Sporting News* led off its September 5th issue with an ominous statistic for the future of baseball in New York City. At the Polo Grounds, as the Giants were going for that 17th straight win, the turnstile count showed that only 8,802 fans were in that cavernous stadium—this in the midst of what was shaping up as an historic drive at the Dodgers. Almost as bad, those in the stands booed the Giants at game's end—after 16 straight wins.[20]

This was the land of McGraw, Ott, Terry and the unjustly vilified Merkle.* But those of us who journeyed up to Harlem could see that the neighborhood was closing in on Horace Stoneham's stadium. The fan base was shrinking as the area became more crime-ridden, and not even the arrival of black players like Monte Irvin, Willie Mays and Hank Thompson could bring back the glory days. Things got even worse, of course, until Stoneman had to move. The truth is O'Malley didn't have to persuade him to leave. Unlike the Dodgers, he was facing eventual bankruptcy and was headed to Minneapolis when San Francisco beckoned. But, as Red Smith often said, the calamity the Giants were facing was in large measure Stoneham's own fault.

In his book More Than Merkle, *David W. Anderson makes the case that by not touching second as the winning run scored—the famous "Merkle boner"—Fred was following the custom of his times. The rule was there but always ignored until Johnny Evers called it and the umpire backed him up, against tradition.*

In his October 15, 1957, column, Smith wrote, "Horace Stoneham stood still for 20 years watching the deterioration of the wonderful organization he had inherited. When at long last the noose tightened around his neck, he cried 'All is lost' and scuttled for San Francisco." Red should have added that the Giants' demise was largely because of Stoneham drinking.

On August 29th, Clem Labine in his first game as a starter pitched the first of four straight wins during the next two weeks, beating Cincinnati 3 to 1 at Ebbets Field. Showing great poise for an untested starter who just turned 25, Clem pitched a seven-hitter, walked none and struck out nine. After his fourth win he was benched by Dressen. And as he went to the bench, so went the pennant.

With the lead dwindling, the first doubts started creeping into the minds of Dodger fans on Saturday, September 1st: Maglie against Branca at the Polo Grounds. It wasn't enough that Maglie held the Brooks to seven singles. The final score was 8–1, with Don Mueller hitting three home runs. Worse, in the fifth inning the Dodgers had a rally going: two on, Reese, with two clean hits, at the plate. Pee Wee on a full count hit a hot liner right into shortstop Dark's glove. Dark flipped to second where Stanky stepped on the bag and tagged Furillo as he was turning back toward first base. The only triple play in the National League that year signaled that the gods might be looking kindly on the Polo Grounds.

The lead was down to six games and it was then that many of us felt—just about knew after that triple play—that the scales were tipping toward the Giants. Also another ominous sign: Bobby Thomson hit another homer off loser Ralph Branca. When was Dressen going to figure out that this guy owned Branca? It seemed he was always belting one against Ralphie, as those along Bedford Avenue called him. A lot of fans had another name for him as the 6-foot-3 right-hander kept losing the big ones.

And so it went day after day. Monday, after the triple play game, the Giants routed Don Newcombe, 11 to 2, with Don Mueller hitting two more home runs good for five RBI. The lead was now five and we started to feel that if Newcombe couldn't stop them, who could? Slap-hitting Don Mueller, hitting five home runs in two games at the Polo Grounds? We'll see later what Giant catcher Sal Yvars has to say about that.

The next day Erskine and Labine gave the team a bit of breathing room as they each went the route in beating the Braves at Ebbets Field by identical 7 to 2 scores, bringing the lead back up to six. Campanella led the offense with seven straight hits, including three homers, one a grand slam, off Max Surkont. With his second straight complete game Labine was a starter, relieved of all bullpen duties.

Another sideshow out of St. Louis that week. Veeck, desperate to draw fans into Sportsman's Park, tried another gimmick. This time he put manager Zack Taylor into the stands and let the fans manage the game. There were only 1,115 in attendance—Veeck was truly in trouble—but a select number were given placards with "Yes" on one side and "No" on the other. Coaches had placards with plays on them and the fans would respond. A tabulator figured the majority, which was usually 60 to 40. Taylor said, "Now they know what a manager goes through. That's why we have gray hair."

On the 9th the Brooks finally took Durocher's men 9 to 0, Newcombe beating Jim Hearn on a two-hitter for his 18th win. Those of us who were at Ebbets Field that day saw one of the best feats of base running possible. I was in the upper deck, first base side, and saw Robinson take third after Pafko hit into a double play. Then Robby was on and off the bag, feinting toward home several times. He had Hearn so upset that Leo went to the mound to settle him down, but it didn't work. Another feint and Hearn threw the ball over Westrum's head, Robinson scoring. Hearn was soon out of the game, said by the writers to be still fuming as he sat in the clubhouse. The lead went back to six with three weeks to go.

Then on the 10th came the game that made many Dodgers fans realize that the pennant really could be lost. Maglie at Ebbets Field won his 20th, 2 to 1, backed by Irvin's two-run homer and brilliant fielding plays by Irvin in the outfield and Bobby Thomson playing third base. In the ninth inning Irvin reached far into the stands over the head of fans to catch Gil Hodges foul.

The inning before, Thomson made one of the greatest plays ever by a third baseman, so stunning that 55 years later, as remembered on television, it sticks out in the mind even today. Snider doubled off the scoreboard and Robinson tripled into the center field exit gate, Snider scoring. Then, as Roscoe McGowen wrote, Thomson came up with the "killing play."

With Robinson on third and one out, Pafko hit a hard grounder to Thomson, who staggered back, fielded the ball, tagged Robinson trying to slide back to third and then threw to Whitey Lockman in time to nail Pafko. There was no instant replay in those days so there was only one look at the play but, again, it was unforgettable. Thomson was so fast that he was mainly a center fielder. But during a good part of the season, with Mays in center, he proved he could be a great third baseman.

On the 11th the Brooks left for Cincinnati on their last Western tour of the season. Labine opened the series with his third straight outstanding game, this one a 7 to 0 six-hit shutout. Again the lead was back to six, with time seeming to be running out on the Giants now as they split a double-header with the Cardinals.

On the following night what could be seen as a microcosm of what was going wrong for the Dodgers—and right for the Giants—was a hit by Lloyd Merriman, a Cincinnati outfielder whose five-year career batting average was .242. Coming to bat in the seventh inning with an .058 average against the Brooks, he lined a three-run triple off Erskine for Carl's 10th defeat against 15 wins.

The game started well for Brooklyn when they got rid of Ken Raffensberger early, Ken being one of the few left-handers who always gave them trouble. The win went to Ewell Blackwell, who at 15 and 14 was having his last decent season with the sixth-place Reds. For a few years there he was one of the best in the game, a 6-foot-6 sidearmer who drove right-handed hitters off the plate as his "bullwhip" curveball dipped in for strikes. But recurrent arm trouble hit him in '48 and again in '52 and he finally drifted to the Yankees and then his final stop, Kansas City in 1955, the year it entered the American League. The joke around the league at that time was that with players going back and forth, Kansas City remained, in effect, a farm team for the Yankees. Stengel, it was said, could easily get Blackwell back if his arm recovered.

For a prime example of this we need go no further than Ralph Terry, who should have kept uniforms in both clubhouses. Ralph was traded by Kansas City to the Yankees in June of '57 and, needing more seasoning on the major league level, went back to KC in May of '59. Then he pitched for Cleveland for a spell before going back to KC. Now, he'd had his on-the-job training so the Yankees took him back in 1960. For the next five years we was 74 and 55 in New York.

One more example: when George Weiss thought Roger Maris was ready for New York, the Yanks got Maris from Kansas City in exchange for Hank Bauer, Don Larsen, Norm Siebern and Marv Throneberry. Maris had hit .247 and .240 his first two years in Missouri, but then the next year he improved to .273 and was now up to Yankee standards. He hit .283 with 39 homers and 122 RBI his first year at the Stadium. Kansas City had prepared him well. Only under a do-nothing commissioner could this cozy little game have been going on. The other teams screamed at this Maris deal as another New York–Kansas City setup, but the Yankees prevailed, as usual.

On the 15th, Preacher Roe went up against Pittsburgh and won his 20th, 3 to 1 with Pafko driving in the winning runs with a two-run homer. His opposition was Murray Dickson, a terrific knuckleballer. Murray's loss that night put him at 18–14, but he would finish the season a 20-game winner, 20 and 16, for a seventh-place club.

Later in the week Labine won his fourth straight, 6–1 over the Cubs at Wrigley Field. In those 36 innings he gave up just four runs, an ERA of 1.00, thanks to one of the best curve balls in baseball, plus Hubbell-like control. The Brooklyn writers were leading the fans in praise of this rookie, knowing that he was a key to the pennant. Charlie Dressen didn't agree, until it was too late.

As the Giants staggered to a 6–5 win over Cincinnati, the Dodgers lost 7–1 to the Cardinals at St. Louis, bringing their lead down to a dangerous three games. The Brooks were in the game until the sixth, when Branca gave up five runs after a Reese error on what should have been the third out.

The lead increased a bit when Roe shut out the Cardinals 3–0 on the 20th but two days later Dressen benched Labine in a fit of pique after Clem disobeyed an order while pitching. Remember again, this involved a young guy with a 1.00 ERA, and one of the worst men at handling pitchers in the league, as attested to by Clyde King and others.

Clem was facing the Phillies going for his fifth straight win and, although he loaded the bases in the first, had hardly been hit. A bad-hop grounder over Rocky Bridges' head was followed by Ashburn's beating out a bunt. Then Rube Walker threw wildly, trying to pick the runner off second, both runners advancing. Dressen ordered Bill Nicholson walked to set up a double play with Willie Jones at the plate.

On a 2 and 1 count Jones hit a grand slam into Ebbets Field's left field stands. Out came Labine for the next 12 days, or three regular starts. No one off the field could know what was happening when Dressen went to the mound, of course, but we could see on television that Dressen was gesticulating in his angriest manner.

Charlie Dressen, a divisive figure now best remembered for a pitching change he made in 1951. With his Dodgers leading 4–2 in the ninth, the manager brought in Ralph Branca—who then gave up Bobby Thomson's "Shot Heard 'Round the World."

"He wanted me to use a full windup with the bases loaded," Labine explained recently. "I went into a stretch. He took me out and decided that I should sit on the bench, not go to the bullpen, just sit until he wanted me to pitch again."[21] Dressen's ego kept Clem on the bench until the second Giants playoff game.

The next day disaster struck in Boston as Brooklyn lost a double-header while the Giants were beating the Phils 5–1. The 13-game lead was now down to just one, and two in the lost column. In the first game Branca was driven from the mound in the very first inning as the Braves scored six off him and reliever Clyde King. In the second game Boston scored six early again as, in Roscoe McGowen's words, Brooklyn played "sandlot baseball," which included two wild pitches by Erskine.

That was typical honesty from McGowen, a beat writer unafraid to offend, even on a day when the Dodgers had to be edgy and uncertain. Roscoe was a hard-working reporter, rarely scooped, since his start with the *Daily News* in

1922. Seven years later he went to the *Times*, where he worked for the next 29 years, mostly covering the Dodgers. He's the beat writer who in 1934 asked Bill Terry, the Giant manager, how Brooklyn would do that year. Terry's answer: "Is Brooklyn still in the league?"—now legendary since Brooklyn caused his Giants to lose to the Cardinals at the end of that season.

The following day Roe lost his chance to hold his percentage record when the Braves, helped by a hotheaded umpire, took a 4–3 game. Bob Addis and Sam Jethroe had singled in the eighth, bringing the Brooklyn infield in for a play at the plate. Earl Torgeson grounded to Robinson, who threw to Campanella for the out. It was a good throw and, from the perspective of television, seemed an out, but umpire Frank Dascoli signaled safe, bringing Campanella up screaming.

Campy and coach Lavagetto were thrown out of the game and minutes later Dascoli cleared the bench, aided by second base umpire Jocko Conlan. There had to be provocation, of course, but it seemed Dascoli had lost control of himself. To throw out a key player like Campanella and then to clear the bench was unprofessional in a pennant race so close and so near the end.

The Dodgers exploded after the game and a few were fined the usual $50 and $100. They were especially bitter because Reese had doubled in the ninth inning and with one out Campanella would have gone to bat. Instead, Wayne Terwilliger, a .240 hitter, grounded to third. There followed the then famous door-kicking episode, with Robinson blamed for knocking out some panels of the umpire's dressing room door.* The Brooks were now in a first-place tie with the Giants. Two separate wins the next day drove the suspense up a notch.

In a day game at Boston the Giants actually took first place alone when Maglie won his 23rd against six losses, shutting out the Braves 6–0. But Brooklyn came back that evening in Philadelphia as Newcombe also pitched a shutout, 5–0, another of his tight pitching in clutch games.

It was now Sunday, September 30, and in a must-win game Jackie Robinson played the game of his life, a performance so stirring that Roscoe McGowen was at a loss for superlatives. Robinson, he wrote plainly and simply, made the most vital play and hit the most important home run of his career. But it was more than that. Those of us who saw it on television as night began to fall in Philadelphia knew it was the play of a lifetime, one that, in the circumstances, would never be seen again.

The Giants had already won in the afternoon as the Dodgers went into the eighth inning, so they knew on every play that if they lost the game the pennant was gone. As the lights were turned on in the gathering darkness the game was tied at eight in the 12th inning with Newcombe in as Dressen's sixth pitcher. Philadelphia loaded the bases with two out, Waitkus up.

Eddie hit a line shot just to the right of second base for what looked like

---

*Years later losing pitcher Preacher Roe admitted he did the kicking.

the game winner, but Robinson, with a flash of his old college quickness and speed, raced over and dived for the ball, clutching it just before it hit the ground. Umpire Lon Warneke's arm went up and the game went into the 13th inning.

Robinson had hurt his shoulder in diving for Waitkus' liner but, after a timeout and treatment by the team trainer, played through the scoreless 13th inning. He came up in the 14th to face Robin Roberts, who had retired Reese and Snider on pop-ups. On a 1–1 count he hit the ball into the upper left field stands for the 9–8 winning score. Newcombe finished it off, completing five scoreless innings, under the most intense pressure, after having shut out the Phils the day before. Thus, the Dodgers and Giants ended the season in a tie, 96 wins and 58 losses, setting up the first playoff in major league history.

It started the next day, Branca against Jim Hearn at Ebbets Field, with Labine still chained to the bench. Branca pitched a decent enough game but two home runs did him in as he lost 3–1. Brooklyn scored first when Pafko homered in the second inning, but the Giants scored what proved to be the winning run in the fourth when Bobby Thomson, Branca's nemesis, hit a fast ball into the left field seats with Monte Irvin on base. The Giants' insurance run came in the eighth when Irvin hit a Branca slider out. Ralph was always a dollar short in the big ones. In this game he was decent on a day when Hearn was brilliant.

The next day Dressen swallowed his stubborn pride and started Labine, who then pitched the game of his life, a 10–0 shutout in the Polo Grounds. Under overcast skies, the Dodgers simply teed off on three Giants pitchers: Sam Jones, George Spencer and Al Corwin, starting with a Robinson two-run homer in the first inning.

Labine, with the poise of a veteran, held the Giants off as they had five hits in the first four innings. In the third with the bases loaded and two out he struck out Thomson for the most dramatic moment of the game. Labine said later the ball was off the plate and would have been a ball if Bobby hadn't swung. Bobby later agreed.

Brooklyn scored three more in the third on Hodges' homer with two aboard. Then the overcast turned to rain, forcing a 41-minute delay of game. Many pitchers are ineffective after a wait like that, but Labine went through the next four innings smoothly while Pafko and Rube Walker, playing for the injured Campanella, ran the score to 10–0 on their home runs. The rookie, finally given his chance, had shut out the Giants on their home grounds in one of the most important games ever played.

Clem was born in Lincoln, Rhode Island, in 1926 to French Canadian parents, and has lived all his life in the Ocean State. He came to the Dodgers in a lucky move by Chuck Dressen. Labine was in Boston to try out for the Braves but their dressing room was locked, preventing him from changing. Dressen, then a coach with the visiting Dodgers, came along and persuaded him into a Dodger tryout. Soon there was a call and a $500 bonus check in the mail.[22]

His career started in 1946 after he got out of the Army, where he volunteered for the paratroopers and served 2½ years in the European Theater. He reported to Jake Pitler, manager at Newport News, but was sent down to Ashville. For the next four seasons he worked his way through Pueblo and then St. Paul and a brief stop in Brooklyn before making the team in 1951.

His final season was just three games for the Mets in 1962, ending a 13-year career, during which he was 77 and 56 with 96 saves. Those who knew him during his playing days were confident that he was one ballplayer who would not have to worry about a pension, since he was one of the most intelligent and articulate men to ever play the game. After baseball he started designing sports clothes and then became the general manager of the firm that manufactured Deerfoot team jackets in Woonsocket, then a Rhode Island mill town. Now 80, he is an easy and articulate interview and even when answering questions by mail is not shy with the truth.

The weather had cleared overnight for the deciding game, with the magic number now one for both teams. It was Newcombe versus Maglie, the best versus the best.* The Dodgers struck first as Maglie opened the game by walking Reese and Snider, followed by Robinson's run-scoring single. Newcombe then shut out the Giants until the seventh when Irvin doubled, moved up on Whitey Lockman's sacrifice bunt and scored on a Bobby Thomson sacrifice fly.

The Dodgers seemed to have wrapped it up with three runs in the eighth on singles by Reese and Snider, a wild pitch allowing Reese to score and another walk, as Maglie was getting wild. With runners again at first and third, Pafko and Cox singled, two more runs scoring.

Big Don pitched a strong eighth and now needed just three outs for the pennant. By now, though, he was obviously tiring. The fateful ninth began with single by Dark and that's where, as events proved, Dressen probably lost the game, and with it the pennant.

There were none out, a man on first and the Dodgers ahead by 4 to 1. Charlie ordered Hodges to hold Dark on first, Dark who at the time was a meaningless run when you're ahead by three. The space between Robinson and the foul line was now gaping and, sure enough, Mueller lined a single past Hodges to put men on first and third, none out.

If he had been in position, off the bag as Dressen should have left him, the double play would have been automatic, with Gil, one of the best first basemen in the game, easily making the first-to-second-to-first play for two outs. In the light of Thomson's historic homer, this incompetence by Dressen is mostly overlooked, but when you think of the outcome, it turned the game around.

*At this time Maglie was going through one of the best three-year stretches the game has ever known. He arrived back from Mexico in time for the 1950 season and for the next three seasons was 59 and 18.

Mueller's hit put runners on first and third. Irvin popped out, affording some relief to the Dodger Faithful, grateful so see such a dangerous hitter out of the way. But Lockman then followed with a double, scoring one and putting both other runners in scoring position.

Time was called when it was found that Mueller had seemingly broken his ankle sliding into third, an injury that proved to be torn tendons. When the game resumed, Clint Hartung, the much-balleyhooed rookie of some years back, was sent in to run for Mueller. Dressen called time again to relieve Newcombe, whose shoulders now appeared to be sagging.

There was a discussion in the bullpen on whether to go with Erskine, Labine or Branca. Clyde Sukeforth said there wasn't enough time to tape Labine's ankles and that Erskine's curve was sinking into the dirt. Sukeforth recommended Branca, a decision that was said to cost him his job. In truth, Clyde was the scapegoat for Dressen's mistakes. O'Malley was reluctant to fire a first-year manager so the coach had to go, an ideal firing from Walter's point of view, since Sukeforth was the last of the Rickey loyalists still with the team. A lot of us thought he should have picked Labine, taped or not. Labine: young, rubber arm, and he seemed to have Thomson's number, something Branca surely didn't.

Dressen explained his reasoning to Joe King of *The Sporting News*: "I had Erskine and Branca warming up in the bullpen and I asked Sukey which one was throwing better and he told me Branca. That's our usual system and that's how it was." That system, with a catcher as pitching coach, was the cause of many of the team's problems, Erskine said years later.

Sukeforth was the coach out there in the bullpen because Dressen didn't want anyone with true pitching knowledge giving him advice, Erskine told writer Jim Sargent almost 50 years later. Most of Brooklyn's pitching coaches — Sukeforth, Bobby Bragan, Joe Becker — were catchers, he added, who couldn't really help if the problem was in a pitcher's motion, striding or any other mechanical fault.

"They couldn't help a pitcher," Carl said. "The only thing a catcher could tell you was whether your stuff was good when he caught it. Later the Dodgers hired Ted Lyons, a future Hall of Famer, but he got discouraged because Charlie Dressen would rarely talk to him. Dressen didn't want any advice about pitching so he did not accept advice from a pitching coach, and that was typical."[23] Years later, however, Carl considered himself lucky that the catcher Sukeforth was out in the bullpen that sad day in the Polo Grounds. "Whenever I'm asked what my best pitch was, I say: 'The curveball I bounced in the Polo Grounds bullpen.'"[24]

When time resumed, Willie Mays was on deck as Thomson stepped in and took a first-pitch strike. On the second pitch he hit a fast ball, up and in, on a line out toward Pafko in left field. Usually balls headed for the seats out there struck the upper-deck overhang but this was hit so hard it carried into the lower seats, perhaps even rising a bit. It's still hard to tell even today because replay technology didn't exist then. There is always, however, that poignant picture of Pafko looking up as the ball disappears. Then seen scoring are the runners that wouldn't have been on if Dressen had left Hodges alone.

Of one thing there is no doubt: It was a waste pitch, somewhat high and inside. After the game Thomson was quoted by James Dawson of the *Times* as saying: "If I was a good hitter I'd have taken that pitch. It wasn't a good pitch. It was high and inside, the kind they've been getting me out on all season."

So apparently Branca knew what he was doing out there but his pitching mechanics seemingly failed him again. A waste pitch at that time was the right move, but not a waste pitch fastball that was hittable. It simply wasn't high enough or inside enough.

In recent years, however, the possibility has been raised that Ralph's mechanics didn't fail him, that Thomson knew exactly what pitch was coming, moreover, that the Giants, while playing at home, knew exactly what the opposing pitchers were throwing to each of their hitters.

Sal Yvars, a catcher on the Giants for seven years, told me during a telephone interview that it wasn't just a possibility that Thomson knew what was coming, but a certainty. The story originally broke in the *Wall Street Journal* back in early 2001, but surfaced again in August of 2005 when Yvars went on John Vorperian's TV show *Beyond the Game* in White Plains, New York, near where Yvars lives.

According to his story, and whispered comments from others through the years, the Giants pulled off the greatest comeback in history—a 37–7 streak down the stretch—because at every game in the Polo Grounds many of the Giant hitters knew what the opposing pitchers were going to throw them every time at bat. In a telephone interview, Yvars said someone came up with the idea of placing

Bobby Thomson gives it the sweet kiss of success in the clubhouse after hitting the famous homer that won the 1951 pennant for his New York Giants. Was he given help by the Giants' wired signaling system? Yes, according to some teammates.

a spotter with a telescope in Durocher's office in deep center field to relay the catcher's signals to him in the Giant bullpen.

"We had a buzzer system installed between Leo's office and me in the bullpen," Yvars said. "I would sit there holding a baseball, waiting to tell the batter what was coming. Our system was a buzz meant breaking ball, no buzz a fastball. I would hold the ball in my hand if it was a fastball. If I tossed the ball in the air it was a breaking ball. So, our guys were tipped off on every pitch." There is usually a 20-second delay between pitches, he said, so there was plenty of relay time for each sign.

"Have you seen the film of Thomson swinging at Branca's fastball? It was up and in and Bobby leaned into that ball like he never did before. He practically leaped at that ball because he knew what was coming. In fact, we had trouble sometimes by hitting too good. One time Don Mueller hit five home runs in two games. Now Don was a very good hitter but he didn't have that kind of power.* We had to tell Don to take it easy or we'd surely get caught."†

The signs were the key to the Giants' winning that year, Yvars believes. "There was no way we could have won without them," he said. "I mean, we were 13½ games behind a great team in August, and we went on a streak that had never been seen before, or since, for that matter. Without those signs the Dodgers win."

How come Labine shut them out? I asked. "Well, you have to remember Labine had one of the best curveballs around," he said, "and he was a very gutty pitcher. With the kind of curve mixed with the great fastball he had you might know what was coming and still not be able to hit it. And he was at his best that day."

Did Branca know? I asked. "Not at the time but he was told about it later," he answered. "Not long ago I was going to a golf tournament with Ralph from Westchester County where we both live. He asked me why I didn't tell him at the time. I told him that I felt sorry for him when I saw him stretched out on those stairs after the game, that I just didn't have the heart to tell him. Bad enough he lost."

How come you were winning on the road without the signals? I asked. "Those wins at home got us up," he said. "They built up our confidence, made us believe we could make that comeback, could come on to win. The home wins kept us rolling."[25]

Branca told the *Times*' Dave Anderson that he knew for years about the stolen signs but that he never mentioned it to Thomson. "It was a forbidden subject," he said. "Besides, Dressen lost the pennant for us, not that game. He wore our pitching staff out."[26]

**In his 11-year career hit Mueller hit 65 home runs, with 1951, the telescope year, his best at 16.*

†*The Wall Street Journal story (1/31/2001) quotes three Giants as admitting the sign stealing. As for Mueller and his home run streak, he has always "preferred not to comment."*

That picture of Branca's torment is one of the indelible impressions of the game's aftermath, stretched out face down on the clubhouse stairs with his number 13 covered by a sweatshirt, and a shocked-looking Lavagetto smoking a cigarette beside him. Ralph never wore that number again, switching to 12 as the 1952 spring training season began.

Sal Yvars, the Giant who passed on the signals in 1951, in a typical catcher's pose. Yvars was the go-between, taking signs from a spotter with a telescope in center field at the Polo Grounds. He said he would then tip off the batter on what pitch was coming by tossing a ball in the air for a breaking pitch or holding it in his hand for a fastball.

Of course there was pandemonium in the Polo Grounds with Stanky tackling Durocher in joy as Thomson crossed the plate, and Russ Hodges' incessant "The Giants win the pennant! The Giants win the pennant!" over and over again as the Giants fought their way through dancing crowds to the distant clubhouse steps in center field.

Years later, looking dispassionately at the pennant drive, four Durocher moves stand out as prime factors in the Giants' win: moving Lockman to first base, bringing up Willie Mays from Minneapolis, playing Bobby Thomson at third and adding Al Corwin to the pitching staff. All of this with help from the other dugout as Dressen, who often swore he'd never have a "doghouse," stubbornly kept Labine on the bench for those last crucial 12 days.

Of course the stolen signals might have been a huge factor in the Giants' drive. There are doubters, for sure, but Yvars is very believable. He is an articulate and passionate man about his baseball life and would seem to have no reason to make up such a yarn to deliberately tarnish his team and its record. While Thomson is ambivalent and Mueller reticent, there are other players who corroborate the story. According to the *Wall Street Journal*, those who have come forward about the signals are coach Herman Franks, pitchers Al Corwin and Allen Gettel (would an old Newark Bear lie?) and Monte Irvin.

Irvin said the whole team knew, but that he, like some others, did not want to know, some remembering, perhaps, the Medwick beaning and Joe DiMaggio's close call when the signal stealing went awry. About half the team, Corwin said, didn't want to be involved.[27]

It all started, Irvin recalled, during a July 19th meeting when Durocher revealed the scheme, asking each player if he wanted to know the signals. Thus the plan was carried through for the last 10 weeks of the season, against the Dodgers and all others.

The old adage "There is nothing new under the sun" applies here. In the modern era similar schemes were used by the Milwaukee Braves and Chicago White Sox, but they actually go way back to 1898 in Philadelphia. During one game with the Phillies, Cincinnati shortstop Tommy Corcoran got his spikes stuck in the third base coaching box. When he tugged at what he thought was a root, it turned out to be a telegraph wire that ran to the Phillies' clubhouse, where a catcher sat with binoculars, stealing signs and buzzing them to the third base coach.[28]

So it appears that all of those involved, especially the 1951 pennant-winning Giants, owe a tip of the hat to Samuel F.B. Morse, inventor of the telegraph and the Morse code.

Immediately after the Series, Brooklyn fans, in letters to the editor of the *Eagle*, began on Dressen. Their main complaint was about Labine: where was he during those last days and what was the reason for his disappearance until the playoffs? Many of the writers expressed the thought that was eating at the entire Borough: if their hottest pitcher had not been benched there probably would have been no need for a playoff. There were also the complaints that the entire pitching staff, especially Newcombe and a tired Preacher Roe, had to take up the slack left by Labine's enforced absence. It was true. They were, as Branca said, worn out.

This was especially hard on Newcombe, who was viciously maligned as a "choke" against the Giants. Here was a man who down that stretch pitched his arm off. On September 26 he went nine to beat the Braves. On the 30th he went the route again, shutting out the Phillies. The next day he relieved in that Robinson game, going 5 and ⅔ innings to beat the Phils in 14. After pitching 14 and ⅔ innings in two days he went 8 and ⅓ against the Giants before Branca relieved him. This is not choking. This is magnificent pitching and those who didn't realize it were whiners with no knowledge of the game.

Big Don was just that, 6-feet-4 and 220 pounds, born in suburban Madison, New Jersey, in 1926, and later grew up in nearby Elizabeth. As the first great black pitcher in the majors he was subject to some of what Robinson went through, the unjustified "choke" charge, for example. He had been pitching since he was 13, even then big enough to play with the men.

He came to Brooklyn out of the Newark Eagles, one of the stars whose leaving doomed the Negro Leagues. He had a great fastball, excellent control and also became one of the best-hitting pitchers in the league, a career .271 hitter with 15 home runs.

His career ended in Cleveland after 10 years and a 149–90 record, which was respectable but, for a man with Don's talents and size, should have been much better. He had been fading since 1957 and the next year the Dodgers gave up on him. The problem was drinking that he could not control and that finished him at age 31, the only pitcher ever to win the Rookie of the Year, Cy Young and Most Valuable Player awards.

When he conquered the bottle he went back to the Dodgers as a counselor, helping young players avoid alcohol and drugs. He told players of friends who died young because nobody cared, adding, "The Dodgers care, I care. You can come to me."[29]

As has been pointed out, Don's pitching all during September was a key factor in the Dodgers' even making the playoffs. The rest, who would have done what, and what if Labine had been allowed to pitch, is speculation, of course. One thing nobody could argue with: the Giants won 37 of their last 44 games, a drive unequalled in the history of the game. And, being contenders, they did it against the best pitchers the other teams had to throw at them: Spahn, Roberts, Raffensberger, Dickson, Blackwell, Roe, Newcombe and the like. Not even confessions of sign stealing can take anything away from such an incredible team effort.

Lost in the excitement of that effort was the attendance at the Polo Grounds for two of the most crucial games in baseball history. In that first game, Labine's shutout, there were 38,609 paid, and in the finale 34,320. How could the writers have failed to mention that huge park, seating more than 55,000, half empty for both games? Not one gave that lack of attendance the prominence it deserved in their stories and roundups. Thomson's home run, the most historic single feat in all of sports, was hit before a half-empty house. The writers didn't notice, or chose not to notice, but you can bet Horace Stoneham did. After those two games he must have known that his franchise, inherited from his father, was in trouble. Not even two playoff games, against the Dodgers no less, could fill that huge, horseshoe-shaped monstrosity.

The year ended on a sad note for all of baseball. Joe D, the great DiMaggio of the hitting streak, of the destruction of the Red Sox just two years before, of the three-brother baseball family, the man of the song "Joltin' Joe DiMaggio," was retiring.

He was offered the usual $100,000 to play another year, but refused, knowing he didn't have it anymore. *Life* magazine tells why. A report on the Yankees by Dodger scout Andy High, made when the Dodgers expected to make the World Series, evaluates DiMaggio, some of which follows:

Fielding: He can't stop quickly and throw hard. He won't throw on questionable plays, and I would challenge him. *Speed*: He can't run and won't bunt. *Hitting vs. Right-Handed Pitchers*: His reflexes are very slow and he can't pull a fastball. *Versus Left-Handed Pitchers*: Will pull left-hand pitchers a bit more. Don't slow up on him.[30] The report left out one vital fact: Joe D, one of the flawless center fielders in baseball history, got old.

Everybody gets old. Gary Cooper, Captain MacGregor of *Lives of a Bengal Lancer*, got old. Cary Grant, Sergeant Cutter of *Gunga Din*, got old. Clark Gable, Rhett Butler of *Gone With the Wind*, got old. Joel MacRae, the *Foreign Correspondent*, got old. Like them, DiMaggio proved mortal after all.

So, the Yankee Clipper would roam no more. He would be replaced by Mickey Mantle, he of the baleful stare, the superior sneer and the self-abusive lifestyle. And the poor writers had to put up with him, and the drinking that finally killed him, for the next 15 years.

In his retirement he blamed DiMaggio for the damaged knee he suffered in his first season, the knee that hampered him all during his career. "DiMaggio always wanted to look good out there," Mantle told Roger Kahn. "That was important to him. So he waited to call Willie's fly so he could be damn sure he could reach it in stride. That's why I had to stop so short. If DiMaggio called for it earlier, or if he had backed off and let me take it, I don't believe I woulda hurt my knee."[31]

The sequence is impossible to corroborate, based only on Mickey's statement. It also runs counter to conventional outfield play in that the outfielder called off a fly ball simply turns and runs around the play rather than risk injury by stopping short. If he didn't go around Joe it was his fault, not Joe's. Pictures in the newspapers show Mantle sprawled on his stomach as Joe makes the catch. It was Mantle's inexperience that caused the damage.

I saw at first hand the antics of Mickey Mantle and what I saw turned me off from becoming a sportswriter. I was with the *Newark Evening News* doing part-time high school sports on Saturdays in the spring of 1953. Being from Newark and relocated to East Orange, I was assigned the Essex-Union baseball roundup. My third Saturday, Charley Hamberger, on the copy desk, asked me if I'd be interested in joining the sports staff, that Hy Goldberg had asked about who was writing the Essex-Union roundup.

I spoke to Hy with hesitation because I saw myself as a general assignment/feature reporter. There were some sports staff retirements coming up so we agreed that I should go with him to two Yankee day games that weekend. I was to just stand and watch, no questions allowed.

I spent about 30 minutes with Hy in the clubhouse after both games, and was horrified at how Mantle and Billy Martin, with Mickey the ringleader, treated the sportswriters. Others joined in, imitating Mantle and Martin in sneering at men old enough, some of them, to be their grandfathers, making fun of their questions, and generally acting like boors.

It was the young ones who were the villains here. I noticed Bauer, Rizzuto and Berra looking on in silent disapproval. Even Whitey Ford, young as he was and as close as he was to Mantle, did not approve, staying in the background, saying nothing until asked a question.

That Sunday evening while driving back to New Jersey I asked Hy if that sort of thing always went on. "It does, and especially with the Yankees," he replied. " I'm a columnist so I don't have to take it, but I'm not going to lie to you. If you become a sports beat man that's the way it is and Stengel never does anything about it. He's too busy drinking after the game. Beside, he doesn't give a damn."

A week later Paul Horowitz came up to me and asked if I'd like to visit the Dodgers clubhouse before I made up my mind. I remember saying: "Paul, I'm a Dodger fan, and after visiting the Yanks I don't want to know what the Dodgers are like. I'll still root from the stands."

Just recently, Dave Anderson, who covered the Yankees occasionally back then, told me I might have made a mistake, that the Dodger clubhouse was much different, perhaps because they were constant underdogs, not worshipped by the Manhattan press as the Yankees were.

"You have to remember," he said, "the Yankees were a mixture of youth and constant winning. There was an arrogance to that team. It was mainly young. Guys like Mantle and Martin were not mature enough to be able to handle all the winning and the adulation. Anyway, the Yankees have always been arrogant. It goes with New York."

Several things confirm this, including a classic remark made by someone years ago, when we were atop the industrial world: that rooting for the Yankees is like rooting for U.S. Steel. Then there is the experience related by Roger Kahn when, as a young beat writer, he was interviewing Casey Stengel. Raschi and Reynolds got on each side of him and started ringing his shoes with tobacco juice, their way, it turned out, of intimidating a green reporter.

Later he asked Reynolds about such behavior. "We knew who you were and it was nothing personal. We were just making sure you knew who we were."[32] That was, and always has been, the New York Yankees.

I declined the job and have never been sorry, especially since the exodus of the Dodgers and Giants. But I made some lifelong friends in the sports department, especially Hy after he went to work for ABC. We'd have lunch about twice a month on my AT&T expense account and it was like a seminar in sports knowledge on past games and personalities. Much of the background I use for this book comes from my close association with Hy and that fine *Newark Evening News* sports staff.

The writers would soon be sorry this 20-year-old Mickey Mantle replaced Joe, that Joe was gone. Joe D: 13 years a Yankee, three years in the Army and a right-handed hitter condemned to hit into that Grand Canyon called left center field in Yankee Stadium.

Sadly, he would someday be Mr. Marilyn Monroe and then Mr. Coffee.

◆ THREE ◆

1952
Dressen Survives His Mistakes

Months after the Series, during the dead winter days of early 1952, the Labine question was still being asked. Some writers were still furious, especially those from Brooklyn or who covered the Dodgers beat.

The Sporting News led the way, with Joe King using that old trick: quote some non-existent fans to get the point across. For example, as Dressen is bringing in Branca, King has people shouting: "Why not Labine? He was in the bullpen and he fanned Thomson yesterday."

King's fans were merely props for his story but the question was legitimate and still being asked by people all over Brooklyn. And just as legitimate was: why Branca in that ninth inning? People who knew the Branca/Dressen history were wondering about Charlie's sudden faith in Ralph. Back in the mid–1940s when he was a coach with the Yankees, Dressen all but called Branca a "choke" because of his failures in the '46 playoff and in the '47 World Series. Ralph responded, calling Charlie "dreck," Yiddish for garbage, or worse.

And then, during that fateful previous September, Dressen kept handing Branca the ball, even toward the end, after the Braves had driven him from the mound with six runs in the first inning. Still, Charlie gave him the ball to start the playoff and, almost predictably, he lost on a home run to, yes, Bobby Thomson.

Labine recently commented in his hometown paper on that Branca pitch Thomson rocketed over Pafko's head. "On that first pitch [fastball] he got away with one," Labine said, wondering why Branca didn't use his curveball next, instead of the second fastball that ended the game and the pennant race. "I wouldn't give him two fast balls in a row no matter what in that ballpark."[1] Again, if it had been more up and more inside the count would have been 1–1 and who knows what would have happened?

After that dismal performance by Dressen as the '51 season ended, O'Malley signed him anyway, showing that he was still the lawyer and not the baseball man he thought he had become. Rickey was missed but no one on the team or in the front office would dare admit it. With O'Malley replacing him in all baseball decisions, the Montague Street offices were left brainless.

Rickey probably would have signed Charlie because that fatal mistake of benching Labine never would have happened. He was close to the team and would have heard of Labine's absence from the rotation within days, and would have ordered his reinstatement, thereby winning the pennant, no matter what the Giants were doing.

On second thought, though, Rickey could not have prevented Dressen's ordering Hodges to hold the bag. He wouldn't have been in the dugout.

Rickey had been the brains of the Dodgers, not O'Malley, nor Dressen after Rickey left. Charlie, for all his bragging and that "I'll think of something" attitude, was just another manager, and many who have followed the game for years feel that players, not managers, win ball games. The estimates of a manager's effect on team wins has been as low as four games a year, to Solly Hemus' 10 a year when he was manager of the Cardinals.

Tommy Henrich and Bucky Walters, both heady ballplayers respected throughout the game, shared their opinions during a 1956 cocktail party for newsmen in New York. They were both asked what a manager means to a ballclub. Walters: "The main thing he can do is get the most out of his players." What about strategy? someone asked.

Henrich: "I don't think there's much difference between managers as far as strategy is concerned. I've always believed that everybody who wears a major league uniform, except for the young kids and the real few knotheads, knows just about everything there is to know about baseball tactics. The game isn't quite as complicated as some people like to let on."

Walters: "That's a fact. Hell, if this game was half as complicated as some of these writers make out it is, a lot of us boys from the farm would never have been able to make a living at it."[2]

After signing Dressen, O'Malley explained why he had replaced Shotton: window dressing, plus pressure from the *Daily News*. Walter wanted "more color" from his manager, someone who would coach at third and "be seen by the fans," instead of Shotton, who managed in street clothes from the dugout.

He also admitted he had been swayed by the relentless campaign against Shotton by *Daily News* sports columnist Dick Young, author of KOBS, in reality a sarcastic reference standing for Kindly Old Burt Shotton. Shotton had his faults but he didn't have an ego so large that it cost his team a pennant. Dick Young was not popular with many in baseball, but O'Malley never realized this, since he was insulated in a way Rickey never had been.

The team had to start spring training without Don Newcombe, who had been inducted into the Army on February 26. This would leave a hole in the pitching staff, losing its ace with the 20 games he won in '51 and his magnificent pitching in that losing cause. They brought up Joe Black and Johnny Rutherford as replacements and they helped—Black at 15 and 4 with 15 saves, and Rutherford, hampered by injuries, with a 7 and 7 season.

As March was ending, with spring training in full swing, Ty Cobb set the baseball world buzzing with an article in *Life* magazine stating that the modern ballplayer could never compete with those of his generation: the age-old cry of elderly gentlemen that things were better in the old days, when storms were snowier, people were smarter and girls were prettier.

What stung was that Ty got specific, criticizing star players by name. He griped about DiMaggio, Williams, Robinson, Minoso and lesser-knowns like Sam Jethroe. His main thesis: they don't play baseball anymore because "they don't learn the fundamentals, they don't practice, they don't train. Their sole object, encouraged by the lively ball and shortened fences, is to hit home runs."

He singled out DiMaggio and Williams in this vein, accusing both of going for the home run instead of hitting to the opposite field, and then piled on DiMaggio because he never bothered to hunt or fish in the off-season to stay in shape. "Nobody in the major leagues today," he added, "not even Jackie Robinson, Minnie Minoso or Sam Jethroe is a first-class base runner. The old time pitchers and catchers wouldn't have let them steal often."

In his opinion only two players of the modern era, Phil Rizzuto and Stan Musial, would have been able to compete in his day, the early part of the century. "The greatest disgrace in today's baseball," he said, "is that few batters know how to lay down a good bunt. Most of them don't even try."[3] It is true that Rizzuto was one of the best bunters ever to play the game, but does that put him in a class above a Joe DiMaggio or a Ted Williams? Ty as a ballplayer was surely great, but always a little off center in his rages and fights.

Ty was diagnosed over the years by psychiatrists, from afar, who agreed that he was psychotic, with a personality disorder that made him genuinely antisocial. Many attributed his problems to the fact that his mother shot his father dead one night when he was coming through their bedroom window. She was found not guilty on her claim that she thought he was a burglar. Town speculation, however, was that he suspected her of being unfaithful and was sneaking home to check on her. Cobb was said to have never gotten over it.

Arthur Daley in his *Times* column quoted Eddie Lopat, among many others, as being furious at Cobb for "having the supreme gall to rap us. I'll bet he wouldn't steal 96 bases today." Jimmy Dykes predictably defended his generation, as the vast majority of those from another age often do. "Yes he could," he said to Lopat. "He'd steal more. He was the best." Daley wrote that Cobb's main fallacy was in comparing two very different eras, that of the strategy built around the dead ball and, with the coming of Ruth, the free-swinging home run style the Babe brought about.

Rogers Hornsby, then manager of the Cincinnati Reds, bided his time but then came back at Cobb with an article "It's Still Baseball, Cobb" in *Look* magazine. His rebuttals were succinct and telling. Williams and DiMaggio, he said, know their fans come out to see them hit the long ball, not singles to the opposite field. "Williams and DiMaggio," he pointed out, "make $100,000 a year for hitting the long ball. Billy Goodman of the Red Sox is a fine hitter who hits singles and doubles. He makes $20,000 a year."

The long ball rules when it comes to base running, he said in defense of Robinson and the rest. "Today base runners don't steal as much as the old-timers because they don't get the opportunities from their managers. Managers today play for the big inning." He then got personal, calling Cobb "supremely selfish," worrying more about his own accomplishments than his team's.

As the coup de grace to Cobb's immense ego, he said "DiMaggio over Cobb would be the choice of any manager interested in winning pennants and not individual batting championships. I still say all, or almost all, of those [Yankee] pennants couldn't have been won without DiMaggio."[4]

On April 2nd, anyone with common sense would have said the Marines did a terrible injustice to Ted Williams and Jerry Coleman by calling them back for more service. Baseball's wise men were predicting the end of Ted's career as, at 34, he was recalled for Korean War service. He did some two years as a fighter pilot, one time almost killed as he was forced to crash land a flaming plane. The injustice: Ted had already served three years as a Marine pilot instructor during World War II. And again, he was 34 years old and a family man.

The same for Coleman, and even more. At 27 he should have been immune if only for his record during the big war. Jerry, a Marine fighter pilot, was in for four years, fighting from the Solomons campaign to the Phillipines, including 57 missions as a dive bomber pilot. Jerry had enlisted in the Marines when he was 18. Now they took him again, even though he and his wife had one daughter and were expecting another child. But through it all neither Ted nor Jerry had one word of criticism about going back in.

The day after that injustice, the Giants suffered a serious blow to their hopes of repeating as pennant winners when Monte Irvin suffered a broken ankle while sliding into third base in an exhibition game in Denver. A usually faultless baserunner, he hooked one of his spikes on the bag, causing a compound fracture and dislocation of the right ankle.

The medical report said the bones were in "good condition" but doctors predicted that Monte would be out for some two months, most of the time with his leg in a cast. They were right, since he was able to play in only 46 games during the entire season, severely hurting their chances to repeat as champions. The Giants knew there was really no way to replace him, since he led the National League in RBI with 121 in 1951. Some expected Clint Hartung to fill in but the Giants gave up on Clint the following week, sending him down to Minneapolis on waivers after no team claimed him.

The Brooks opened the season in Boston, beating Warren Spahn 3–2 with

Roe pitching a three-hitter. The only long ball was Sam Jethroe's homer in the third inning. This would be Sam's last full season in the majors, to the surprise of a lot of people. Sam was a terrific centerfielder, fast and sure-handed. He was only up for three years, during which he led the league in stolen bases twice. But his average went from .280 down to .232 when he was traded to Pittsburgh. The suspicion here is that Sam, whose baseball age was listed as 34, was older than that. Remember, in his day it was far more difficult for a black man to make the majors, so it's understandable that a lot of them shaved off a few years. Robinson, like Monte Irvin, was one of those who couldn't do this because there were college transcripts and Army records available.

The Giants came into Ebbets Field the next day, the 19th, and were in the 14th inning tied 6–6 when Pafko hit his second home run of the day, what today would be called a walkoff, this one a homer over the scoreboard. In his column Red Smith cited a surprising statistic supplied by Dodger statistician Allan Roth: in 52 years in the National League, the Dodgers that day won their 3,928th game against 3,928 losses—.500 ball over half a century.

After more than five years' silence, former baseball commissioner Albert Chandler held a news conference April 29th to explain why he banned Leo Durocher for a year while he was Dodger manager. "I wanted to protect him. I had to keep him from killing somebody," Chandler said. "In 1947 he was in such a mood that no one knew what he would attempt to do next. I was vilified at the time, but I think Durocher will be the first to tell me that the suspension made him a credit to baseball rather than a detriment."

Chandler went on to relate Durocher's constant association with known gamblers and his slugging (with a blackjack) of a fan under the stands at Ebbets Field in 1945 for "taunting and insulting remarks that he made" as the two basic reasons for the banishments. "I was afraid that at any moment there might be a far more serious incident."[5] Chandler was well aware that although Durocher was acquitted in less than half an hour by a star-struck jury, in the civil case involved he paid out $6,750 to his victim, John Christian, a medically discharged veteran.

The second week in May, O'Malley brought the double-header back to Ebbets Field and drew a full house, 31,777 to the twi-nighter. The baseball wasn't a success, however, with Robin Roberts and Karl Drews taking both games to knock the Brooks out of first place. The two-game idea didn't last and didn't spread, the Lords of Baseball not liking two games for the price of one.

The Dodgers were slumping on the 21st when Cincinnati came into Ebbets Field for one of the wildest, most one-sided games since Abner Doubleday. At the start of a 19–1 thumping, 21 Dodgers went to the plate in the first inning, scoring a record-setting 15 runs, 12 after two were out. No one could stop them, not Blackwell, Bud Byerly, Herm Wehmeier, Frank Smith nor Joe Nuxhall.

The batting was so unreal that the pitcher, Chris Van Cuyk, got four hits and scored three times. Only Rocky Bridges and Hodges failed to hit as Van Cuyk pitched one of the few complete games in his brief career. The 21 who went to bat in that first inning broke the record of 14 held jointly by the 1922 Cubs and the '48 Red Sox.

The owners were fearful again in mid–May as they awaited the report of Rep. Emanuel Celler's House subcommittee studying antitrust violations and baseball's reserve clause. On May 23 they breathed a sigh when reading that the committee, after 10 months of study and millions in expenses, decided to do nothing, ruling that baseball needed some kind of reserve clause, and advising owners to solve their own antitrust problems.

The committee was wary of tampering with the clause because it feared that its removal would benefit clubs in the major markets, those who would be able to outbid smaller cities for the service of star players. This is exactly what has been happening since the clause was outlawed: The Yankees and Red Sox, for example, can always outbid clubs like Kansas City and Minnesota.

"Baseball's history shows that chaotic conditions prevailed when there was no reserve clause," the report stated. "Experience points to no feasible substitute to protect the integrity of the game or to guarantee a comparatively even competitive struggle."[6] That committee was far-seeing, predicting today's situation when Yankee fans and writers, for example, start whining when their team goes four whole years without winning a World Series.

Thus the owners stumbled along depending on a clause that everybody knew was weak, as the Gardella case and bribery proved. The owners needed a Marvin Miller to help plan the game's future, but they didn't have the collective wisdom to hire such a labor expert. As we know, the players hired him and he subsequently helped destroy the owners' antitrust immunity. As a result, the day would come when the players would control the game, play where they want and draw salaries undreamed by the likes of DiMaggio and Williams.

The Cardinals, probably egged on by Eddy Stanky, started up again with Robinson in early June, resorting to racial slurs at Jackie, and now a new victim, Joe Black. They were angry because the Dodgers came from behind in the last two innings to beat them 6–2, upping their league lead over the Giants to five games. Joe Black took over in the eighth for his second win.

Since he had left the Dodgers for the Giants in 1950, Stanky made Robinson a target for racist taunts, sometimes directly, sometimes through his team. He often hid behind his players because everyone knew that at 5-foot-6* (his real height) he wouldn't stand a chance if Jackie came after him.

It all ended quickly and peacefully for a change when the next night

---

*For years I have not trusted team bios. I was out of the Navy four days in 1946 when I went to a day game at Ebbets Field. Coming up out of the subway I saw this little bow-legged guy in front of me, Stanky sure enough, taking the subway, common for ballplayers in those days. I was 5-foot-8 at the time, Eddie's listed height, and I was looking down at him. He may even have been 5-foot-5 or so.

Robinson went up to Cardinal owner Fred Saigh's box saying that "he was sorry the whole thing came about," as though it was his fault. Saigh had previously said he knew nothing of the matter but that if what was told him was true he'd "throw him off the team," whoever he was. Yeah.

O'Malley expressed outrage the next day saying his players "should be protected against such insults." Saigh apologized personally to Robinson even though he said that from his box he heard nothing unpleasant. Stanky, as usual, "didn't hear a thing. Of course there was the usual jockeying but that was just routine." Yeah.

Rogers Hornsby—nasty, outspoken, martinet Rogers Hornsby—was fired on the 11th as manager of the St. Louis Browns, replaced by Marty Marion. Owner Bill Veeck told the writers that Hornsby doesn't "consider players people, just things to be manipulated." Veeck had called Rogers some days before the firing to tell him to protest an umpire's decision. "Nobody's going to tell me how to run my ballclub on the field," Hornsby told the press before leaving for his home in Chicago.

The Browns later presented Veeck with a 24-inch silver trophy engraved with: "To Bill Veeck for the greatest play since the Emancipation Proclamation." Hornsby was certainly a difficult man to get along with—documented by many players down through the years—but the presentation seemed a bit much, something, as Red Smith wrote, "only small men could have thought it up."

Carl Erskine took the mound at Ebbets Field June 19 and pitched a no-hitter against the Chicago Cubs, an almost perfect game marred only by a walk to the pitcher, Willard Ramsdell, in the third inning. He had to wait out a 41-minute rainstorm before getting his sixth win against one loss. Time of game, not counting the rain delay: 1 hour 48 minutes, an unheard-of time today.

At the end of June, Satchel Paige was named to the All-Star team, fulfilling, as he said, one of the dreams of his life. At the age of 42, so he said, he had made the major leagues with the Cleveland Indians, much too late, as his fellow Negro League teammates always maintained, to be appreciated for the great pitcher he was.* But even late in life, as everyone knew, he was a star for the Indians, a 12–10 pitcher with a 3.10 ERA. Making the All-Stars, he said, completed his major league ambitions: first, make the majors; second, pitch in a World Series; and then be one of the Stars.

Satch didn't get to pitch in Philadelphia that day because the field was already sodden by game time, and the game was called because of rain after five innings The Nationals won their third straight, this time by a 3–2 score on a solo homer by Robinson off Vic Raschi and one with a man on by Hank Sauer off Bob Lemon.

---

*There could another side to that. The Cleveland Indians owner who eventually signed Paige said he had tried to sign him much earlier, but that Satchel wouldn't consider it because he was making so much money barnstorming.

A week after the All-Star game Jimmy Piersall started his slow slide into madness. He was only 22 and had been sent by the Red Sox down to the Birmingham Barons for more experience. His truly erratic behavior began in the second inning of a game against Atlanta when he used a water gun to spray home plate in celebration of a home run by Milt Bolling.

In the same inning he was called out on strikes and protested so vigorously that he was thrown out of the game, his fourth ejection in two weeks. He then climbed to the stadium's grandstand roof, where he continued to heckle umpire Neil Strocchia. In 1957 Jimmy was the subject of the movie *Fear Strikes Out* starring Tony Perkins as the outfielder under treatment in an asylum, and Karl Malden as his psychiatrist. He recovered and continued his 17-year career with the Red Sox, but was at times zany, as when with the Mets he hit his 100th home run and ran the bases backwards.

The Dodgers won a sweet one against Cincinnati toward the end of July. Tied 2–2 with the Reds going into the 10th, Joe Black gave up four runs in the top of the inning. Brooklyn came back with five, the winner coming in when Blackwell hit Rube Walker in the arm with the bases loaded. Blackwell, victim of sporadic arm trouble since leading the league in wins and complete games in 1947, was almost through, one of the great pitchers of the 1940s suffering his 10th loss against two wins.

The first week in August the Brooks went into the Polo Grounds for a night game that turned out to be one of the most agonizing a Dodger fan ever had to sit through. The 15-inning game took 4 hours 59 minutes and ended at 1:31 in the morning before what had started as 43,373 paid attendance.

Ordinarily, a ballpark would be half empty by that time, but the game was so well played and tense that the vast majority hung on till the end. After a grand slam by Hodges in the sixth the Giants tied it up when George Wilson hit a home run batting for Jim Hearn in the seventh. The game then went six scoreless innings until Brooklyn scored on a Pafko sacrifice fly in the top half of the 14th. The Giants came right back with another pinch-hit home run, this one by Bob Elliot batting for George Spencer.

The Brooks went ahead again on an unearned run in the top of the 15th, but then were done in by some freak baseball in the Giant half, with Chris Van Cuyk pitching. After a one-out double by Bobby Hofman, Robinson bobbled a Dusty Rhodes grounder, putting men on first and third. Bobby Thomson then drove in the tying run with a single to left, tying the score. With Monte Kennedy running for Hofman, Don Mueller hit a fluky chop single that hit the front of the plate and soared so high that Van Cuyk, 6-feet-6, could not catch it in time to get Mueller as Rhodes scored the winning run. As all of us Dodger fans left the park the memories of the previous autumn—the Giants' tremendous comeback, the Thomson homer and resultant pandemonium—came rushing to mind. A chopper off the plate cut the Dodger lead over the Giants to 5½ games. Those who were with me driving home said later that I didn't say a single word all the way from the Polo Grounds to East Orange, a suburb above Newark.

The next evening Satchel Paige, who seemed to be truly ageless, pitched a 12-inning shutout against the Tigers' Virgil Trucks, winning 1–0 on a bases-loaded single. When he was first signed back in 1948 Paige gave his age as 39 but his mother told the Associated Press that he was actually 44, which would have made him fairly close to 50 when he went those 12 innings. And there were a number of people, his mother notwithstanding, who felt he was much older.

Ebbets Field, always a magnet for many visitors to New York, hosted the 17-year-old King of Iraq, Faisal II. According to the *Times'* page-one story he was the guest of O'Malley and when he smiled warmly as Bobby Thomson hit one for the Giants, Walter answered the smile with a pained expression before explaining the Thomson home run of the previous autumn.

The king replied, "Maktoob" (It is written). It was his first baseball game, and when Durocher charged the home plate umpire after a call, screaming so that could be heard all over the park, the king asked, "What is he shouting about?"—a question us native-borns had been asking for years.

Edmundo "Sandy" Amoros, a key figure in the Dodgers' future, arrived from St. Paul on the 21st as Chris Van Cuyk was sent down. It's hard to imagine now that the likes of Billy Herman were comparing Sandy to Pete Reiser and Willie Mays. He was fast, that's for sure, and played outstanding ball in the minors, but those comparisons for a 19-year-old out

Edmundo (Sandy) Amoros, highly-touted rookie out of Cuba, never lived up to his early promise, but paid off later as one of the key players in the Dodgers' first winning World Series. His speed and right-hand glove enabled him to catch Berra's fly to deep left and then turn it into a double play, killing a late-inning Yankee rally.

of Cuba were made, perhaps, for trade purposes. Another Reiser? Another Mays? For one thing, Sandy at 5-foot-7 and 170 was too small for really consistent power.* His speed, however, at times made him invaluable, even though he was only a .255 career hitter.

Brooklyn closed out August with a 9–1 win over the Giants, mainly on another Hodges grand slam, giving the 22-year-old Billy Loes his 13th victory of the year. Their lead was comfortable—nine over the Giants and 12 over St. Louis—but there were those lingering doubts. Those playoffs, after all, were fewer than 12 months before.

Sure enough, the Dodgers went on a losing streak and by September 6th—in just a week—the lead was down to four after Jim Hearn and Bill Connelly took a double-header at the Polo Grounds. The writers got out their '51 clippings, a few predicting another Dodgers collapse against the "charging" Giants.

It looked like it for a while as the lead dropped to three on the 14th—nine full games in just two weeks. On that day the Giants took Cincinnati 3–2 while Brooklyn, on their home grounds, lost to Stu Miller of the Cardinals. Three games was the smallest Brooklyn lead since the 4th of July. By this time the Dodgers were having pitching problems, making for an even more panicky situation. They tried Kenny Lehman against Miller but he was bounced out early and soon back in St. Paul.

But the writers soon put away their year-old clips, for on the very next day the Dodgers started proving, against the best pitchers in the league, that this was another year. After beating Cincinnati 11–5 on five home runs they went up to Boston to face Max Surkont, Warren Spahn and Jim Wilson.

It was a three-game sweep, assuring them as they headed home of at least a tie for the pennant. Surkont lost the opener 4–2 when he wild-pitched Campanella home with the winning run in the eighth inning. The umpires, realizing the importance of the game, kept it going through three rain delays and often driving rain during play.

The second game was a classic 1–0, 10-inning win by Erskine over Spahn. Warren wasn't having a good year in wins, for the Braves were down in seventh place, way below .500. This superb performance, however, brought his ERA below 3.00 to 2.98, good on any team. Both he and Erskine went all 10 innings, with the lone run off Spahn the result of Robinson's fourth hit, scoring Cox from second.

Joe Black, making his first big-league start, also pitched a three-hitter the next day, beating Jim Wilson 4–2. It was Joe's 15th win against four losses, his one great year before Dressen started tinkering with his deliveries. His

---

*Not that lack of height means lack of power. Hack Wilson, and others, was around 5-foot-6 but he usually weighed between 190 and 200 pounds. Mel Ott, for another, was a slight man at 5-foot-9, 170, but as a strict pull hitter was aided immensely by that short right field line in the Polo Grounds.

ERA was 2.15 and would certainly have taken the league leadership if he had been able to get in 154 innings. But he took the Brooks home knowing they could win the pennant in the next few days.

The Yankees were also in a tight pennant race that day as the Cleveland Indians closed to within one game of them by beating Detroit 6–3 behind Early Wynn. It was Early's 23rd victory, bringing the totals of that superb trio that won the '54 pennant — Wynn, Mike Garcia and Bob Lemon — to 77 wins against 34 losses.

Johnny Rutherford, the future doctor, clinched it for Brooklyn two days later, September 23, against the Phillies at Ebbets Field in the first game of a twi-night double-header. Johnny survived a grand slam by Granny Hamner in the third but pitched shutout ball the rest of the way to win 5–4 as his team came from behind against Karl Drews. The Dodgers had scored in the first inning when Snider walked and Robinson doubled him home. Shuba, filling in for the injured Furillo, hit one over the scoreboard in the fifth for the second run. The winning three runs came in the next inning.

Hodges singled, Rutherford was safe on an error but Cox bunted to Drews, who forced Hodges at third. With the two on, Reese singled to center, scoring Rutherford. Snider cleared the bases with a long double off the right field wall for the winning runs. The second game was a 1–0 Phillies win but nobody cared.

It was the sixth pennant in modern Brooklyn history and the crowd was restless during that second game, waiting for celebration time. So it went 12 innings, building the impatience of the 24,408 paid. Then came the bells, foghorns and general hysteria as all the Brooks descended on Rutherford while the crowd kept cheering wildly, forgetting the disappointments of the last year and the year before.

It was a supreme moment of glory for Johnny and it was his last. He was a pitcher of great promise, his 7–7 record being the result of injuries most of the year, some that could be attributed to Dressen's handling of the bullpen staff. He thinks his greatest mistake was agreeing to be long man in the bullpen.

"As the long man with a nervous manager you warm up a lot but don't get in the game that often and it wears you out," he said, echoing the complaint of Clyde King, whose arm went dead in '51 from the same unnecessary overuse. "After I pitched the pennant winner in '52 I went to spring training the next year and told Dressen my arm was hurting again. Instead of taking me on to Brooklyn with the team he shipped me out. I found I had a ruptured rotator cuff, so after trying for three years I quit and went to medical school."

The Rutherford story around Ebbets Field in those days, though untrue, was much more dramatic than that. The word was that Johnny quit right after the '52 Series and that no amount of persuasion by the Dodgers would sway him from med school. Some of us smelled a Hollywood touch there, a bright and talented young man turning his back on major league glamor to struggle through medical school. Of course Johnny would naturally give it another shot after Dressen sent him down. He knew with his brains and background he still had time for med school.

In his opinion the size of the Brooklyn organization with its more than 600 players was the problem with many pitchers, not the size of the park. "If a pitcher couldn't pitch he was shipped out rather than treated, left to recover or not on his own." That, as we will see, is the reason Carl Erskine kept quiet about his sore arm all during his career. Johnny let his problems be known to an impatient Dressen who, he said, "was of the old school and not very resourceful."[7]

Clem Labine remembered Johnny as a pitcher who had it all. "He was only with us that one year and had a number of injuries that raised his earned run average," he said. "But with all his stuff he would have had a bright future if his arm had recovered."[8]

Before the Series started *The Sporting News* announced the results of its poll of players and managers to pick the Rookie of the Year. In the National League it was Joe Black, a shade ahead of the Giants' Hoyt Wilhelm. Their records were close enough that either could have won, but Black was chosen because without him the Dodgers could never have won the pennant. Joe was 15–4 with a 2.15 ERA and Hoyt 15–3 and 2.43. Other close contenders were pitchers Wilmer Mizell and Stu Miller of the Cardinals and Pirate shortstop Dick Groat.

Looking back over the season, Black led a bullpen that was the most prolific in the game that year, one that recorded a record 38 wins: 14 by Black as a reliever, five from Labine and five from Loes, among others. The three also had 24 saves, led by Black with 15. The team as a whole won the pennant by their play against the second division, particularly Cincinnati, Boston and Pittsburgh, winning 54 out of 65 games against those three.

Luck and the U.S. Army also played a part. The Giants finished only 4½ games back without Willie Mays, who was drafted, and for most of the season without Monte Irvin, a terrific hitter and the National League's RBI leader, out until late summer with that ankle he broke sliding into third base in the exhibition season. Durocher was platooning 36-year-old Bob Elliot and shuttling Bobby Thomson and Hank Thompson between center and third. They didn't quite make it but they were what the Victorians would have called "a gallant crew."

In the American League Rookie honors, Browns catcher Clint Courtney, famous later for his fights with Billy Martin, was chosen over Sammy White, catcher for the Red Sox. Courtney hit .283 and White .281. With averages that close many thought White should have been chosen for, although both teams were in the second division, Boston was a much better club and faced tougher pitching.

Just before the Series, George Blaeholder was finally given some recognition for his discovery of the slider, a pitch that along with the curveball has baffled major league hitters and driven many a rookie back to the minors since Blaeholder first threw it in 1928. Back during the war Bob Feller credited the pitch to George but in the rush of battle news and stateside wartime emergencies he was ignored.

In a column by George Cobbledick, sports editor of the *Cleveland Plain Dealer*, Blaeholder was described as a "good-natured Californian" generous with his discovery. "He taught the slider to other members of his team, and through trades and conversation it soon spread throughout the majors," Cobbledick wrote. At the time Blaeholder was 24 and one of the better pitchers in his league. Batters were soon complaining that "every fast ball he throws is a curve."[9] His 104–125 record over 12 years is deceptive in that he pitched for more than eight years with a team that was never in contention. There should be some kind of recognition, a niche somewhere near the players' plaques in the Hall of Fame, for a man who discovered a pitch that has so affected the game.

The slider is often called the nickel curve, since it breaks at the very last moment, throwing the hitter off. There are a hundred versions of why a ball curves, for me going back to Newark's Central High School when Mr. Bernstein, our general science teacher, told us that the side of the ball's rotation draws air from the other side, causing a spin that becomes a curve. I lost some faith in this later, since Mr. Bernstein's two immutable rules, that the atom could not be split nor could matter be created or destroyed, proved to be false. However, of all the theories I've heard, Mr. Bernstein's is as good as any. Whatever its scientific explanation, it is a pitch that has sent many rookies packing, as in Ring Lardner's *You Know Me Al,* the "busher" writes home: "See you soon Ma. They're starting to curve me."

Of all the theories, the one that drew hoots from all over the baseball world was a *Life* article in September of 1941 "proving" that a baseball could not be made to curve. Yankee Vernon Gomez, the always clever Lefty, spoke for his fellow pitchers when he moaned: "Here I am trying to make a comeback and they tell me my best pitch is an optical illusion."[10]

Of course they all knew the ball curved, just as they knew the difference between it and the slider. As the pitcher throws the curve the spin slows it up as it reaches the plate. The slider is thrown with velocity, just like a fastball, but its late dip or swerve often causes foul tips and strikeouts as the batter realizes too late that he has been fooled, as Blaeholder's opponents complained that "every fast ball he throws is a curve."

The Yankees clinched their fourth straight pennant on Friday, September 26, when Johnny Sain, relieving Eddie Lopat, won his 11th game, 5–2, beating Harry Byrd, Philadelphia's fast-balling rookie. Billie Martin drove in the winning run in the eleventh inning. As Yogi Berra crossed the plate there wasn't much excitement in Shibe Park except for those fans who came down from New York. The team celebration started and, of course, continued in the clubhouse, but the shouting and horseplay seemed forced and the pictures staged. Blasé after four in a row, and hated by underdog lovers throughout the country.

To no one's surprise, Joe Black, the best reliever in baseball that year, was named to start the World Series. On October 1st a paid figure of 34,861 jammed Ebbets Field, one of the largest crowds in that small park's history. Black was facing Allie Reynolds, at 20 and 8 the Yankees' only 20-game winner.

Joe, 28 and from nearby Plainfield, N.J., was a gamble by Dressen, for although he had a sensational year as a reliever this was only the third start of his career. It paid off as Joe went all the way for a victory that was the first time the Dodgers had ever won the first game of a Series—six of them, dating back to 1916.

He gave up six hits in outpitching Reynolds 4 to 2 as Allie went seven innings before giving way to Ray Scarborough. Joe was backed by home runs by Robinson, Reese and Snider. John Drebinger wrote that from tavern to tavern in Brooklyn went the cry, "This is the year." As the joke says, not so fast, Robinson.

The Yanks evened it up the next day as they banged Erskine and Loes around in a 7 to 1 win for Vic Raschi. Vic pitched a three-hitter, all in the third inning, and was so in control that the game was, in essence, over after Billy Martin's three-run homer during the five-run seventh inning. Raschi was one of the best money pitchers of all time and, the war aside, has the highest win percentage in Yankee history, 132 and 66, a .667 total.

The official Yankee leader, as proclaimed by their media relations people, is Spud Chandler at 109 and 43 (.717), but Spud pitched through the war and between 1942 and 1945 was 38 and 10. There is no comparing wartime ball and the caliber teams Raschi pitched against during his eight years as a Yankee.*

The Series moved to Yankee Stadium the next day and the Preacher came through with a 5 to 3 win in that big park, ideal for his slow curves and spitters. The only real shots off him were homers by Berra and Mize, Johnny's as a pinch-hitter in the ninth when it was too late. Eddie Lopat went 8 and ⅓, relieved by Tom Gorman. Roe said later his pitch to Berra was high, "just where I wanted it." Roe and Newcombe, among others, were learning there was no way to pitch to the man. The Yankees, like many other teams, knew Roe was throwing the spitter, as he revealed years later, but could never catch him at it. Teammates like Reese helped by rubbing up the ball at opportune moments, like when the umpire asked to see it.

---

*Raschi was 13 and 6 in 1953 and asked by George Weiss to take a pay cut. He refused and was traded to the St. Louis Cardinals for $85,000. That 13 and 6 on many clubs would call for a raise but not from "Lonesome" George.

The Dodgers' winning runs came in the top of the ninth when singles by Reese and Robinson drove Lopat out. Then with Gorman pitching they pulled a double steal, winding up on second and third. The critical pitch, with Pafko up, was a passed ball by Berra, allowing Reese and Robinson to score the winning runs.

Preach said after the game that he was "wild, really wild. My curve either broke six feet or six inches and I couldn't get it over the plate." That occasional spitter he threw was often off the plate but it was one of his most useful tools. Like Lew Burdette, he used it enough to keep the hitter guessing. After he retired he publicly admitted he threw the spitter to keep the hitters off balance, but he also referred to it as his money pitch.

Reynolds and Black faced each other the next day and Allie got his revenge for the first-game loss. He threw a four-hit, 2–0 shutout and had to be that good, for Black in eight innings also pitched a four-hitter but one was a fourth-inning home run by Big John Mize. The other came off Rutherford in the eighth on a triple by Mantle and an error by Reese. Reynolds by now was truly a nine-inning pitcher. He was often ridiculed in the late '40s as writers would quip that the day's battery would be Reynolds/Page, since Allie was relieved by Joe so many times. But that was Stengel, really. Casey was apt to go to the bullpen when he had Page, an all-time great when off the bottle.

Although the next day's game was a 6 to 5 win, a not impressive score, it was one of the gutsiest games ever by a Brooklyn pitcher—or by any standard, any pitcher. Carl Erskine was ahead 4 to 0 in the fifth inning when the Yankees scored five times, three on a Mize homer with two on.

Ewell Blackwell had started for the Yanks, a Stengel hunch that didn't work out. When Sain relieved him in the sixth inning he had given up four runs, but the Yanks were still up by one after Mize's homer. Many pitchers would have been discouraged at that point but with Dressen sticking with him Carl "bowed his head," as pitchers used to say, and held the Yanks scoreless until the eleventh, when Snider's single drove in the winning run. On the way, terrific catches by Pafko and Furillo, both preventing home runs, helped save the game for Erskine.

Only a few of his teammates knew what Erskine was going through, what he went through practically every game he pitched as a Dodger. In answer to a series of questions I put to him he referred to the injury, saying that in pitching to Bill Nicholson back in '48 he pulled a muscle and never got over it. "It was my first start and I was pitching in the rain. It dogged me for twelve seasons and to this day I have never gotten rid of that problem in the back of my shoulder." Things got worse in his next start when the muscle pulled away from his right shoulder bone, starting a scarring in the area of the tear. He was ambivalent about the park's effect on his pitching. "Ebbets Field was so small it was a tough park to pitch in. But the Dodgers scored a lot of runs there so I had my best games there."[11]

He was usually able to pitch around the injury, he told writer Jim Sargent recently. "Some days I couldn't get loose but I took my turn anyway. The trainers, the front office people, the managers, I don't think any of them ever had a clue what I was battling. I didn't say much. The Dodgers had a bunch of pitchers, hard-throwing young guys in the minors. When you faltered you're gone. I never wanted to be known as a sore-armed pitcher so I gutted it out. And I'm not the only guy who's ever done that."[12] Twelve years as a major league pitcher with a 122–78 record, all that time with a sore shoulder. Through it all Carl was a terrific curve ball pitcher and had a good fast ball even after the shoulder injury. He left the game with that 122–78 record and an ERA of 4.00, not bad for a sore-armed guy pitching mostly in Ebbets Field.

Carl Erskine, one of the most remarkable pitchers in Dodgers history, pitched an almost perfect game in his first no-hitter. He worked 12 years with a sore shoulder suffered as a rookie, an injury he covered up for fear of being shipped out to make way for a healthy young arm down in Montreal. He covered it up well in compiling a 122–78 record.

Carl was a small-town boy all his life until he got to Brooklyn. Born in 1926 in Anderson, Indiana, he went into the banking business there after baseball, eventually becoming vice president of the local bank. During his 12-year career with the Dodgers he was always articulate and cooperative, friendly to the fans and helpful to the beat writers. But what many of us find strange, even now so many years later, is his posing for a publicity shot with the wrecking ball as it started demolishing Ebbets Field in 1960.

He had put the Dodgers up 3–2 in the Series and as they headed back to their home park they needed just one of the final two games for Brooklyn's first World Series in its history. Vic Raschi, Eddie Lopat, Allie Reynolds and Bob Kuzava stood in their way. *Bob Kuzava?*

The sixth game was a 3 to 2 Raschi win that featured excellent pitching and four home runs, two by Snider and one each by Berra and Mantle. But for a balk by Billy Loes the game would have gone into the 10th inning tied. But Billy looked somewhat unnerved in the seventh after Berra's home run. He balked a runner to second base and then Raschi's hit up the middle went for a single that scored the winning run. Thus, Snider's second home run went to waste.

After their deadline pressure let up, the writers interviewed Loes, who told them he lost Raschi's drive in the sun. This brought almost universal derision, mostly from those who didn't know what they were making fun of or what they were talking about. Of course he lost it in the sun, and through no fault of his own. Anyone who has played the infield in a roofed grandstand knows about the sun, when the shadow creeps across the diamond until it is halfway between home plate and the mound. The ball comes out of that shadow into bright sunlight in a blinding fashion, easy to lose sight of.

Part of the derision was that Loes was what ballplayers then called a flake, good newspaper copy but a little off. He often said he'd rather be hanging on the corner with his Long Island buddies than pitching in the major leagues. He also used to say that he didn't want to win 20 games in a year because "afterwards they'd always expect you to." Billy was known to be hard to manage at times. For example, during the crucial seventh game, Dressen asked him to start warming up in the closing innings. Billy protested that he was "too tired." Yes, he had worked the day before but he was only 23 years old. At 6-feet-1 he seemed smaller, but he was a big man and with the stuff he had he should have been a "big" pitcher, willing, like many others, to pitch when "tired." After 11 years, 80 and 63 aren't bad, but Billy should have won more, should have been more serious, more of a team player.

The finale was another sad one, 4 to 2, with Joe Black the loser again as the Yanks took their fourth straight World Series. Only a Joe McCarthy team, Yankee of course, had ever done that. One of the crucial plays was a mere popup to the infield that caused a great stir because the bases were loaded in the seventh and all the Yankees were watching the ball come down without moving toward it. Finally, Billy Martin realized what was going on, charged at the mound and at the last split second caught the ball off his shoelaces for the third out.

The Yankees had used their big-gun pitchers through the first seven innings—Lopat the starter, relieved by Reynolds, relieved by Raschi. The Yankees scored first in the fourth on Rizzuto's double and run-scoring single by Mize. Brooklyn came back in their half, knocking out Lopat when he loaded the bases with none out on singles by Snider, Robinson and Campanella. Reynolds relieved and the best the Dodgers could do was a Hodges liner to left that Snider scored on after he tagged up.

The Yanks took the lead again on a Woodling homer but Brooklyn bounced back again to tie it as Billy Cox doubled off the right field wall and scored on a single by Reese. The winning run came on a home run by Mantle (who else?) in the sixth inning.

Then came the dramatic seventh. With Raschi now pitching, Cox singled and Furillo and Reese walked with one out. Then Stengel beckoned Bob

Kuzava from the bullpen. Kuzava was a journeyman now with his fifth team in a career that eventually had him on three more. Before he joined the Yankees in 1951 he had been a 24 and 21 pitcher with ERAs in the 4.02 to 4.15 range. As he walked in from the bullpen he was 29 years old, 6-foot-2 and 202 pounds, an ideal age and build for a pitcher but, as the crowd reacted, seemingly not an ideal pitcher for this bases-loaded situation and one out.

But, as usual in his Yankee years, Stengel's luck held. Snider popped weakly to third base and then Robinson hit that high pop-up to the right of the mound with Martin's hat flying off as he made the shoe-top grab. Kuzava, to the surprise of just about everyone in the park and watching on television, retired the next eight straight batters to sew up the game and the Series. There used to be a saying on the Newark sandlots: Luck will overcome all skill.

And it was largely luck, that whole Kuzava thing. Casey is credited with genius on using Kuzava but when you look at his roster and the pitchers he had been forced to use in his last desperate moves to tie up the Series you see he had little choice. All of his star pitchers—Raschi, Lopat, Reynolds, Sain— were worn out, not "tired" like Loes, but truly worn out. It was either Kuzava, who was 8 and 8, Tom Morgan, 5 and 4, Bill Miller, 4 and 6, or Bobby Hogue, 3 and 5. Casey went with Kuzava and lucked out again.

He was now hailed as the greatest manager in baseball. With the Braves and Dodgers he was called a clown, once coming out to hand in his lineup card with a bird in his hat, which he let loose. With the Mets there was no telling. They were so inept during his years that no one could have done anything with them, a crew so bad that it was sad seeing Richie Ashburn surrounded by such castoffs and minor leaguers. But with the Yanks, Case had the horses and, with luck at times, won with them.

The Series ended on a very sad note for a very nice man. Gil Hodges, the Dodgers' home run guy and usual RBI leader, went hitless in 21 trips. He hit the ball hard at times, as he did against Lopat in game seven, but not often enough and in the wrong directions. "I hit a few of 'em pretty good," Gil said after the game, "but I couldn't seem to hit one safely."

Even God couldn't help him, such was his bad luck. For the first time in memory the churches of an entire city prayed for one baseball player. Priests, ministers and rabbis throughout the Borough used part of their Saturday and Sunday pulpit time to urge their flocks to "pray for Gil Hodges." To no avail.

The partisan Brooklyn crowd was also especially kind to Gil as he struggled. He drew the loudest ovation of the Series during his at bat in the seventh. He hit a long ball to straight center but Mantle caught up with it. Brooklyn's souvenir venders weren't as kind, though. During that seventh game they were going through the stands shouting: "Souvenirs, souvenirs here. Hodges half price."[13]

George Shuba, after a decent Series—three for 10 with a double—headed home for surgery on his troublesome left knee. Like a lot of knee operations it was only partially successful, since some things cannot be replaced. However, he managed to get three more major league years out of it as a part-timer and retired after the 1955 victory. A good man in a difficult role: coming off the bench as a pinch hitter and playing the outfield part-time.

Shuba told me in our telephone interview that the knee didn't affect his hitting very much but that it did hurt his fielding. Having the exact same knee problem, I believe the fielding part but I can't believe his hitting wasn't affected. I watched the man for seven years, in person and on television, and have always been convinced, seeing that swing and those shotgun line drives, that he would have been a .300 hitter with two good knees.

Looking back at the Series, Chester Smith of the *Pittsburgh Press* was quoted by *The Sporting News* in asking the most pertinent question of all the post–Series analysts: "How could the Dodgers have carried this thing all the way to seven games," he wrote, "when the pride of their power had batted only a collective .129? Roy Campanella hit .214, Jackie Robinson .174 and Gil Hodges .000. The answer is that Snider and Reese caught fire and that the Brooklyn defense, especially in the outfield, was much superior to the Yankees, and that Preacher Roe and Carl Erskine did a stretch of superlative pitching." Mr. Smith was correct as far as he went, but he should have spread the blame around a bit more. Two of their other key hitters had a dismal Series, Furillo at .174 and Pafko at .190.

George Shuba, known as "Shotgun" for his line-drive hitting, was a favorite at Ebbets Field, affable and well-liked by teammates. He played six years for the Dodgers, mostly on the bad knee that prematurely ended his career. An excellent clutch hitter, he is one of the few men to pinch-hit a home run in a World Series, against the Yanks in '53.

His conclusion: If Campy, Jackie and Gil had hit their averages the Series would have been shortened by two days. Maybe so, but the Yankees of those days always seemed to know how to win. As Al Abrams of the *Pittsburgh Post-Gazette* put it: "They're champions, a team that doesn't know how to lose." It certainly was true in that Series. Mr. Smith pointed out Brooklyn's failings, hitting just .214 as a team. But the Yankees hit only one point higher, .215, and still won. Some of their key hitters, Bauer, McDougald and Rizzuto, had an awful Series. But power made the difference. Berra, for example, hit only .214 but had two home runs that drove in three important runs.

Towards year's end O'Malley announced the signing of Dressen for 1953 at a pay increase to an estimated $35,000, serious money for a manager in 1952. O'Malley also said that Joe Black was the first Dodger to sign and that he would be given a bonus of $1,000 on top of his salary, a reward for his great year. Joe had all the tools he needed to be a winner for some years yet, but they weren't enough for the great handler of pitchers. Charlie tinkered and, as we shall see, that was the end of Joe Black.

Jackie Robinson ended the year undiplomatically, as usual, and got himself in the middle of a furor over his answer to a question on the Yankees' failure to bring a black player up from the minors. He was on Faye Emerson's radio program *Youth Wants to Know,* Sunday, November 30. He had answered a number of questions about baseball when one youngster asked: "Mr. Robinson, do you think the Yankees are prejudiced against Negro players? I'm a Yankee fan and I'd like to know."

Robinson was said to have audibly gasped but quickly regained his composure, answering: "Yes, I think they are. I don't mean the players. They're a fine bunch of fellows and sportsmen, but I think the Yankee management is prejudiced. You asked the question and I answered it honestly. That's my opinion."[14]

George Weiss, Yankee general manager, answered Robinson's charge the next day, calling it unfair since there were "numerous Negroes in our farm system, and our scouts are instructed to make every effort to land good prospects, but we will not bring one up just for exploitation."[15]

In hindsight it's obvious that Weiss was lying. This was, after all, five years after Robinson, Bankhead, Doby, Irvin and Hank Thompson were brought up, and by the time Robinson made his comments there were blacks scattered throughout the majors. Two teams, George Weiss' Yankees and the Red Sox, remained lily-white the longest, the Yankees until 1955 when Elston Howard made the team, and Boston until 1959 with the signing of Elijah (Pumpsie) Green.

The truth is that while Weiss was denying Robinson's charge, the Yankees had a great prospect on their Triple A team, the Kansas City Blues. Vic Power, a 21-year-old first baseman, was down there waiting but was not promoted until they traded him to the Athletics in 1954. It wasn't that they couldn't have used him. Joe Collins was a decent ballplayer but not exactly a fixture at first base.

The word around the press boxes was that Weiss thought Power wasn't a "Yankee type, too flashy, a showboat." However, what registered most heavily in Weiss' mind, it was said, was that Power consistently dated white women, a no-no in Yankee land and, to be fair, in most other places in 1952.

The Robinson furor did not die quickly. Almost three weeks later Jackie announced that Commissioner Frick had asked him to refrain from further discussion of the Yankee/Negro question. "Frick asked me to avoid the issue in the future if I could," Robinson said, "and I said certainly. But I also told him, while I was not looking for any arguments with the Yankees or anybody else, I would give the same answer if I were asked the same question again. There are thousands upon thousands of people in Harlem who feel the same way. Maybe we're wrong."

He wasn't wrong, though, and he knew it. But what he didn't realize was that thousands upon thousands outside of Harlem, white people from all over, agreed with him. Frick's role in all this was the first sign since he replaced Chandler that he would be largely a do-nothing commissioner, almost always on the side of the power structure. He called Robinson to task but George Weiss was allowed to go along with his lying for three more years.

And it wasn't that Weiss gave in easily even three years later. He knew, as the entire Yankee organization realized, that there was no way to keep Elston Howard down in the minors. As it was, of the 16 major league teams, they were the 13th to bring a black player, Howard, up. Elston must have had a thick skin, for Casey often used the "N" word. In fact, he was quoted, but not in the daily press, as saying about Howard: "When I finally get a nigger, I get the only one in the world who can't run."[16] Weiss brought up Harry (Suitcase) Simpson in 1957, but as late as 1964 they had only two blacks on their roster, Howard and pitcher Al Downing. Perhaps their lack of black players contributed to their decline in the 1960s.

For years even after there were many blacks, baseball executives were uneasy with the question of how many to have on a team, of making sure that there was at least a 5 to 4 majority of whites as teams took the field. It reached the point where in 1962 Pumpsie Green, a .231 hitter at the time, asked for help from the NAACP when he was traded by the Red Sox to the Mets. The trade went through.

The time would come, however, when blacks would outnumber whites on the field and no one would even notice. The ultimate occurred at Forbes Field in Pittsburgh on September 1, 1971, when the entire Pirate lineup was black: Al Oliver, Rennie Stennett, Jackie Hernandez and Dave Cash in the infield, Willie Stargell, Gene Clines and Roberto Clemente in the outfield, Manny Sanguillen catching and Dock Ellis the starting pitcher.[17] The *Times*, in its baseball roundup the following day, didn't even mention it.

Jackie Robinson died in March of the following year. He had been in bad shape for a long time with diabetes and heart problems. His wife, Rachel, said years later that he was happy to have lived long enough to read that lineup.

♦ Four ♦

1953

Race Was Always a Problem

The year 1953 started off with one of the worst trades in Dodger history, one that even now, many years later, is puzzling since it was never explained rationally. On January 17 O'Malley traded Andy Pafko, one of the premier outfielders of his time, to Milwaukee for second baseman Roy Hartsfield and $50,000.

Pafko had been the answer to Brooklyn's years-long search for a top-quality leftfielder when they got him in 1951. He had everything, the arm, speed, power and batting eye that had been lacking at that position. He had an off year when they got him in 1951, but he still hit 30 home runs and drove in 68. In '52, his only other year, he hit .285, with 19 homers and 76 RBI.

Andy was as baffled as anyone else about the trade. "That January when they sent me to Boston," he told Roger Kahn years later, "Walter O'Malley wrote [me] a letter and said someday he'd explain why. [He never did.] I started to wonder. Two trades in three years. I don't know. Is something funny here?"[1]

Nothing the Brooklyn brass said or did regarding the trade made any sense, with Hartsfield a big part of the puzzle. He was immediately sent down to Montreal and never played another game in the majors. Vice president Buzzy Bavasi, a company man all the way, explained to newsmen that they regretted letting Andy go, parting with a man "who always gave his best," but that a youth movement was underway at Ebbets Field.

"We sold him for the reason that we've got to make room for a lot of young fellows," he said. "What's the use of maintaining an expensive scouting system if we're not going to believe our scouts when they tell us these boys are ready for the majors?"

A youth movement? Total craziness. Pafko was only 31 years old and played and hit well for another six years. What youth movement? Dick Williams, Don Hoak, Wayne Belardi, Walt Moryn, Don Thompson? Not one of them anywhere near Pafko's level. But apparently to some nitwit in the Brooklyn hierarchy, Sandy Amoros was, so Andy was traded. Amoros eventually took over left field but was never the hitter Pafko was.

Bringing up Gilliam was another matter. Jim had impressive credentials, but he wasn't worth risking tearing the club apart for. For that's what almost happened and it's a wonder the team won the pennant with the dissension that seethed below the surface. Andy's question about something funny going on was more true than he knew, and it was Walter O'Malley at his worst.

Follow this sequence: Gilliam replaces Robinson, who goes to third base, replacing Billy Cox, and Amoros is called up to play left field. That was the announced plan but it didn't quite come off, but that didn't matter. The announcement itself created unrest on the team, especially among the pitchers, knowing that one of the best gloves who ever played third base was going to the bench to be a utility man.

Andy Pafko seemed to be the answer to Brooklyn's perennial left field problem until, in a senseless trade, O'Malley sent him to Milwaukee for Roy Hartsfield and $50,000. Pafko will always be remembered for that moment he watched Bobby Thomson's homer disappear into the Polo Grounds' left field stands in the deciding 1951 playoff game.

Part of the problem was that Gilliam was a good glove man too, not on Billy's level, but few were. Jim was also a decent hitter. He came out of Nashville, born there in 1928, nicknamed Junior when he was the youngest player on the Baltimore Elite Giants. In his five years with Brooklyn he hit .272 and was durable, coming to bat an average of 592 times a season.

He wasn't the flashy type so he didn't get much attention from the beat writers. Although he hit .300 in 1956 and was the All-Star second baseman, he never became one of the Brooklyn Dodger cult figures, no doubt because he spent nine years playing in hated Los Angeles. Even today, some baseball record books describe him as a utility infielder for the Brooklyn Dodgers. It's a mighty unusual utility infielder who goes to bat 592 times a year.

But before his skills were known, and even after, Cox' going to the bench did not sit well. "The morale problem created by the switch of Jackie Robinson to third base is delicate now and may grow worse," Kahn, then Dodger beat man for the *Herald-Tribune*, wrote when it was announced that Buzzy Bavasi, O'Malley's vice president, would fly down to Vero Beach to get Billy's reaction. "Right now Dressen thinks his strongest team must use Junior Gilliam at second, Jackie Robinson at third and Cox as utility man."

Kahn was cautious about the race issue, referring to it only once. He must have felt he had to be, since the year before, when he championed Robinson once too often and used his fiery quotes, he got a teletyped message saying: "Note to Kahn: *Herald-Tribune* will not be a sounding board for Jackie Robinson. Write baseball, not race relations. Story killed. Sol Rogow, night sports editor."[2]

Toward the end of this story Kahn took a chance. "When Don Hoak and Bobby Morgan worked out at third base nothing was said by the other players. When Gilliam moved to second and Robinson to third,

An undercurrent of racism shocked Brooklyn fans as a result of Billy Cox' being benched to make room for Junior Gilliam at second base. They couldn't keep a glove like Billy's on the bench for long, but the overtones of the move lingered long after, bringing the realization that the problem of blacks in organized baseball was yet to be resolved.

resentment grew. The reason is nearing the surface and remarks by some Dodgers in the clubhouse and at their hotel indicate that the problem of Negroes in baseball is still to be finally resolved."[3] This time he got away with it.

Dressen's, or O'Malley's, plan didn't really work. No one could keep a glove like Cox' on the bench, especially since he was a .260 hitter and excellent with men in scoring position. Robinson played left field much of the year while Cox played 100 games, mostly at third, and hit .291, some 29 points above his career average. But the resentment never really went away. Billy was a quiet sort, but well liked, even by the opposition.

As it turned out, the year was not much different from his past seasons. He never was a 154-game third baseman. His problem dated from his 18 months' service on Guadalcanal, where he was involved in the most vicious combat, sometimes hand-to-hand. While on the island he contacted malaria, from which he never fully recovered, and as a result, although he was 5-feet-10, he never weighed more than 150 pounds.[4] His highest game total was 142 in 1951, but years of 100, 116 and 119 were more his norm.

Billy was from Newport in central Pennsylvania, where he played high school ball. In 1940 he was signed by the Harrisburg Senators but wasn't with them long. He was only 21 but good enough to be called by the Pirates the next spring. Those were the days when baseball was THE game—no National Basketball Association, no National Football League or the golf tour to speak of—so the competition was fierce and it was not unusual for players to spend years in the minor leagues. A great hitter like Hank Sauer, for example, was 31 before he became a regular with the Cubs in 1949. And the George Shuba story would be funny if it weren't so sad.

"I'm in Mobile, it's '47 and I hit 21 homers and drove in 110 runs," he told Kahn for *The Boys of Summer*. "Next spring at Vero Beach Rickey says he's sending me back to Mobile, that I have fine power but not enough average. I shorten up. It's '48. I bat .389. The spring after he sends me to Mobile again. Nice batting, Rickey says, but your power fell off. We need someone who can hit them over that short right field wall in Ebbets Field." By the time he was brought up, the knee that dogged his career and finally ended it came up with him.

Billy was luckier than that, thanks to his marvelous glove and the power he had before the war and the malaria. He was called up by the Pirates in early 1941, but with the war looming ahead, after 10 games he was drafted and ended up on The Canal. When he was discharged he was a scrawny 130 pounds and never really got over the recurrent fevers, although they lessened as the years went by. The plays he made, however, were magic. Casey Stengel once called him an acrobat at third base. And the arm: he would grab a hot one on the baseline, look the ball over and then gun it to Hodges for the out.

The racial overtones behind Billy's shift shook up Ebbets Field. We fancied ourselves as the most liberal of all baseball fans. Didn't we open our arms to Jackie Robinson? And didn't we have a team that proves the races can intermingle on the ball field and in the clubhouse amicably? The obvious white resentment on the team came as a shock.

What was not obvious from all the coverage the Dodgers got in the press and other media at this time was that Robinson and Campanella didn't see eye-to-eye on these racial issues. Roy often told Robby that he "was no crusader" as Jackie certainly was. There was no feud, but there were differences between them, Robinson being a college graduate and Campy coming from a poor section of Philadelphia, and a professional catcher since he was 16 years old.

That was the year, 1938, he was signed as the first-string catcher for the Baltimore Elite Giants, a team founded in 1918. He often described how tough life was in the Negro Leagues, relating how one Sunday he caught four games: a double-header in Cincinnati and another in nearby Youngstown that night. There were no team doctors, either, he recalled. "You didn't get hurt in those leagues. You played no matter, 'cause if you didn't play you didn't get paid."

His first Dodger assignment was Nashua up in New Hampshire, where he and Don Newcombe were the outstanding battery in the league. After stops in Montreal and St. Paul, he took over the Dodger job when Bruce Edwards came down with arm trouble. After all those years on old buses and in cheap hotels, Roy loved being in the big leagues and wasn't about to risk it all by becoming a firebrand.

He and Jackie looked at life from different perspectives, Robby being the fiery black ever ready to take offense, and Roy being easygoing and more patient in his dealings with the world and with the way things were going for the Negro in America. But at bottom they were friends and caused no split among the team. Roy, in fact, often acted as a rein on Jackie, sometimes with the remark: "Robinson, you are not only wrong, but LOUD wrong." Jackie in his autobiography said he was glad that those who tried to divide him and Roy were unsuccessful, even though the two had serious differences of opinion on racial matters.

The nationally known black sportswriter A.S. "Doc" Young described Roy as wanting to be "getting along," while Jackie, he said, "is an aggressive individualist who is willing to pay the price and does not believe that effusive thank you's are necessary."[5]

Roy's position on not being a crusader offended Jackie somewhat in that he felt that all black players should be crusaders, as he was, for decent accommodations and respect. His opinion after Roy's paralyzing accident are somewhat confusing. He wrote how his "respect for Campy deepened" after Roy admitted he "might have been wrong in his thinking about the right of a black man in sports to express himself."[6]

But he later told writer Roger Kahn that Roy "had a little Tom in him" but if he went into that he'd be "hitting a cripple."[7] There are millions of us, white and black, who feel that one man's Uncle Tom is another man's Roy Campanella, minding his business and seeking the good life for his family.

Jackie and Roy's formative years and home life were strikingly different. Roy dropped out of school and from 16 on didn't have much of a home life, being on the road so much with the Elite Giants. Jackie was born in Cairo, Georgia, in 1919 but grew up in Pasadena, where his mother migrated after his father ran off with another woman. After that, life was hard as his mother went out to do washing and ironing, often able to feed her five children only two meals a day. In Jackie she was doubly lucky. He turned out to be a combination scholar/athlete, highly intelligent and recruited by UCLA, where he was the first four-letter athlete in the school's history.

But, strong-minded as ever, he dropped out after two years, telling his classmate and future wife, Rachel Isum, that no amount of education would help get a black man a job. He wanted to play football, but because of segregation had to play for the Honolulu Bears while working for a construction company near Pearl Harbor. With all that behind him, plus his experiences as an Army Second Lieutenant, he seemed the ideal candidate to help Rickey break the color line.

Branch knew that Jackie was given an early honorable discharge from the Army just to get rid of him. Always ready to stand up for his rights, he had refused to move to the back of an Army bus in Fort Hood, Texas. He was, after all, an officer and no buck private was going to order him around. After a firestorm among his black brother officers, and publicity in the powerful black newspaper, the *Pittsburgh Courier*, the Army backed down and settled on the honorable discharge. Rickey's aides told him of all this, warning him to be careful.[8] But Branch went with his instincts and, as usual, was proven right.

Pee Wee Reese played a vital role in the acceptance of Robinson, both on the Dodgers and with the league in general. It could not have been easy for a native of Louisville, Kentucky, to accept a black man as a teammate back in the 1940s, but Harold Reese, always the gentleman, did it publicly and gracefully.

Reese first heard of Robinson when he was in the Navy, at sea coming home from the war. Southern-bred as he was, he had doubts about playing alongside a black man, wondering what the folks back home would think. But when he first met Robinson the doubts disappeared. After Jackie joined the team, Pee Wee, like some other Dodgers, tired of the racial taunts and insults direct at Robinson, so one day, in front of hostile fans in Boston he walked over to Robinson, put his arm around his shoulder and talked to him. He was signaling publicly that Robinson was accepted on a now color-blind Brooklyn team.

The Captain, Harold Reese, held the Brooklyn infield together for 15 years, with time out for World War II service in the Navy. "Pee Wee" was a misnomer, a nickname that refers to marbles; Reese had won a tournament in his native Louisville. He was 5-foot-9, 175 pounds and a great clutch hitter, especially with two strikes on him.

"I don't even remember what he said," Jackie wrote in his autobiography. "It was the gesture of comradeship and support that counted. As he stood there talking with me with a friendly arm around my shoulder, he was saying loud and clear, 'Yell, heckle, do anything you want. We came here to play baseball.'"[9]

Pee Wee, now in the Hall of Fame, was the captain and Grand

Old Man of the Dodgers by this time, dating back to 1941, with three years away in the Navy. He was originally the property of the Red Sox, but when Joe Cronin, the Sox shortstop at the time, scouted him in the minors he told his boss, Tom Yawkey, "The kid will never make it."[10] After 20 years Joe was still protecting his job. Reese got his nickname as a boy in Louisville when he won a marble championship, but soon outgrew the name. As a player at 5-foot-9 and 160 pounds, Harold Reese was never small in any way.

Going into April, the racial unrest seemed to have quieted down and Dressen began concentrating on his pitching staff. Thus began the ruination of Joe Black, his star pitcher of the year before. As has been said, Dressen considered himself the smartest man in baseball. He was going to make Joe Black even better than the 15 and 4, 2.15 ERA of the year before.

Joe's limited repertoire, a fastball and quick little curve, had made him one of the best relievers in baseball, but now Charlie was going to have him learn the change-up, screwball and big curve. Joe pointed out that his index and middle finger curved downward because of faulty tendons and were therefore not suited to such pitches. His two pitches had served him well because he threw them with supreme confidence and control, two things that are more than half the battle in a pitcher's life.

Joe was born in 1924 in Plainfield, New Jersey, where he was an all-around athlete, excelling in just about every sport. He had the build for sports even then, a high-schooler at 6-foot-2 and around 200 pounds. He was late coming to the majors, Rookie of the Year at 28, after his superb 15 and 4 season in 1952.

He always wanted to play baseball and, being one of the best in the state when he graduated from Plainfield High in 1940, he found there was no place for him in that pre–Robinson age. But he didn't believe it when he was told by scouts, "Colored guys don't play baseball." He replied, "Are you crazy? You've seen me play." It was seven years after he got out of the Army, where he served in World War II, before he got his chance.

Dressen must have known that he had messed up a great pitcher, for during the exhibition season on the way north he changed his mind, telling Joe to go back to his old ways. But it was too late. Black's faith in his pitches had been undermined and his confidence was gone. Once that happens to a pitcher he is done. Confidence is vital out there on the mound facing nine batters who want to knock you around. One of the saddest things to watch at Ebbets Field during 1953 was the slow disintegration of Joe, from his magnificent year before to a 6 and 3, 5.33 ERA reliever. He never found it again. In one sad conversation with Roger Kahn he summed it all up: "I did everything the man said. Fast ball high. Curve ball low. Now I been throwing so many damn things I don't know if I can control anything."[11]

But Dressen had a replacement for him and for Newcombe, now serving his second year in the Army. Clem Labine became the principal reliever and

Russ Meyer became one of Dressen's starters. There was some apprehension when Meyer first entered the clubhouse, there being that feud with Robinson and a number of other Dodgers. But, as with Maglie in '56, everything went smoothly as Russ changed uniforms and allegiances. Winning, of course, is what counts in the pros, not old animosities.

Meyer's win in his first start at Ebbets Field was no surprise but his mound opponent was. Big John Lindell, the former Yankee outfielder, was trying for a comeback at age 37 as a pitcher with the Pirates. Any old International League fan would remember John as a star pitcher for the 1941 Newark Bears, a 23-game winner in what was then tough Triple A competition.

He was now a 37-year-old, 6-foot-5 knuckleballer as he gave the Dodgers eight hits and walked a fatal 10 in losing 4–2. Russ also gave up eight hits but scattered them, walking but one. Johnny didn't have a bad year considering the last-place Pirates lost 104 games. He went 5 and 16 on a staff that had six other pitchers who didn't reach .500.

Both Meyer and Labine were brilliant all year, Russ 15 and 5 and Clem 11 and 6. The Monk had three seasons in Brooklyn and won 32 against 13 losses. Labine's 11 and 6 with his 2.77, the lowest ERA on the staff, gave an indication that one of the great relievers in baseball had arrived. Dressen had been screaming for more pitching and finally got what he wanted.

A smiling Walter O'Malley after his 3-hour meeting with California Gov. Earl Warren at Ebbets Field, August 28, 1953. Neither man ever revealed what they talked about.

The fans of Milwaukee and Lou Perini also got what they wanted. The owner of the Boston Braves got permission to move his club to the beer capitol in the first team shift in the major leagues since 1903. It was obvious to all that Perini was in desperate financial shape, as attendance had fallen dramatically since the team's heyday in the 1940s. Unlike O'Malley's phony attendance figures, Perini's were true. From the pennant year of Spahn and Sain, when the Braves drew 1,455,439, they were down to 487,475 in 1951 and 281,278 in '52.

Perini and everyone else knew that the Braves without a

contender never could compete with the far more popular Red Sox. There was never a Boston Braves Nation and even during the many years the Sox were also-rans they outdrew the Braves. Not even a Braves pennant could change things, as was proved in 1948 when they won the pennant and the Red Sox still outdrew them. The American League pennant race that year was so close that the Sox were in a playoff with Cleveland. But even so, the Braves were winners that year and should have drawn better. So Perini left and hit a Midwest gold mine, for a while. The Braves of Milwaukee drew over a million for nine straight years until the beer turned flat. For four years attendance dwindled until 1965, it went down to 555,564. Although the gypsies had to move again, team shifts were now fairly common and new teams were springing up all over the place.

One shift was delayed, however, while the Lords of Baseball took out their revenge on Bill Veeck. His St. Louis Browns, like the Braves in Boston, were also in bad shape, with attendance running from some 300,000 to 500,000 a year. But the owners remembered all of Veeck's promotional antics, particularly his sending up a midget to bat against Detroit. He applied for a transfer to Baltimore but was turned down, the transfer finally approved six months later when Veeck was gone, bought out by a syndicate for $2.475 million.

The following week the Dodgers were trying to regain their interracial image as Bavasi claimed to have talked to a number of players who told him "there is no such problem, never has been and never will be." Newsmen went for Robinson, hoping, of course, for a controversial story. They were disappointed, however, by a genial Robinson saying that everyone knew "there was nothing personal" in his move to third base, that he knew Cox was naturally upset about losing his job. "I just hope he's not angry at me, and from what I heard from players who came and talked to me today, he's not."[12] A shadow of doubt creeps in, however, when the thought occurs: why didn't Jackie go directly to Billy and talk to him?

On April 6th the Dodgers confirmed that Gilliam would start the season at second base, with the anticipated move of Robinson to third. On that same day the Cotton States League threw out the Hot Springs, Arkansas, club because it had signed two Negro players and refused to release them. The move was made, the league's president said, because the Negroes would "disrupt the league and cause its dissolution." There was no follow-up to the story.

On April 19th the Hall of Fame came calling on Mickey Mantle in but the third year of his career. The day before, Mickey had hit an announced 565-foot homer off Chuck Stobbs in Washington's Griffith Stadium. The Hall wanted the bat and ball for display, even though many baseball historians insisted that longer balls had been hit, particularly by Babe Ruth and Jimmy Foxx.

Nevertheless, the ball and bat went up to Cooperstown as Arthur (Red) Patterson, Yankee publicist, got away with another one. Since the ball was hit out of the stadium no one could prove that the actual ball was produced, but no matter. In those days Patterson got a lot of newspaper ink by running around with a tape measure whenever a Yankee, especially Mantle, hit a long one. Red was also the master of the long, long injury list, the poor Yankees suffering from split fingernails and the like.

Carl Furillo's simmering resentment against Leo Durocher and his Giants came closer on the 24th to the explosion that occurred later in the year. Carl was up against Sal Maglie, despised by all Dodgers, when The Barber threw one over his head. On the next pitch Carl swung viciously and let the bat fly out of his hands toward the mound. Maglie sidestepped the bat, but by that time players and umpires swarmed around both men, preventing a fight and possible team brawl. When order was restored Maglie struck Carl out. Furillo remembered, though, and was not a man to just simmer forever.

On May 5th Brooklyn announced that Jackie Robinson would move out to left field, sharing the position with George Shuba and, at times, Dick Williams. The idea appears to have been Robinson's, with Dressen going along. Jackie said there were two reasons for the move. First, to prolong his career, and then to have Cox return to third base. McGowen wrote in *The Sporting News* that Robby was never happy about moving Cox off third, feeling that "I can't carry his glove and neither can anybody else."[13]

In mid-month Dressen finally had to bench Gil Hodges, who was in one of the worst slumps of his career, one studded with slumps. Gil had just gone 14 for 76 and Charlie felt he needed time off to "get back on the beam," the popular aviation directional signal of the time. Gil's nemesis was the low outside curve, a pitch that possibly has kept him out of the Hall of Fame. His problem seemed to be a stance too far from the plate, and it dogged him for much his career.

It was common knowledge throughout baseball of this weakness. Giant catcher Wes Westrum in evaluating hitters for his pitching staff would tell them: "Hodges? Keep the ball away. He'll give you the outer third of the plate."[14] Of course, it took a pitcher with the curve ball of a Sal Maglie to get him out consistently, for his 370 home run total shows that anything up was often gone. Plus, left-handers had no such advantage. But we always wondered why he didn't step in closer. If he had he might have hit .300 with the 500 homers that automatically mean Cooperstown.

Gil was a 19-year-old out of Princeton, Indiana, when he played one game for the Dodgers in 1943 during which, he recalled later, Johnny Vander Meer struck him out twice. When he signed with Brooklyn he dropped out of St. Joseph's College in Rensselaer, Indiana, where, at 6-foot-1½, he was a sophomore on a basketball scholarship. He then went into the Marines where he spent 2½ years in combat in the Pacific Islands campaign where, according to Don Hoak, a later Marine, he sometimes had to kill Japanese soldiers with his bare hands, such was his strength.

He came up as a catcher but Durocher moved him to first base early in 1948 because of Campanella's obvious skills behind and at the plate. Gil's chances of making the Hall are fading by the year but his career numbers might someday still get him in through the Veterans Committee: 370 home runs, seven consecutive seasons of more than 100 RBI, 14 grand slams and a .273 batting average. Lesser men have been in the Hall for years. There was one year he would have made it had not his buddy Campanella been too ill to attend the meeting. Roy's vote would have swung it.

June started with Russ Meyer putting on a unique show of pitching against the Phillies at Ebbets Field. There are no gradations of the word unique. It is or it isn't. Judge for yourself. Meyer had been jawing at umpire Augie Donatelli on ball and strike calls as the fourth inning started. With Ashburn at the plate it got worse on everything not called a strike until, after he walked Richie and Johnny Wyrostek, he could barely control himself. When Donatelli called ball three with Mel Clark up, Monk stalked toward the plate, about to rush Donatelli as Dressen turned him back toward the mound. Then things got hilarious.

When Meyer got to the mound he reached for the rosin bag and

Russ Meyer was known as "The Mad Monk" for his explosions on the field. But behind all the antics and tantrums was a great pitcher. During his three years in Brooklyn he was one of the most productive pitchers in Dodger history. He was traded to the Dodgers by the Phils in February 1953 and from then until 1955 he was 32 and 13, a .711 percentage.

threw it high in the air. He turned toward the plate as the bag came down, smack on his head. The fans were up and roaring, watching Meyer flinch and look around thinking someone from the stands had thrown something at him. Without exaggeration, it was probably the most hilarious scene in the history of Ebbets Field, if not any field. By now Donatelli had had enough and waved him out, but as he walked into the dugout he made an obscene gesture at the still-laughing fans.

When a number of complaints from those watching on television reached Frick, rather than chastise Meyer he voiced strong disapproval of television cameras nosing into baseball dugouts. "A fellow has certain private rights," he said, "and the dugout is his home while he's at the ball park, and the TV cameras have no right focusing on things that occur there." Those, remember, were the good old days when the TV networks didn't have baseball by the throat.

Meyer was born in Peru, Illinois, in 1923 and his temper was such that Roscoe McGowen once named him "The Terrible Tempered Mr. Bang." After his 32 and 13 record for his three years in Brooklyn, at age 32 he was traded, having virtually nothing left. But he was fascinating to watch. It was almost like watching Jack Paar on television. When Russ pitched, anything could happen; he could blow at any moment. After he left baseball he remained Brooklyn Dodger Blue for the rest of his life. In 1981 he, Erskine and Amoros returned to Brooklyn to promote a movement to have the Dodgers brought back to New York. Russ' visit was frightening as well as unsuccessful. One evening he was held up at gunpoint at Lexington Avenue and 25th Street and had his 1953 and 1955 World Series rings stolen. Yes sir, the Big Apple, Fun City.

The day after Meyer's blowup Ralph Kiner was traded by Pittsburgh to the Cubs, bringing to baseball lore one of the great quotes, accurate or not, of the modern game. Newsmen quoted Rickey as saying to Kiner when he told him of the trade: "We finished last with you and we can finish last without you."

Kiner has a different version, close and almost as good. He quotes Rickey as saying, "We can finish last without you." The trade brought Rickey six journeyman players, $150,000 and the enmity of most Pittsburgh fans. Ralph knew he was to be traded months before the deal because "I was making a lot of money and we were a lousy ballclub." To pacify the fans, he said, Rickey blamed him for demands he didn't make—like moving in the walls. "I kept copies of my wires and [in them] there were no demands at all on my part."[15] What it all came down to was the Pirates needed money and Kiner was expendable because he was one-dimensional, a slugger without the arm, speed and fielding skills of the ideal Rickey player.

Branch told the *Times'* Arthur Daley that he had to proceed warily in any dealings involving Kiner. "He had market value and gate appeal, and I dared not destroy them [in contract haggling]," Rickey said. "But Ralph met my requirements in only one respect—as a home run hitter. To me it wasn't enough."

On the 7th, the Dodgers won a game at Ebbets Field in the sweetest possible way. Down 4–2 in the ninth against Stu Miller of the Cardinals, Robinson singled to left, Campanella singled on a double play ball that bad-hopped over Solly Hemus' head at second base and Hodges followed with a homer to left for three runs and the game.

What some noticed watching the game on television was the double standard on the part of some umpires. Before Hodges' homer, a ball was called, causing catcher Del Rice to go into a frenzy. He yelled at umpire Bill Engeln, kicked dirt on him, threw his mask to the ground, threw his cap away and finally tossed the ball high in the air as he walked to the mound.

He was not thrown out of the game. But if Jackie Robinson had done half of those things he would have been in the clubhouse within five minutes. Bill Stewart, senior umpire working first base, said Rice would be the subject of a report to the Commissioner's office. Yeah.

On July 10 Ralph Branca left the Dodgers, sold to the Tigers for $10,000 after all seven other teams finally allowed him to be waived out of the National League. Ralph had one great year among a number of disappointing ones in his eight years with the Dodgers. In 1947 he was 21 and 12 with a 2.67 ERA. But that same year he fell apart against the Yankees in the World Series. In '46 he blew sky high in the first playoff game against the Cardinals and then in '51 came the Thomson home run heard, they say, around the world.

A very disappointing young man, since he had all the natural equipment any pitcher could ask for: 6-foot-3, 220 pounds, great stuff except for an ordinary curveball. He was even a member of the Dodger official family, having married Jane Mulvey, of the Mulveys who owned 25 per cent of the club. But an 80–58 record as a Dodger just never seemed enough from a man who looked so imposing out there on the mound. In later years his most memorable failure made him a celebrity as he and Bobby Thomson appeared at shows and on television in an act that centered around — what else? — the 1951 home run.

Another pitcher, of far greater stature, was released two weeks later. Hal Newhouser, a 207-game winner, was waived off the Detroit roster and picked up by Cleveland after 15 years with the Tigers. Hal later made the Hall of Fame in a vote that has always been puzzling, considering the number of better players who have not made it. Many pitchers, for example, with more than 207 wins are not at Cooperstown. Two that come immediately to mind are Bert Blyleven with 287 wins and Jim Kaat with 283. Why these guys have not been elected is a mystery, especially since they were with teams not often contenders.

A look at wartime statistics reveals the weakness in the Newhouser choice. Of his 207 wins, 62 came during the years 1943–1945, years of all-out war when baseball was manned by kids and castoffs, or men too old for the service. Newhouser was aware of this, of course, and tried to enlist more than once but was turned down each time because of a heart condition. Still, 207 wins alone should not be enough for the Hall, and when you subtract 62 because of wartime, 143 is a disgrace. However, unlike many other wartime ballplayers, Hal was a good pitcher after the war, winning 97 games between 1946 and 1950.

As July wore on, the Dodgers were described by the *Times* as "sizzling," having taken double-headers from the Cubs and Braves. Hodges was hot again and Johnny Podres, with his sixth straight win, was emerging as a pitcher of consequence, as was Erskine, heading for a 20-win season. The lead was 7½ over the Braves and 8 over Philadelphia. The Giants, in fifth place, were 9½ out but not enough for us in Ebbets Field, as we habitually kept a wary eye on Durocher's team. Furillo, the always overlooked Carl Furillo, was also a hot hitter. While Snider and Hodges got most of the headlines, Carl was third in the league at .323, in this, to be his Batting Champion year. He was points behind Schoendienst and Irvin but was moving up daily until he finished the year injured at .344. Many a Hall of Famer was never a batting champion.

Robinson and Burdette almost went at it on July 26 as the Dodgers were sweeping a double-header from the Braves in Brooklyn with Burdette, making his first major league start and taking his first loss. Lew was upset in the very first inning when he walked Gilliam, Reese singled to left and then Robinson was safe on a bunt down the third base line. Burdette, ostensibly offended by Jackie's successful bunt, shouted something that Robinson said later was "you black bastard." Both men started toward one another but before any confrontation umpire Babe Pinelli stepped between them and broke it up.

The race business came up again as the Dodgers went into Milwaukee in early August. It was always there under the surface but it took loudmouths like Stanky or Burdette, the one from Alabama, the other West Virginia, to make it public. This time it was claimed that Burdette called Campanella a "black [MF]," which, Roy said later, "was the worst thing I've been called since I've been in the big leagues." This, on top of the incident with Jackie Robinson little more than a week before at Ebbets Field.

Dave Anderson, writing for the *Eagle*, said the way it started and the reaction of the Milwaukee fans at first indicated "it could have developed into the most violent racial incident since Negroes entered organized baseball." In the eighth inning Roy was knocked down twice by Burdette and, after striking out, went for Lew with a bat in his hand after what he said he heard. As both teams emerged from their dugouts and swarmed around third base, Furillo grabbed the bat from Campy's hand and helped drag him off the field.

Fans by this time were throwing cushions and other things at Roy as he was hustled off. Burdette didn't deny saying something, but said he made the remark after Campy yelled a curse at him. Whatever Burdette said, the usually mild-mannered Campanella had taken a step toward the dugout, stopped, turned and charged the mound.

After a night's sleep both players said they just wanted to forget the whole thing, even though umpire Tom Gorman was filing a report with the commissioner's office. This set off *Eagle* columnist Tommy Holmes, who quoted Gorman as saying "nothing would have happened if Campy had kept going back to the bench after striking out." Gorman, he wrote, "seems to have confused cause and effect. Twice during his time at bat Campanella had been turned upside down by pitched balls flying at his skull. Burdette then piled insult upon injury by hurling a racial slur at the Brooklyn slugger."

Tommy, often confused with the outfielder, was a meticulous reporter who Red Smith once described as "the best baseball writer of his time." He covered the Dodgers for the *Brooklyn Eagle* starting in 1924, and then the *Herald-Tribune* when the *Eagle* folded in 1955. He was scrupulously fair, never a "homer" in his coverage and was much admired for overcoming his handicap. Tommy, like Pete Gray, lost an arm in a childhood accident, but learned to type with one hand. He retired when the Dodgers moved to Los Angeles.

"The stand of the umpires is fairly typical," he wrote, "established policy for them to hear no evil, see no evil, speak no evil except when their job of administering order on the field is concerned. So from the point of view of the umpires nothing Burdette did made them look bad. But the racial aspects of this particular flare-up obscured the other basic cause of the unpleasantness, the beanball."

The next day, O'Malley, tired of his black players being constantly thrown at, announced that at the next league meeting he would introduce a rule making it mandatory that a "wild" pitcher be removed from the game at the discretion of the plate umpire. With "dusters" being part of the game for a hundred years, it never surfaced.

By coincidence, Robinson got into this act through a piece he had signed off on weeks before for his magazine *Our Sports*. It just happened to come out right after the Milwaukee incident and the July 26 ruckus at Ebbets Field when he said Burdette called him a "black bastard."

He violated the O'Malley code of silence when he wrote "there may be some resentment on the Dodgers to this day" about Negroes, and then referred to other teams such as the St. Louis Cardinals yelling "porter" and "shoeshine boy" at him and Joe Black. We weren't insulted, he went on, "if a great many Negroes must earn their living that way we know where the fault lies, and it is not with the Negroes themselves."[16]

After the Dodgers beat the Giants on August 8th Chuck Dressen added another page to baseball literature when he said: "The Giants is dead," Durocher's men being 16½ games out at the time. He was furious the next day, mostly at Dick Young for playing the remark up in the *Daily News*. "I coulda give it to him the other way," he said, "I can say the Giants ARE dead, and next time that's what I'm gonna do."[17]

The Brooklyn Board of Education came to Charlie's rescue, saying through a spokesman that he was grammatically correct. "You wouldn't say the United States are the best country try in the world, would you?" the spokesman asked. "Then how can you say the Giants are dead? The Giants is dead is perfectly proper."[18] Maybe so, but it just doesn't sound right.

Ted Williams, two weeks back from air combat in Korea, pinch-hit a home run, number 325, in the seventh inning of an August 8th loss to the Cleveland Indians. Williams had served 16 months as a fighter pilot and once was almost killed on that occasion when he had to crash-land his burning plane. Again, many celebrities served but few were called back a second time, and fewer still ever saw action as a combat pilot. Again, to his credit, Ted never complained.

August 28 was the evening of California Governor Earl Warren's visit to Ebbets Field where he and O'Malley sat together in Walter's box for the entire 2½ hours of play on a Friday night. Walter denied the visit had anything to do with gathering rumors of a Dodger shift to the West Coast, seemingly affirming his remark two days before that "the Dodgers are mighty fortunate to be in Brooklyn."

He would have had the world believe that the governor of California, one of the busiest men in the country, came to Ebbets Field just to spend an evening with Walter O'Malley. What else could they have discussed but the Dodgers? It is reasonable to assume that on that August 28 the future of the team was decided, and that future was California.

When reporters asked the governor about future baseball in California, he replied: "We don't want to steal the champions [Dodgers]. Any big league team will do." He added that both Los Angeles and San Francisco could support big league baseball and that the people of California were anxious for it.[19] Note that when speaking of a team he didn't use the word transfer, or purchase. He used the word *steal,* and when it happened that's actually what it was, the theft of a ball team by one city from another.

It was strange that Warren would get involved in all this messy Dodger business. This was a man who obviously still had political ambitions, even though he was Dewey's running mate in an embarrassing Republican defeat in 1948. In his role as emissary for Los Angeles, he could be sure of hostility from the voters of New York, then the most powerful state in terms of electoral votes. But then again, in 1953 he was 62 years old, and with Eisenhower in his first term, he gave up politics and all participation in Dodgers affairs when Ike named him Chief Justice.

As August was ending there was some bench jockeying between two enemies, Robinson and Stanky. It was their usual banter, sometimes cruel, but it has been turned into a vicious episode of race baiting.

It was the seventh inning with Stanky's Cardinals trailing 6–3, Robinson up. Jackie was having trouble with his left knee and stepped out of the batter's box to flex it. In his book, *Brooklyn's Dodgers*, historian Carl Prince writes that Stanky "crudely and publicly imitated an ape in the dugout, taunting the limping Jackie Robinson." The *Brooklyn Eagle*, he claims, "caught Stanky in a series of photos showing the Cards manager in action: fists under armpits, lips out, jaw thrust forward, grunting, shuffling and scratching as he moved from one end of the dugout to the other whenever Robbie came to bat."[20] This is a gross exaggeration of what really happened.

Kahn, ever ready to spring whenever Robinson was wronged, wrote in his *Herald-Tribune* account that Stanky and Robinson "turned comics" with Stanky getting laughs as he limped around the dugout imitating Jackie with the bad knee. In the *Eagle* Holmes had Stanky "limping over to the water cooler" several times, making fun of Robinson's knee problem. McGowen, in the *Times*, wrote that "the Cardinal manager, ridiculing Robby from the bench, finally got up, wrapped a towel around his leg and went back and forth to the water cooler with an exaggerated limp." Not a word in any of the coverage about ape-like movements. And there were no follow-up stories the next day.

The *Eagle* photos show nothing except Stanky limping. In one shot, with Hilda Chester waving a handkerchief at Stanky, he is not doing ape moves, as Mr. Prince claims, but is stepping down into the dugout with his right hand on the dugout roof. Stanky was often an open target with his sometimes race baiting but not even he would dare do an animal routine in Ebbets Field.

Finally, Dave Anderson, then with the *Eagle*, was with Holmes covering the game and said there was no ape imitation at any time. Then there is the matter of television, which had cameras trained on Stanky during his antics. I saw no animal act, nor did any of my friends. The camera, remember, never lies.

Anderson, like Holmes, was another *Brooklyn Eagle* writer to be trusted unquestioningly. He grew up in Bay Ridge, Brooklyn, came out of Boston College and joined the *Eagle* covering the Dodgers, going over to the *Journal-American* when the *Eagle* folded. He joined the *Times* sports department in 1966 and such were his writing skills that he has for years now been one of their sports columnists, covering all aspects of sports. As a result of his columns he won the Pulitzer Prize in 1981 for "distinguished commentary."

On September 6th, fans at the Polo Grounds saw one of the more ferocious on-field battles within memory. Carl Furillo was at the plate when, he said later, he heard Durocher yell "Stick it in his ear" to pitcher Ruben Gomez, who then hit Carl on the right wrist. There had been bad blood between Carl and Durocher, dating back to 1950 when he was hospitalized after being struck by a pitch from Sheldon Jones.

This time Carl's resentment boiled over and, leaving first base, he charged the entire Giant bench to get at Leo. Before anyone could

Carl Furillo was "The Reading Rifle" in recognition of one of the best arms in baseball history. He was not only one of the best outfielders of his era, he had credentials that many at Cooperstown lack: a Batting Championship, .299 career average and 1,058 RBIs. He was blackballed by O'Malley after he won an injury-based suit against the Dodgers.

stop him he had the Giant manager on the ground with his hands around his throat and was throttling him before Monte Irvin and Jim Hearn went to Durocher's rescue. In the melee and struggle to free Durocher, someone stepped on Carl's left hand, breaking a bone and ending his season.

Even later when his hand was being treated he was still enraged, vowing further revenge. "I have heard him threaten to fine pitchers who didn't throw at hitters," he said as they were bandaging his hand. "I will get him. The first time I see him, the first time we come face to face, on the street or anywhere, I will get him. He has crossed me once too often." Leo countered that by saying "wherever or whenever he wants to try it I'll be ready." It was over, really, since Durocher, brave words and all, wisely never "crossed" Carl again. But, as Louis Effrat wrote in the *Times*, "It was a long time coming."[21]

In his attack on Durocher, Carl had something going for him unknown to those not in on the secrets of the clubhouse. As his hand was being bandaged he was asked how he thought he could get through the entire Giant team to get at Durocher. "I wasn't worried about the other players ganging up on me. A lot of Giants hate him too."[22]

Some days later in a telephone conversation with National League President Warren Giles, Carl admitted that he made the threat to get Durocher in "the heat of anger" and he had no intention of carrying it out." The incident, Giles pronounced, "is closed."

Durocher always feigned innocence in the matter, and the surprise to many, like Arthur Daley, was not that Carl went after Leo but that it took him so long, since he had never hidden his loathing for him. "Leo speaks with a viper's tongue," Daley wrote, "and his fang marks are in every hide in the league, and he is still the most provocative bench jockey in the league."

Daley, another of the *Times*' many Pulitzer Prize winners, came out of Fordham and joined the paper in 1926. For 31 years he was a sports columnist, eventually one of those following John Kieran in writing the daily "Sports of the Times." He was the first of the paper's sportswriters to be given a foreign assignment, the 1936 Berlin Olympics. His Pulitzer was awarded in 1973, the first sportswriter to be so honored.

With Furillo, Daley is being forgetful. Others of us who watched Carl over the years remember that he did not have a short fuse, that when offended his resentment built over a period of time—in the case of Sheldon Jones' hitting him on Durocher's order, three years. But when he lost control he was as tough as anyone in the league, a powerfully built man with a 6-foot, 190-pound frame. Leo's mistake in crossing him yet again was that he thought he had his team to protect him, never thinking that Carl would be able to charge through all of them to get at him.

Furillo was of Italian stock, born in 1922 in Stony Creek Mills, Pennsylvania, near Reading, thus the nickname Reading Rifle in recognition of one the best arms in outfield history. As a rookie his arm was so strong, his throws so fast, that they tried him as a pitcher. But, like Rex Barney later, he had the velocity but no control. He was a proud man who would stubbornly stick up for his rights, even against a power like Walter O'Malley.

In 1959 he was injured and the Dodgers released him. Carl sued on the grounds that you can't release an injured player, and won $21,000 back pay, not realizing that O'Malley would blackball him, making it impossible for him to get another job in baseball through all the years until his death in January 1989. He left a legacy that many in the Hall of Fame do not match: a batting championship, a .299 career average, a team leader in seven World Series, 194 home runs and 1,058 RBI. Given his skills and experience there was no doubt of O'Malley's influence.

Carl Erskine pitched the Brooks to their 10th pennant on September 12, the earliest clinching date in modern National League history. Erskine played a major part in the race by going 14 and 2 for the last half of the season and 20 and 6 overall. He, like the rest of the team, wasn't too excited about winning the flag, since they had been so confident for so many weeks. The only clubhouse displays were when they put on a show for the photographers.

On September 29 the new game of major league musical chairs went into its second round as the transfer of the St. Louis Browns to Baltimore was approved, again, after Bill Veeck's departure. It was the second shift since 1903 but soon would be followed by so many franchise moves that to this day it's hard to remember where certain teams were from originally.

Baltimore had been in the International League for years, but many younger fans didn't realize that it was going back to its major league days of glory when, starting in 1871, it had been the home of some of the most famous teams and players, among them John McGraw, Wee Willie Keeler, Wilbert Robinson and Hughie Jennings. After finishing last in the American League in 1902 it dropped out of the major leagues, later to become the New York Yankees.

Another Dodger/Yankee World Series opened September 30 at Yankee Stadium, the 50th anniversary of the "fall classic." This one looked like the breakthrough, with the Dodgers more powerful than they had been since the war: 105 wins and a team batting average of .285, highest in years. But again it was the Yankees in six, as they beat Labine twice.

Not only was Labine belted around but Erskine was knocked out in the very first inning of the opener. This was disheartening for the entire Borough, expecting much in that opening game, with Erskine being the team's ace, a 20-game winner. Instead, Carl gave up three walks and two triples, one with the bases loaded by Billy Martin, for four runs, then gave way to Jim Hughes.

Reynolds started for the Yankees and lasted into the sixth, relieved by Johnny Sain, the eventual winner. Sain went the rest of the way and it's not that the Brooklyn fans begrudged him. The thought was that his day was past, the great days of Spahn and Sain in Boston, and now here he was a reliever for the Yanks, another of their reclamation projects that always seemed to work out—like Johnny Mize and Johnny Hopp. Labine took over in the sixth and was the loser when Joe Collins homered for the winning run in the next inning.

Martin did it again in game two as Eddie Lopat and Preacher Roe both pitched complete games. Preach almost had it won until Billy tied the game with a homer in the seventh and Mantle hit a two-run shot the next inning for the 4–2 Yankee win.

Game three was at Ebbets Field and was all Erskine as he struck out 14, a new World Series record. It was tight, though, as Raschi took the loss in a 3–2 pitcher's battle. Campanella homered in the last of the eighth for the winning run. I was sitting with fellow reporter George Wilson in *Newark Evening News* seats in a temporary press box section, enjoying the moment, seeing the record set as Johnny Mize struck out as a pinch hitter, the last out of the game. Figure it: Carl gets knocked out early in huge Yankee Stadium and then pitches one of baseball's classics in that little stadium on Bedford Avenue.

The Dodgers scored early off Whitey Ford in the fourth game, with Snider driving in four runs on two doubles and a homer for a 7–3 win. Billy Loes, unpredictable Billy Loes, went eight innings, relieved by Labine in the ninth.

Johnny Podres was next and he was rocked for six runs in the first three innings. It was an almost total rout, 10–2 before the Dodgers scored five in the late innings to bring the score to a more respectable 11–7. The Yankees teed off on four Brooklyn pitchers as Mantle, McDougald, Martin and Woodling homered.

The final game was tight, 4–3, Labine again the loser and Reynolds in relief of Ford the winner. Furillo tied it with a two-run homer in the ninth but Martin again drove in the winner on a single with two men on.

Billy was the Series' hottest hitter, setting a then-record 12 hits in 24 at bats and eight RBI. There was a stark difference in attendance as, even with capacity crowds at Ebbets Field, the Yankees outdrew them 198,530 to 108,820. A 90,000-plus attendance represents a lot of money and was a reminder to many that the Dodgers needed a new and bigger park—either in Brooklyn or nearby Flushing Meadows.

Nine days after the Series, Dressen was gone, the victim of his own stubbornness in refusing to accept a one-year contract. But with O'Malley you never knew. He announced it, explaining that "Charlie understands that we will not deviate from our policy of one-year contracts." Dressen had asked for three years but would have settled for two, not realizing that O'Malley wanted to get rid of him. Walter announced on the very next day that he "very definitely" had been considering a replacement for Dressen.

Charlie headed for Oakland, where he bought stock in and signed up to manage the Oakland Oaks of the Pacific Coast League, at that time not far below the majors in salaries and a much better league for travel. He had been a manager and coach in the majors since 1934 and would be up there again.

Charlie was born in Decatur, Illinois, in 1898. In his playing days he was the Cincinnati Reds' third baseman for eight years and spent his last season with the Giants, retiring with a .272 career batting average. He must have been a tough young man, for before baseball he had been a quarterback for two early National Football League franchises—professional football at just under 5-foot-6 and 146 pounds. As has been pointed out, his ego was as big as a clubhouse and finally did him in as Brooklyn manager.

The year ended well for two Dodger regulars when Campanella was chosen Most Valuable Player and Gilliam Rookie of the Year. Roy had his career year: .312, 41 homers and 142 RBI, the league leader. Gilliam hit .278 and led the league in triples with 17.

In early December, O'Malley chose Dressen's successor, Walter Emmons Alston, a career manager in the minors and a native of Venice, Ohio. They decided to call him "Smokey," a nickname from his high school pitching days, in deference to O'Malley, who thought there might be too many Walters around. It took time for Alston to gain the respect of his players and the rest of the league, since he was viewed as a career minor leaguer because, in 1936, in his only at bat in the majors, he struck out and then was sent back to one of the Cardinals' farm teams.

Walter solved that problem soon enough as word got around that this former first baseman was 6-feet-2, 200 pounds, and physically very tough, not afraid of anyone. He must have had extraordinary mental strength also, for he eventually signed 24 one-year contracts, more than 20 of them with Walter O'Malley.

Yes, a very strong man who would prove to be the Dodgers' most successful, if not liked and admired, manager. He would also prove to be a factor in the end of Jackie Robinson's career.

◆ FIVE ◆

1954
Behind the Giants Again

From the start of the '54 training season Robinson and Alston did not get along. None of the writers knew why and neither man would spell out the trouble directly. It couldn't have been color, for Alston managed in several towns where black players were totally accepted, and earlier was the manager at Nashua, New Hampshire, when Rickey assigned Newcombe and Campanella to play up there.

Some writers thought the problem was that Alston was O'Malley's man and would therefore automatically dislike Jackie. But Dressen was O'Malley's man and Jackie had little trouble with Charlie. The most reasonable cause was probably temperament, Robinson being so outspoken alongside the quiet, almost taciturn, man that Alston was.

Some of the Dodgers who played for him at St. Paul and Montreal knew what they were getting, but many others didn't. They soon learned that he was probably the strongest manager in the game, and one of the toughest. There were times in his career that a disagreement with a player led to an invitation, not to the dance, but to a physical confrontation.

Buzzy Bavasi told some writers a few Alston stories to get them familiar with the man, to give him a good press. Buzzy recounted a time in the minors when Alston, confronted with youthful insolence, invited each team member to get off the bus with him and have things out with fists. It was the same in the majors. If at an impasse, players always had the option of having things out in Alston's office. There were never any takers.

Carl Erskine expanded on this. "If a player rebelled," Carl said, "Alston would say 'Let's see who's managing this team. Do you want to step outside?' No one ever did."[1]

Again, Robby and Walter were almost direct opposites in temperament and their approach to the game. Alston depended a lot on his mere physical presence, a big dominating man. He would argue with umpires occasionally but was never the Durocher/Robinson type, ever ready to go on the attack.

Walter inherited Jackie at probably the worst possible time. Monte Irvin and others, noting Jackie's increasingly volatile outbreaks, were sure they were a result of his enforced silence that first two years, and the insults and physical abuse he suffered because of his promise to Rickey that he would not retaliate. They noted that many of his actions as his career was winding down were in revenge for those early insults, particularly those that continued through the years from Stanky, Durocher and the like.

Jackie, unlike his manager, could not contain his feelings for long. Early in the season Snider hit a ball into the left field stands that went for a double after it bounced back onto the field. Jackie raced out of the dugout to argue, something that is a manager's prerogative. Alston, coaching at third, made no move toward the plate umpire, later calling the episode "Jackie's temper tantrum."

Silent and strong Walt Alston finally broke the Brooklyn jinx in 1955 with the Series win over the Yankees. The man was so self-assured and confident that he worked 24 years under one-year contracts, most of them for Walter O'Malley, not the game's easiest boss.

Jackie had insulted his manager by his actions, and to make matters worse, was quoted after the game as saying: "The team might be moving somewhere if Alston had not been standing at third base like a wooden Indian."[2] He later explained that he thought the whole team would follow him out of the dug-out in protest. "Unfortunately, none of my teammates followed me," he wrote in his autobiography. "I became aware that Alston was standing at third base, hands on hips, staring at me. It was a humiliating moment."[3] Afterwards they had words at times but it never went beyond that. Alston, like many others who disliked Robinson, had a grudging respect for his now somewhat eroding talents, but even more for what he went through in breaking the color line, for the years of abuse and insults while he had to keep silent.

It's always sad to see a grown man cry but in the case of Enos Slaughter it was heart-rending. Enos was traded by the Cardinals to the Yankees on April 11th for Bill Virdon and Mel Wright. He had been in the St. Louis organization

17 years, with time out for three years in the Army. But the Cards, in the midst of a youth movement, thought he was too old.

He was 37, and there he was pictured in the *Times* sobbing forlornly into a handkerchief. "This is the biggest shock of my life," he said. "I've given my life to this organization and they let you go when they think you're getting old. I've got some good baseball left in me." And he did. Many in Brooklyn were not sorry to see his tears, remembering his deliberate spiking of Robinson when Jackie first came up and was playing first base. Enos, a North Carolinian, consistently denied the spiking years later, but Robinson always insisted he knew Slaughter went out of his way to get him, and that he still felt the pain days later.

The Dodgers and Giants opened the season with two games dominated by Willie Mays and Don Newcombe, both back after almost two years in the Army. It was Maglie against Erskine in the opener, with Maglie the winner, 4–3, on a long homer by Mays. Newcombe evened things up the next day, winning 6–4 as a triple by Mays was wasted when a two-run rally by the Giants fell short.

That same day the biggest crowd in the history of Baltimore, some 500,000, flooded the downtown streets to welcome their new Orioles, about to play the first major league game in that city since 1902. Bob Turley, in his only year with Baltimore, won the opener 3–1 over the Chicago White Sox. As with most expansion teams, the Orioles finished deep in the second division this first year, but they didn't improve themselves for 1955 by selling Turley, one of the league's most promising right-handers, to the Yankees, no surprise.

Baltimore, playing in the shadow of the Washington Senators, drew 48,000 for their opener and has drawn well since the start, despite playing for years in a stadium not up to standard. It was a strange rebirth, for the old Orioles left Baltimore in 1902 and surfaced the next year in New York as the Highlanders, then years later the Yankees. So the old Baltimore Oriole club was the grandfather of today's Yankees. New York got the club because Ban Johnson, American League president, wanted a team in the city and got it there despite the opposition of John McGraw's powerful New York Giants.[4] Until they got Ruth, a Baltimore native by the way, the Yanks were also-rans or worse, finishing one year 55 games behind the Red Sox.

On the 21st Alston made the moves that shook up the Borough and the team: Amoros to left field, Robinson to third base and Cox to the bench. Walter had his reasons, mainly that Robinson was not a good outfielder, and Amoros was, speedy and sure-handed. Billy was still rated the best third-base glove around, but time was catching up. He was 35 now and this would be his last season with Brooklyn. He only got to bat 226 times and his average dipped to .235, but for this final year his main value was as a defensive replacement in tight games. He was traded to Baltimore in '55 but was unhappy there and retired after 53 games.

The Yankees' Billy Martin is sent flying and called out by umpire Art Gore after a home-plate collision with Dodger catcher Roy Campanella. Watching the 1953 World Series action are Joe Collins and Gene Woodling. After the game Campanella told reporters "no little guy like that is gonna get by me." Martin was six feet tall, embarrassed but unhurt.

Roy Campanella also had to sit for a while, making way for Rube Walker. Roy was down to .167, constantly troubled by a bone chip fracture in his left wrist, the result of its being hit by an Allie Reynolds pitch in the first game of the previous World Series. The injury restricted his hitting for the entire year, even after an operation in early May. He was out for three weeks and afterwards was limited to 397 at bats for a .207 season average, 69 points below his career number.

In mid–May Ted Williams came back to baseball in a spectacular fashion, even for him. He had missed the first 18 games of the season and all of spring training after falling and breaking his collarbone March 1st while running down a fly ball. In his first game in 2½ months he went 8 for 9 against Detroit in a double-header, including two home runs in the second game. Ted was now 35, an age when injuries don't heal that quickly, as he found out. After the games he said his shoulder pained him every time he swung. Boston, true to its fashion, lost both games.

The next day, Joe Page, the Brooklyn nemesis in two World Series, was released by the Pittsburgh Pirates, a Rickey reclamation project that failed after fewer than two months. Joe had been dropped by the Yankees in '52 when his arm went dead, but after an operation and a year off he persuaded Rickey to let him try a comeback. Page's problem through the years wasn't just his arm on the mound but his foot on the bar rail. DiMaggio, often saying you couldn't help liking the guy, tried to straighten him out, even made him his roommate. But reportedly Page would often drink till he was blind, a 6-foot-3 bad drunk. DiMaggio after a while got sick of his drinking and late hours and requested a single room on the road.[5] Page was 36 when he was through and died at 63 in Latrobe, Pennsylvania.

Joe Black was also finished, age 30, the victim of a manager's meddling. After his miserable season in '53, just one year after he was named Rookie of the Year, the Dodgers gave him every chance, hoping the former best reliever in baseball would come around. But in seven innings of relief he gave up 11 hits and nine runs, three of them homers. After trying to regain it playing for Cincinnati and then Washington, he dropped out of baseball, no fan of Chuck Dressen.

One Saturday at the end of May a bad experience I had at Ebbets Field resulted in a change of the Dodgers' ticket-office policy. I had worked a morning shift in the *Newark News'* Orange office and wanted to go to that afternoon's Dodger-Giant game in Brooklyn. I called the ticket office to ask whether it was a sellout and was told it was against Dodger policy to give out such information.

I took a chance and drove into Brooklyn, drove around until I found a parking space, and walked to the ticket office, where I was told it was a total sellout, even including standing room.* I got home and wrote a scorching letter to Walter O'Malley, pointing out that word from the ticket office would have saved me a long round trip and that such information would take only a minute or so, if that.

To my surprise I got a personal reply from O'Malley a week later, apologizing for my trip and saying that my letter was posted in the main ticket office, instructing personnel to give out the game's seating status to callers. Also enclosed were two box seats to a future game.

The letter is lost but if I had been alert I would have picked up its greater import. After his apology, O'Malley went through a litany of ills: lack of parking, the deteriorating ball park, and limited seating, among other things. I felt I was apologized to, but also chided, and for things I had no control over. Why O'Malley would write such a letter to a private citizen still surprises me. As to being alert to his later intentions, this was the spring of 1954. The fact then that the Dodgers would ever leave Brooklyn was unimaginable.

As June began, Robinson's temper got him in trouble again, this time in

---

*I would have gone down into Newark to pick up a press pass but I didn't have time.

Milwaukee with three people hit by a bat he flung in anger. Robinson had been thrown out of the game by umpire Lee Ballanfant, and as he approached the dugout he flung his bat in disgust. It bounced along the dugout roof, hit an usher and then a man and his wife sitting in a box seat. All three had minor injuries, not bad enough to be treated.

Robby, in apologizing to the three, said he held the bat too long and when he finally let go its trajectory carried it onto the dugout roof and then to the area of the box seat. Warren Giles, National League president, later ruled the incident accidental. Afterwards the couple filed a $40,000 damage suit against Jackie but, since there were no further reports on it, probably settled out of court.

June was a bad month for the Dodgers, a lot of them unhappy over the hidden racial unrest. Robinson, the team leader, was hitting well, but was discontented with his manager and the fact that he was being shunted from third base to the outfield and back, positions he couldn't play nearly as well as his natural second base.

Cox, of course, was brooding about his secondary role behind Gilliam and Robinson, as was Don Hoak, an excellent glove man wondering why he was brought up to play behind Robinson and at times Cox. Roe, Billy's best buddy, was griping around because Billy wasn't a regular, an unexpressed feeling among the entire pitching staff. They didn't care how he hit, which had been never been a problem. They missed his glove, still the best in the business at killing doubles and preventing runs.

Then there was the constant concern about Campanella hitting some 70 or 80 points below his average because of his recovering wrist. Alston didn't help matters with his frequent silences. This team was used to Charlie Dressen, clapping his hands and chirping around the dugout, often bragging about his managerial skills. This big quiet man was taking some getting used to.

The age factor was setting in as well. Aside from youngsters like Amoros, Gilliam and Hoak, the team was aging. Roe, their former ace, was 39, Reese 36, Robinson and Cox 35 and Campanella 34. There would be one great moment to come, but this '54 team, regardless of how the world saw it, was discontent both racially and over playing time.

The wonder of it is they went into July only 3½ games out, but they hated the team they were chasing, Durocher's Giants. As Red Smith wrote: "There is no balm in Gilliam." Junior was too young to be part of the Durocher haters but the feelings were contagious, especially with Furillo still aching to get Leo, no matter what he promised the commissioner.

The hitting of Snider, Hodges and Robinson and pitchers Erskine, Meyer, Podres and Loes were keeping them close, along with their continued ability to hit in the late innings. On the fifth they were in Philadelphia, against Roberts going into the 10th. Starting with a triple by Walt Moryn, they scored four runs to win it. And this was a team with some new faces: Moryn in left, Gilliam at second, Hoak at third and Don Zimmer at short.

At this point Moryn comes to mind for one reason: a crack about him written by one of the New York writers, name forgotten after all these years. Walt was big, 6-foot-2 and 205 pounds, with the Dodgers only two years. He wasn't fast, but one night he made a good play on a fly to right field. The writer, possibly Roger Kahn, wrote in his overnight story, "Walt Moryn got hit in the glove by a fly ball." Funny, but then again, not. Why would a writer, whoever he was, a man who couldn't even make a Class D League team, make fun of a man who was hitting .275 and playing the outfield for one of the best teams in history? This sort of thing explains why many ballplayers dislike many sportswriters.

The insult might not even have been original. Dave Anderson recalled that during Babe Herman's time with the Dodgers some sportswriter, identity unknown but obviously one of the anti–Herman brigade, wrote the same thing about the Babe out there in right field. Again, sportswriters feeding on one another through the generations.

On the 8th Alston was furious with the team for having lost six straight to the Giants even though, strangely enough, he said there was "no lack of hustle." That's breaking a cardinal rule of managing: lack of hustle is the deadly sin. Not hitting and poor pitching are inevitable in a 154-game schedule.

Don Newcombe had also just broken another cardinal rule when he sided with an opponent against one of his own teammates in the matter of Russ Meyer and Monte Irvin. The latest loss to the Giants had seen some beanballs, not unusual for these two. In one sequence Irvin was at bat after Mays had hit a three-run homer in the first inning. Meyer then knocked Irvin down and then, in one of his tempers, hit him. Irvin admitted later that as he got to first base he was shouting insults at Meyer, who responded predictably. Monte was justifiably angry, of course, but though he was totally in the right, he started the insults.

Later in the clubhouse Irvin said he expected the knockdown pitch, but "it was right at my head and the next one hit me on the leg. He was throwing to hit me. I could tell that. I never talked to a pitcher before but this got to me. When I got to first base I called him a gutless son of a bitch."

Newcombe, not knowing the sequence but irate since Irvin was a close friend, verbally jumped Meyer as he came into the dugout, knocked out of the game. It was said that Newcombe resented a racial remark by Meyer and, although no blows were struck, there was a heated argument between the two. Both Meyer and Newcombe later denied there was any kind of scene, but both were lying. The cameras were on the dugout when Newcombe went at Meyer, and it looked for a few moments that there would be a fight. Later Meyer admitted his role, saying, "Can't he be thrown at? This is baseball, not tea and crumpets. This has been going on for a hundred years and now he wants to make something of it."[6]

Newcombe, just out of the Army, was having an excellent year on the pitching mound, eventually 20 and 5 for the year. But he was at times acting erratically, perhaps because the drinking that later ended his career had already started. As we shall see in the next chapter he was insubordinate twice in early 1955 for a triviality like refusing to pitch batting practice, part of every pitcher's life.

As the All-Star game approached, Alston picked seven Dodgers: Erskine, Robinson, Snider, Reese, Hodges and Campanella. Campy was a strange selection, smacking of "homerism," since he was hitting only .215 and was far from over the wrist operation earlier in the year. Alston's reasoning was said to be that Roy had caught the past 44 consecutive innings of All-Star competition, a streak he didn't want broken. Roy had been judged completely recovered, except for some numbness in his left hand, but still, an All-Star hitting .215? The Americans won for a change in an 11–9 sluggers' battle. After they had hit four homers, the winning runs scored on a blooper by Nelson Fox in the eighth inning.

Brooklyn's first stop after the All-Star lull was Milwaukee, where they lost a game that showed how this 1954 season would be going, and would also never be forgotten by either team. It was a double-header, the Brooks losing a tough first game by 2–0, Bob Buhl over Bob Milliken. In the second they were ahead 8–3 going into the last of the ninth.

The Braves had three outs left when Bruton singled and Mathews doubled. Joe Adcock drove both in with a single, 8–5. Erv Palica came in relief to face Pafko, who after a walk doubled for two more runs. Johnny Logan singled for another, Logan tasking second on the throw home. Pinch-hitter Charley White then singled up the middle off Palica for the sixth and winning run. You can't lose them any worse than that. Charley White was .166 as a pinch hitter and .236 overall.

A milestone in black player participation was reached the next day as Jim Hughes outpitched Lew Burdette 2–1, with Furillo, Hodges and Adcock driving in the runs. The Times took note that for the first time in major league history Negroes outnumbered whites on a major league starting nine.[7]

Except for the *Times*, not much notice was taken by the press, but there was talk around both leagues, mostly from Southerners like Stanky or the number of fringe players who feared for their jobs. Oklahoman Bobby Morgan, for example, was never happy with playing with blacks and, being tough and able to handle himself, wasn't afraid to say so. He once stood up in the dugout and, spotting a black player on the other team, said, for all to hear: "Why isn't he a Dodger? He's black enough." Bobby was a good utility man at several positions but the days for remarks like that in the Brooklyn dugout were gone, and soon so was he, to make room for players like Amoros and Gilliam. Bobby had to go because he was one of the "Klan contingent" and, unlike a few others, he wasn't valuable enough to the team to get away with it.[8]

Actually at th at time it was not unusual for four black position players to be in the Dodgers lineup, for Alston had played Amoros several times with Robinson, Gilliam and Campanella. Newcombe pitching that day tipped the balance. Established players like Reese, Snider, Labine and Hodges had accepted black players for years and couldn't be bothered about who they were playing with as long as they had the skills to be there.

As July was ending the lack of spirit in the Dodger clubhouse was puzzling, starting with Robinson saying the team needed a "lift" and Snider taking a shot at Alston by comparing him disparagingly to Durocher and Dressen in the ability to inspire. McGowen in his *Times* story was quoting answers to what he termed "unanswerable questions."

Reese was saying how much he felt sorry for Alston, Hodges was asking who Alston was supposed to blame, and O'Malley was refusing to blame anyone for the team's slump. "We've simply had some tough breaks," he said, "but I think we're going to come back and snap out of it."

The Dodgers were obviously so used to winning—two pennants in a row—that a little of what seemed to them adversity was getting to them. The only "unanswerable" question was why all the flap, why all the downcast faces and looking for answers. At the time this story was published in *The Sporting News* the team was three games behind the league-leading Giants—three. Imagine what a Senator or Athletics fan would say in that locker room.

Athletics fans would probably have told the Brooks to stop whining about tough breaks like Campanella's wrist, that their team was being forced to leave Philadelphia, playing to empty seats because of poor finishes year after year. A mayor's campaign to save the Athletics was an announced failure at month's end. It was so bad that a report to Mayor Joseph Clark stated that both the business community and the general public were apathetic and sometimes even hostile to the team's staying in Philadelphia. Big league musical chairs would soon start again.

A major problem with this then downcast Dodger team was that it was not a cohesive unit, as in the past, even in the days of Robinson's arrival. Three games behind in those years would not have caused even minor problems. But now the constant unrest surrounding the benching of Billy Cox was aggravated by something new to the team, a language problem.

Edmundo (Sandy) Amoros was brought up from Montreal to solve the left field problem created again when Pafko was traded in 1953. Robinson was not the answer, so the 22-year-old Amoros, with his great speed and good International League bat, was given his chance. One drawback was that Sandy spoke no English, being from Matarzas, Cuba.

This is no problem today as teams now have Japanese interpreters and enough Spanish-speaking ballplayers to help those who speak no English. But this was a new experience to that Brooklyn team: outfielders not being able to communicate verbally, players sitting next to a guy on the bench who didn't speak English, plus all the social situations where a common language is necessary. With some of the players it didn't sit well. The famous catch, made possible only by Amoros' speed and right-hand glove, smoothed much of this over, but that was more than a year away.

Milwaukee came in for a game on August 31 that showed Ebbets Field at its worst, that the old ballpark, built in 1913, was getting too small for the modern game.

Ten home runs were hit in a nine-inning game won by the Braves, 15–7. Joe Adcock not only tied the modern record with four home runs, but went five-for-five, doubling his second time up.

The ball was too hopped up and the bat speed, made possible by the modern slender bats, was too fast for a park with those left field stands and that right field screen. Snider, Hodges, Adcock, Mathews, Musial, Campanella and a host of others found the Ebbets Field a homer heaven that many pitchers dreaded. To this latest barrage the Dodgers' answer was the brushback, of course.

The next day Adcock was sent sprawling by a Russ Meyer pitch and then hit a double to left-center. Later he was struck on the head by a Labine pitch and taken off the field on a stretcher. Both Meyer and Labine were adhering to the pitcher's code of brushing back a hot hitter. Luckily, Joe was wearing his plastic helmet as the pitch struck just above his left ear, and got off with just a headache and a day in his hotel room.

There were several near fights on the field as the Braves came rushing out yelling about Labine deliberately hitting Joe. Clem later said "it goes without saying" that he wasn't throwing a beanball. "I was trying to brush him back, that's all." Adcock took it all gracefully, knowing how he'd be pitched to after hitting four home runs. "I'm not mad at anyone," he said. "What's there to be mad about? I'm just out there making a living."

Things turned around the next day with the Dodgers winning a 13-inning game 2–1, having set a record for leaving 20 men on base before Cox drove in the winner with a sacrifice fly with the bases loaded in the 13th. Two days later they beat the Cardinals 8–7 on Robinson's two-run homer into the upper left field stands in the last of the ninth inning. Those were always sweet, to win with the bases empty and two outs left. But at day's end they were five games behind the first-place Giants.

Tommy LaSorda, one of the International League's best pitchers, was brought up from Montreal that week and made his major league debut in a losing sluggers' battle against the Cardinals. Stanky's men routed Preacher Roe early and then went on to a 21-hit total in winning 13–4. Tommy pitched the sixth inning and gave up two runs on three hits. He appeared in eight games over the next two seasons, and then on to Kansas City for a final unsuccessful shot.*

The next day Brooklyn faced Cincinnati's Joe Nuxhall, who this 1954

---

*LaSorda was known to be the sociable type, profane but with a sense of humor. I was walking the grounds of Vero Beach one spring when I spotted a stocky catcher wearing the number 41. I saw LaSorda approaching in a golf cart and I stopped him. "Mr. LaSorda," I said, "That guy number 41 better be good." He looked and asked why. "That's Labine's number, he better live up to it." He shook his head and said, "I never thought of that," before taking off, laughing.

season would become a front-line pitcher with a 12 and 5 record and 3.89 ERA. Joe had made his name as the youngest pitcher to ever appear in a major league game after he was signed while in junior high school by the Reds during the war years. He was 15 and really got pounded in his first appearance.

The Reds were losing 13–0 to the Cardinals when Nuxhall made his debut in the ninth inning, giving up five runs on five walks, two singles and a wild pitch. His ERA was 67.5 but the Reds management knew what they had, a 6-foot-3 fastballer they nursed along in the minors until his comeback in 1952 at age 24.

Against the Dodgers Joe went 7⅓ innings and managed to make it out of the last inning the winner in relief of Bud Podbielan. There was some excitement in the Dodgers dugout when blonde and beautiful Mona Freeman, another movie star Brooklyn fan, appeared and posed for pictures with a number of Dodgers. George Shuba declined, saying, "I need a shave."

There's no telling how good Shuba would have been if he hadn't hurt his knee down in the minor leagues. He was born in Youngstown, Ohio, from immigrant Slovakian stock and grew into a compact, powerful man at 5-feet-11 and 180 pounds. He came to Brooklyn as "Shotgun Shuba," known for his line drives to all fields.

He was personable, easy to talk to and liked by both players and fans. The trouble was the knee that never enabled him to live up to his great potential. He had a decent career, the second man in history to pinch-hit a homer in the World Series. But a bad knee on the major league level is more of a handicap than in the minors, even Triple A like Montreal. He ended up at .259 and was a good pinch hitter, but after seven years he had to retire. As he used to say, baseball kept him out of the mills, where his father worked all his life.

During a Friday night game on August 13 the Dodgers, all of a sudden, got it together temporarily. They swept the Giants in a three-game series, during which the garrulous Durocher was virtually speechless as he knew the gap between the teams had closed to only one-half a game. Throughout Brooklyn fans were thinking: could this be revenge for 1951? For a while there it was, the old Dodgers, self doubts removed.

It started with Erskine against Maglie. The game was scoreless until the sixth when Reese hit one off the wall after Erskine and Gilliam had singled, Erskine scoring. The Giants came back with two in the seventh as Maglie went out for a pinch-hitter. Brooklyn got the winning runs in their half when Furillo homered with Hodges on first.

During this game it became clear that Robinson was now sometimes almost out of control. At one point an inside pitch crowded Erskine, only crowded him, not hitting him. Jackie bolted out of the dugout again, arguing, as Alston, this time resenting such interference, was coming in from the third base coaching box.

Red Smith, covering the game for his column, wrote that only Robinson sprang from the dugout to argue the pitch to Erskine. "Sometimes Jackie Robinson tries the patience of those who like and respect him most," he wrote. "He is so everlasting competitive, so quick to pop off, so often in wrangles," like the Erskine thing.

In private, talking confidentially, Red was much more outspoken. "I just don't like the guy," he told Roger Kahn. "I'm fed up with his Robinson fights and Robinson incidents and Robinson explanations. He's getting boring. I'm going to heave a sigh of relief when he gets out of baseball. Then I won't have to bother with him anymore."[9]

Smith was entitled to his opinion, but he could not always be trusted when it came to the Dodgers. As Snider and other players used to say, he only went to Ebbets Field when it was necessary, preferring his beloved Yankee Stadium, a nice easy subway ride from midtown Manhattan. He even went so far once as to compare Brooklyn fans with cockroaches during the '47 Series as Dodger fans were jeering Bobo Newsom, then a Yankee, after he was driven out of the game. The Dodger fans, Smith wrote, were "like fauna coming out of the woodwork."[10]

He was awarded a Pulitzer Prize in 1976 for the quality and freshness of his writing, a prize he richly deserved. But to many of us city-bred fans from Newark and Brooklyn, for example, he always seemed to be writing about fishing in the Adirondacks or Wisconsin, perhaps because he was from Green Bay. But worse, he loved horse racing, a sport for gamblers, and wrote of it excessively.

Staying on Robinson, Red's fellow *Tribune* writer Kahn quoted one Milwaukee pitcher as saying: "The reason we have beanball fights with the Dodgers is Robinson. His needling starts things off, and it's too bad. If he didn't needle so much he could be the most respected man in baseball."[11]

Preacher Roe, after he retired to his grocery store in West Plains, Missouri, came to Robinson's defense in his "farewell" article in *The Sporting News*. "Jackie had to take an awful lot of guff in his first few years and keep his mouth shut," Preacher said. "That sort of stuff piles up in you. In the last couple of years he has simply gushed out. Sure he's popping off and scrapping, but I think he feels that's his right after all those years of taking abuse. I can't say that I blame him a bit. Maybe I'd do the same thing in his place."[12]

The best take on Robinson from among the newsmen was from, surprisingly, Dick Young of the *Daily News*, a man who Jackie once described as a racial bigot. "He made enemies," Young wrote, "he has a talent for it. He has the tact of a child because he has the moral purity of a child."[13] What a marvelous way to describe Jackie Robinson, as a man of moral purity. Because that's what he was, a man who fought not usually for himself, but for the integrity of his people and for their right to stay in decent hotels, never for his own gain, particularly monetary gain. He knew this made him unpopular, but it made no difference. But through it all he was admired even by those he offended for what he stood for and what he went through.

The next day things had calmed down for another Dodger win, the score 6–5 as Furillo drove in four runs on a grand slam, giving the win to Jim Hughes and the loss to the Giants' newly-arrived John (Windy) McCall. The lead was now 1½ , with Durocher so upset that all he would say in the clubhouse was, "I don't want to talk about the game." He was second-guessing himself on his decision in the sixth inning: two out, Campanella up with two on, first base open and the pitcher batting next. Leo elected to pitch to Roy, who then drove in the winning run on a clean single to left.

New York was so excited about the next Dodger win, the sweep game, that the *Herald-Tribune* put it on page one. The Dodgers won easily 9–4 behind Loes, who gave up four home runs, one almost unheard of in Ebbets Field— an inside-the-park drive by Alvin Dark. Snider and Hodges also homered as a parade of five Giant pitchers, starting with Jim Hearn, tried to stop the rout. The Giants' recent seven-game lead was now just one-half game.

Then as quickly as the spirit came, it went. The fourth-place Phillies swept a three-game series at Ebbets Field while the Giants took a doubleheader from the Pirates. Roberts gave up six runs but Dodgers pitchers, starting with Bob Darnell—*Bob Darnell?*—gave up nine.

Herm Wehmeier and Murray Dickson combined the next day for the sweep by 6–2 and 6–0. Erskine took the loss in the first game and Meyer the second. In all fairness, it is not unusual for a team to let down after a couple of tense series, especially if victorious. The adrenal level has to come down eventually. The Brooks were unlucky only in that the Giants picked themselves up and started winning again. Suddenly, the gap was back to a comfortable four for Leo.

While all this was going on, Bing Crosby was feuding with Branch Rickey about the future of the Pittsburgh Pirates. Crosby, a 20 percent owner, was refusing to go along with Rickey's long-range plan to stock the Pirates' farm system with prospects in a Rickey plan termed "highly expensive rebuilding."

Crosby succeeded in persuading the club to downgrade Rickey to the position of "advisor and scout," effective in one year. A good part of the problems between the two was that Crosby was also angry on two other counts: Rickey's failure to ever take him into his confidence, and the sale of Crosby's favorite Pirate, Gus Bell, who later became a star with the Cincinnati Reds.[14] Der Bingle could be touchy.

As August was ending, the writers and broadcasters who covered the team voted their choices for the All-Time Dodger Team, a couple of them pretty weird. Five of the present regulars were chosen: Robinson, Hodges, Reese, Campanella and Snider. Then there was Dazzy Vance as pitcher, Zack Wheat in left field, Dixie Walker for right field, Arky Vaughn at third base. Some sentimentalist gave Pete Reiser one vote at center field.

Two selections were debatable. How could they have ignored Carl Furillo in favor of Walker? Dixie was a fine man and player but he played all during the war, when he had some of his best years against that inferior competition. And Arky Vaughn at third is a joke. Arky came to Brooklyn as a shortstop at the end of his career and played just 191 games at third. Ignoring both Cox and Lavagetto was strange.

Out in Detroit on September 17 the Cleveland Indians finally broke the Yankees' hold on the American League pennant, beating the Tigers 3–2 on homers by Jim Hegan and Dale Mitchell against veteran right-hander Steve Gromek. It had been six years, back to 1948, when a team other than the Yankees won, Cleveland having done it that year. The win that day was number 107 for the Indians.

Three days later the Giants beat the Dodgers 7–1 at Ebbets Field, winning the 1954 pennant and making for the first New York–Cleveland rivalry in the history of the World Series. That baseball can be a strange game, often confounding the experts, was proved by those Giants pennant winners. They were essentially the same crew that finished fifth the year before, a full 35 games behind the winning Dodgers. And, in this strange vein, the Dodgers of '54 were essentially the same team as the '53 winners. As the bookies say, "Go figure." Durocher's estimate was that the injuries to Campanella and Robinson were decisive factors in the race.

The Dodgers' pain over losing was eased somewhat by the arrival of Karl Spooner, who, after pitching two games, was given the "phenom" label by the writers, often a sure jinx. He came down from Oriskany Falls, New York, and in his first major league start not only held the Giants scoreless, but struck out 15.

Then in his second start, the final game of the season at Ebbets Field, he shut out the Pirates, striking out 12. That's 18 scoreless innings and 27 strikeouts for a 23-year-old rookie in two starts. The Dodgers were dreaming of another Dazzy Vance, Whit Wyatt, Van Lingle Mungo (when sober). It was not to be, for like many another sure-shot "phenom," Karl's arm went the next year after a mediocre 8 and 6 season. Was it Ebbets Field that did it, those short fences that doomed Harry Taylor, Ralph Branca, Jack Banta and so many others, for whom a waste pitch in that tiny park was fatal? Some can thrive, like Labine and Erskine. Others looked good for a while, then vanished.

As the year ended, Roscoe McGowen and Bill Roeder analyzed the things that caused Brooklyn to come up short, five games behind the Giants. Major injuries to Campanella and Robinson and Carl Erskine's in-and-out performances led their lists. Then there was Johnny Podres' appendectomy, the end of Preacher Roe as a front-line pitcher in this, his final year in baseball, and Newcombe reduced to a 9 and 8 pitcher. They also listed the decline in the baserunning of Robinson and Reese, and the failure of Billy Loes, a potentially great pitcher, to step up to the front rank of the staff, replacing Newcombe and Erskine.[15]

There is a lack of perspective in these appraisals. The Dodgers finished only five games out, in second place behind the Giants. They didn't collapse into the second division. For many other teams through the years a finish like that would be deemed a most successful year. It's hindsight, of course, but this same team, with all those "woes," would soon be World Series winners, for the first time in 55 years.

Cleveland came into the Polo Grounds with one of the greatest four-man pitching rotations in memory: Early Wynn, Bob Lemon, Mike Garcia and Art Houtteman, with Bob Feller as the fifth starter, went into that Series with a team that had won 111 games during the regular season. The Giants swept, 4 games to 0.

The winners in the sweep were the much less-known Marv Grisson, Johnny Antonelli, Ruben Gomez and Don Liddle. The Series also made a star out of journeyman Dusty Rhodes, lucky Dusty Rhodes of the two 260-foot home runs down that right field line in the Polo Grounds.

With its pitching staff, Cleveland was heavily favored: Lemon 23 and 7, Wynn 23 and 11, Garcia 19 and 11, Houtteman 15 and 7, and Feller 13 and 8. The Giants had good pitching but were somewhat nondescript when compared to those five. Johnny Antonelli was their big winner at 21 and 7, followed by Ruben Gomez at 17 and 9.

The shape of the Polo Grounds decided the first game. The big play was Mays' famous catch, with his back to the plate, of a 425-foot drive by Vic Wertz, a home run anywhere but in that misshapen Giants ballpark. The game was actually a pitchers' battle between Lemon and Maglie until Rhodes came up in the last of the 10th inning and with two on and hit one of most disgraceful home runs ever seen in a World Series game, or any other game. A pull hitter, he lined

Preacher Roe, part of the best trade Branch Rickey ever made, warms up in Ebbets Field. At .714, Preach was the highest percentage pitcher in Brooklyn history: 95 and 38 during his seven years with the Dodgers. After retirement he proudly admitted throwing the spitball, saying that with all the restrictions on a pitcher "he's got to help himself."

one down the right field foul line just into the seats, 258 feet away—258 feet for three runs and the game.

Johnny Antonelli and Rhodes dominated game two, another 3 to 1 pitchers' battle. Johnny went all the way after giving up a homer to left fielder Al Smith with his first pitch of the game. Rhodes again came through, this time a two-run pinch-hit single and another Polo Grounds home run, again down the right field line. Cleveland was pretty helpless at the plate, leaving 14 on base.

It was Gomez-Garcia in game three and again Dusty pinch-hit for Irvin in the third inning and with the bases loaded drove in two runs with a single to right, driving Garcia out early. It ended 6 to 2 as Wilhelm relieved Gomez in the eighth and retired the last five batters.

Rhodes, after a pinch-hitting role never seen before in a Series, sat out the last game. The Giants routed Lemon early and were ahead by 7–0 before Cleveland scored in the fifth. The final score was 7 to 4 with Don Liddle the winner as the Giants became the first National League team to win a Series since 1946.

In no World Series until that time was a premier pitching staff such a disappointment. That big four gave up 21 runs in the four games after going through the season with a combined 2.78 ERA. Many of us wanted to see Bob Feller pitch once more, but the Series was too short and Rapid Robert wasn't that rapid any more.

The Saturday the Series ended I got lucky. I was down in Newark doing afternoon sports overtime when, in going to the water fountain, I passed the City Desk and heard the words, "They land at LaGuardia at 7 o'clock." I went back to my desk thinking nothing of it.

Later, Harry Anderson, our Saturday City Editor, came back to our overtime section and went from desk to desk asking, "Are you up?"—meaning are you available for assignment. As he threaded his way everyone said no, thinking it would be just another "Bruce and Spruce," a tenement fire in the Central ward. As he neared my desk it clicked: 7 o'clock, LaGuardia, the arrival of the victorious Giants.

I said I was up as everyone looked at me like I was crazy. Harry, who knew the ropes, looked around in triumph, saying: "Rudy, get your car and you and Luther Jackson go out to LaGuardia and meet the Giants' plane. Call rewrite from the airport and then you can go home. Your overtime continues till midnight." Envious stares followed me as I left.

My principal assignment was to interview Willie Mays about a rumor that he was buying a home in Orange, New Jersey, near where his mentor, Monte Irvin, lived. Sports had set me up well by calling Irvin that afternoon and alerting him to my assignment. Monte was from Orange and had starred in everything at Orange High, so he had been a *Newark News* reader most of his life.

I was on the tarmac waiting for the plane when I was joined by Irvin, as expected, and Laraine Day, wife of Leo Durocher, unexpected. To say her beauty was stunning is a waste of time. We were out there almost a half hour and exchanged small talk, but to this day I can't remember a word of it. And, true to the newspaperman's code, I didn't ask for an autograph.

Freddie Fitzsimmons was the first one off the plane and it was obvious Freddie was having a good time, slightly buzzed and smiling. When Mays arrived we got him off to the side and he was helpful, not the impatient impolite man he was in later years. He told me yes, he was considering buying a place in Orange and would let me know through Irvin if he decided to. I left for home thankful that I had just spent one of the most interesting evenings of my life, all because I heard the words "LaGuardia at 7 o'clock." Willie never bought that Orange home.

The year ended on a sad note for baseball purists when the Philadelphia Athletics packed up and moved to Kansas City. The Athletics was Connie Mack's team, one of the originals that formed the American League in 1901. Why fans turned against such an historic franchise is a mystery. Certainly it had seen hard times for years, but most of the time the Phillies had done no better.

We now know it was the second in a series of dizzying moves that accelerated in years to come with one franchise, those original Athletics, hopping from one city to another across the country: Philadelphia to Kansas City to Oakland. Today it's difficult to remember what teams used to be where, the moves have been so numerous. Judge Landis would never have allowed it, but Judge Landis was long gone.

◆ Six ◆

1955
Finally, The Year of Jubilee

The year 1955, the Year of Jubilee for the Brooklyn Dodgers, started ominously for the Borough itself. Its newspaper, the venerable *Brooklyn Eagle*, ceased publication on January 29 after the Newspaper Guild of New York went on strike the midnight before.

The publisher, Frank Schroth, had previously told the Guild that the *Eagle* could not meet union demands that the paper match the salary levels of those across the river. Schroth argued that he couldn't, because the *Eagle's* benefits, overtime pay, night differential and call-back provisions were so much better, and paid so much better, than the Manhattan papers.

The newspaper's Guild members went on strike as scheduled and the paper, founded back in 1841 and Brooklyn's only daily, ceased publication. In a front-page farewell Schroth told his readers that the paper could not survive financially if the Guild would not lower its demands. They would not, and he prepared to close down. Schroth felt he had gone as far as he could but that the union was adamant and inflexible. He warned them that he had seven weeks' strike insurance and that when it ran out he would shut down for good. It did and he did.

We on the *Newark Evening News* felt the sting of the New York Guild's stupidity and corruption in 1959 when I was one of four who tried to organize the paper. At our first meeting in Newark's Robert Treat Hotel the Guild rep showed up drunk, almost incoherent. At our next meeting his replacement was so stupid as to hand out enrollment cards and then collect them publicly. We soon found out that our publisher knew of our every move and had a list with all our names. The source: he was seen having lunch with our Guild representative at the American Hotel in Freehold in central New Jersey. It wasn't long before he broke us through firings and transfers, and when we tried for redress, legal counsel told us the National Labor Relations Board in those Eisenhower years was conservative and would most certainly side with the publisher. The paper was never organized.

That same Guild later sat by and watched the newspaper business in New York City be almost destroyed by the Printers' and Engravers' Union, led by Tom Powers. Powers-led strikes killed the *Daily Mirror*, *World-Telegram*, *Herald-Tribune* and *Journal-American*. The hundreds of jobs that were eliminated, or the effect the closings had on the city in general, made no difference to the unions, for none of the leaders had the foresight to see what a four-month strike and impossible demands would do to their industry. You could have told them they won a Phyrric victory, but Powers and his stooges would not have known what you were talking about.

The *Eagle's* closing was almost a pattern for the later stupidity. The paper closed, the jobs disappeared and Brooklyn lost its one daily voice. All this was a severe blow not only to the Borough, but to the Dodgers. The team was now left to the Manhattan writers, most of whom gladly covered the Giants and Yankees, but were reluctant on most days to cover Dodger games. They thought the subway trip too long and involved—over the bridge, change at DeKalb, or wherever, and all that nuisance in those days.

Roger Kahn left the *Tribune*, but his place was taken by the defunct *Eagle*'s Tommy Holmes, one of the best sports reporters in the area, one arm and all. Though Kahn had worked for the *Tribune*, he was a Dodger fan at heart and resented the attitude of those from across the river.

"I fault the New York press in its coverage of the Dodgers," he told fellow writer Peter Golenbock. "Red Smith and Arthur Daley should have been there a hell a lot more. But it was a long subway ride to Brooklyn. It was much easier to go to the Polo Grounds or Yankee Stadium."[1]

As spring training was moving along, playing time became an issue again but this time with a difference: to the reader of the sports sections, as the team moved north it appeared that relations between Alston and Robinson had again deteriorated and, worse, both men were acting like children.

Robinson again "popped off" to an unidentified reporter, telling him his arm was better and "I've got as much right to be in the lineup as any man on this team, and Alston knows it." He then made the startling admission that he hadn't told the manager about his recovered arm "because I can't talk to him somehow." What he should have done is at least told his manager his arm was back and that he could again take over third base from Don Hoak.

Alston, almost as bad, griped to reporters, "If Robinson had a complaint why didn't he come to me? I talked to him last night. I didn't know his arm was all right. Now I assume his complaint to the press indicates it is all right."

These were grown men, sharing the same clubhouses, riding north on the same trains. Why the constant circling around each other and going to the press with their troubles? Robinson, though he would not admit it, was wearing down by this time. At 36 he should not have expected to play full time and, as the season progressed, it wasn't possible. Robby was listed as the team's starting third baseman, but for a few years his at bats had been falling off. He was only up 317 times in the coming season, but that wasn't Alston's fault, nor Jackie's. He had given his all for years, played hard and played rough for a long time whenever necessary. He was an old 36.

Earlier in the year he had collaborated on a three-part series in *Look* magazine. Though much of what he revealed was later used in his book, *I Never Had It Made,* he explained in some detail the reasons for his combativeness and why he competed so fiercely. Some of it, of course, dated back to his first two years in the majors when he had to take racial and personal abuse day after day without responding. "Throughout those two seasons I had to keep my mouth shut and take it. I couldn't protest to an umpire and I couldn't get back at players who taunted and insulted me with racial remarks." He was, as we know, keeping his promise to Rickey that he hold himself in check, no matter the provocation.

A good deal of it, however, he traced back to his childhood during the Depression when his abandoned mother had difficulty feeding five children. There wasn't always enough to eat at home but he survived in other ways. "I was the best athlete in the class," he said, "so the other kids gave me sandwiches and dimes to go to the movies so they could play on my team. I had to win from the start if I wanted to eat as well as the rest of my friends."[2]

O'Malley tried to smooth things over between Alston and Robinson, saying he was "delighted" at the way each "blew his top," that it was a "healthy sign." It really wasn't, but at least Jackie was starting to accept his reduced role, though the animosity between him and his manager lasted until his retirement.

The whole affair had become typical Robinson but was totally out of character for Alston. Bavasi had told the press about Walter's silent ways during his first season when Roger Kahn, for instance, named him "Wordless Walt." This year he was more confident in his role and somewhat more outgoing.

Typical of this second-year attitude was his answer when a reporter asked him if he had been offended by something he wrote. "I understand you're sore at what I wrote," the reporter said. "I don't give a damn what you write," Alston replied, walking away.

Brooklyn again opened its season at the Polo Grounds, Newcombe against Maglie. The score was 10–8 and, as could be expected there in Harlem, home runs dominated the game. Both starters were banged around, but Newcombe was one of the hitting stars with two home runs off Maglie. No one was surprised at this, since Newcombe was one of the best hitting pitchers in the game.

From there the Dodgers went on to win their first 10 games, a record for a team opening the season. In trying for their 11th they were beaten at Ebbets Field by Leo's Giants, 5–4 in a game at times enveloped in heavy fog. They knocked out Jim Hearn, but the Giants lumped five runs in the eighth inning, mostly off loser Johnny Podres.

The next day things got so nasty with beanballs and such that there were retaliations from each side, with one of them ending the career of Giants second baseman Davey Williams. Davey, 5-foot-10 and 160 pounds, was literally run over by the much bigger Robinson, who hit him with a shoulder block, thinking he was hitting Maglie.

After the knockdown the umpires faced near-riotous conditions as both teams swarmed around first base and the prostrate Williams. Alvin Dark charged at Robinson from across the infield for what looked to be a fight, but with the umpires intervening, no blows were struck. Later in the game Dark came in very high at third base trying to knock down Robinson, but Robby made the tag, got out of the way and later said he could have rammed the ball down Dark's throat but decided not to. Realizing this, Dark later told reporters to relay to Robinson that it was all over, no need for it to continue.

Some writers interpreted Dark's move as motivated by fear of Robinson, a ridiculous notion, but one that made a headline or two. They ignored the fact that later in the game Dark had thrown a body block as he came into third, jarring the ball from Robinson's glove. The truth is that both men later realized how inane their differences were, especially with Davey Williams in the Giant clubhouse, barely able to walk, his career in jeopardy, as events would prove. Robinson and Dark were mature, college trained, superlative athletes. Dark realized that when Jackie decided not to smash his face in as he slid into third, the rivalry was ridiculous. He also realized that Davie Williams took the hit meant for Maglie.

Later as a manager Alvin's courage in expressing his opinions, misguided as they might have been, was to cost him his job as San Francisco's manager. He confided to *Newsday* sportswriter Stan Isaacs that he thought Negro and Latin-Americans ballplayers were not as alert as others. Such players for him at the time were Mays, Cepeda, Marichal, McCovey, two of the Alous and Pagan. Regardless of what anyone thinks of the others, no manager in his right mind would call Mays anything but the intelligent, hustling ballplayer he always was until those sad days he staggered around the outfield for the Mets at the end of his career.

In the resultant furor Dark maintained that Isaacs "gravely misquoted" him, an argument he used in appealing to Commissioner Frick in an unsuccessful attempt to save his job. In just about every case in recorded history a ballplayer, actor or politician whose mouth gets him in trouble cries foul, I was misquoted.

Isaacs vehemently denied this during a recent telephone interview, saying he happened onto Dark at a time after the Giants had suffered a string of tough losses, with Alvin frustrated to the point where he vented feelings that were part of his upbringing in the South. "He was a nice man but he had this condescending attitude toward blacks and Latins," Isaacs said. "He felt that as much as he tried he could only get so much from them. I remember he was particularly disturbed by Orlando Cepeda making so many dumb baseball mistakes. On their part, the players resented being forbidden to speak Spanish in the clubhouse. This to them was racism. Alvin threatened to sue me for libel but he knew and I knew that he had said similar things to other people. So he never sued, just kept saying he was misquoted."[3]

Robinson's mistaken hit on Williams was in retaliation for several near beanings by Maglie as he was outpitched 3–1 by Erskine. After one such "duster" Robinson indicated to Maglie that he would bunt down the first base line, which he did two pitches later. He barreled down the line, naturally expecting Maglie to cover first. But Lockman fielded the ball and seeing Sal was not covering, Williams ran over from second and got to the bag just as Robinson arrived, hitting Davey a heavy blow in the midsection.

Another Dodger-Giant tense and hateful game, but this time with grave consequences. Davey Williams left the game with a severe back injury, from which he never fully recovered. He played in 82 games that year but retired at season's end and never played again.

Robinson apologized, saying that he regretted hitting Williams but could not understand why Davey made the play. It was clearly Maglie's job to cover the bag, he said, and as he was speeding head down toward first he assumed it was Maglie he hit, adding that if he had known it was Williams nothing would have happened.

"So you see, it wasn't Williams I was after, it was Maglie," he told *The Sporting News*. "He'd been throwing at us and someone on the bench, looking at me, said we should do something about it. Well, whenever there's something like that to be done the players expect me to do it. I went to the batter's circle and our batboy said I should let someone else do it. I didn't agree with him."[4]

The Dodgers began May facing big Gene Conley of the Braves, a 6-foot-8 right-hander who played for the Boston Celtics in the off season. Conley and Erskine battled through 11 scoreless innings until in the bottom of the twelfth Carl Furillo hit a two-run homer with Robinson on base for the ball game. The game had but two minutes to go as Furillo approached the plate. He hit the winner just in time, for the game would have had to be called at 11:15 so the Braves could honor their travel commitments.

Conley was unique in baseball circles, a successful major league and National Basketball Association player for a number of years, many as a reserve center for the Celtics. He had a good baseball career, considering the physical pounding he took season after season. He ended up 91 and 96 with a 3.82 ERA after 11 years.

That week Newcombe was suspended for the silliest of reasons. He refused to pitch batting practice because, he said, he wasn't being started often enough. Alston, not a man to mince words, called him into the clubhouse and told him to take off his uniform and go home, suspended indefinitely.

Newcombe had pulled this before and Alston had gone easy that first time. But this time Walter wanted an apology and an understanding: when to start pitchers was his business, he said, "but Newcombe seems to be making it his." Newk told pitching coach Joe Becker he had a sore arm, but the entire club knew this was not true, that the trouble was "Don's head, not his arm." It was suspected the drinking that would eventually ruin his career had started, for he had turned moody and irascible since coming out of the Army.

The suspension lasted only one day, for Big Don, after spending some thinking time while driving home to Colonia, New Jersey, returned to Brooklyn and apologized, taking a $250 fine. This was good for him and for the team. He went on to have one of his best years, 20 and 5, leading the league with an .800 percentage. Fittingly, he relieved the next day against the Phillies and got the win, pitching two scoreless innings as the Dodgers won in the twelfth, 6–4.

What brought him back so soon was money, Don revealed later. "When I first left the clubhouse I didn't give a damn," he said. "But then I was driving home I got to thinking a bit. I asked myself what was I thinking. You can't play ball anywhere else [the reserve clause] and you can't make that kind of money at any other job. So by the time I got home I felt different."[5]

The Dodgers continued hot there in Philadelphia, winning their 20th game against two losses, 6–3, Erskine beating Roberts. Typical of Philadelphia, fans showered the field with empty beer cans after umpire Al Gore cleared the bench of Earl Torgeson, Roberts and pitcher Jack Meyer. The team and the fans were in an ugly mood, the team on its way to an eighth defeat that would drop them down into last place. Roberts was particularly upset because his record would fall to 5 and 16 against Brooklyn in his home park.

On to Chicago, where there were all smiles between Newcombe and Alston after Newcombe pitched the finest game of his career, a one-hit, 3–0 win during which he faced the minimum 27 batters. Cub second baseman Gene Baker lined a single past Newcombe's head in the fourth inning, one of only five balls that went into the outfield. A masterpiece, 96 pitches in one hour and 55 minutes.

As May was ending, a tremor shook Brooklyn, especially around the area of Ebbets Field, as the Borough got its first hint that the Dodgers might be leaving. There had been signs: O'Malley's whining based on false attendance figures, the almost three-hour conversation between O'Malley and Governor Earl Warren of California in O'Malley's private box at Ebbets Field, and the marauding delegation from Los Angeles that was trolling through Eastern cities trying to steal a team. But this was concrete evidence: the story in the *Times* on Los Angeles floating a $5 million bond issue to build a 63,000-seat stadium.

The story noted that there wasn't a big league facility out on the coast, the nearest large-capacity stadium being the 100,000-seat Coliseum. That, *Times* writer Gladwin Hill pointed out, "will not accommodate a good baseball park layout because of its oval design." Little did he know Walter O'Malley.

Things quieted down later in the week when word came that the voters of Los Angeles had voted down the proposal by a 160,000 to 131,000 count. The baseball world was shocked at the result: a Coast city turning down the chance for a big league franchise, even knowing that it would probably be the Brooklyn Dodgers.

Preacher Roe started July by selling the story of his spitter to *Sports Illustrated*, startling his teammates and the rest of baseball. The surprise was not that he threw it—many did—but that he admitted it after not getting caught for so many years. All the Dodgers knew it, as Furillo revealed years later. "When Preacher went to his cap with two pitching fingers together that was our signal. If he went to his cap with fingers spread he was faking."

In the story, he confessed that it wasn't his "little ol' sinker" that had been his money pitch. It had been the outlawed spitter. "I threw the spitter the whole time I was with the Dodgers," Preacher said. "Seven years in all. Conscience? Hell, it never bothered me none throwin' a spitter. If no one is gonna help the pitcher in this game, he's got to help himself." He always maintained he had three pitches, "my change, my change off my change, and my change off my change off my change."

He revealed in the article, "The Outlawed Spitter Was My Money Pitch," that he often had help loading up the ball. "I wasn't always the one to load up the spitter. Once in a while, after the ball had been tossed around the infield, Pee Wee or my buddy Cox, would come up to the mound, drop the ball in my glove and say 'There it is if you want it.'"[6]

He defended the pitch, feeling that with the many rules favoring the hitter, it was a way to even things up. Among his targets were the three-second stop rule on the pitcher, the smaller strike zone, bringing in the fences, the lively ball and the batter, unlike the pitcher, being allowed to take almost as much time as he wants at the plate: stepping out, adjusting his cap and going through all the other quirky mannerisms many batters have. Mike Hargrove, who retired in 1986 as Cleveland's first baseman, was nicknamed "Rain Delay" Hargrove, he took so much time.

Roe always passed himself off as a hick, a hillbilly from Arkansas who talked slowly and with that twangy drawl. He really had a sharp intelligence and in the off season often taught high school mathematics. And his family was hardly of the Hatfield/McCoy stripe. His father was a medical doctor and his brother a school superintendent.

Preach was born in Ashflat, Arkansas, in 1915, and for all his adult life was a stringy 6-foot-2, 170 pounds. His hillbilly image was always shattered when people found out he attended Harding University in Searcy, Arkansas. Also his attitude on race relations was that of the literate man he was, not the image he projected.

He was a pitching star at Harding, where he was known by his middle name Charles, from 1935 until 1938 when he signed his first professional contract with Branch Rickey and his St. Louis Cardinals. During Homecoming Week on October 25th, 2002, he was named Outstanding Alumnus by Harding's College of Sciences.[7] Hillbilly indeed.

At the age of 88 he was interviewed by eighth-grader Michael Harrington, winner of a *Weekly Reader* contest. When the boy asked him about Jackie Robinson he replied: "Well, I'm proud of my career at that time. It was a step for civilization and I'm part of it. I just felt that if Jackie hit a home run off me it counted as much for me as if Pee Wee Reese or some other white guy hit it. It didn't matter to me. I'm proud of my space in history then."

There were those who doubted his confession. Umpire Larry Goetz, for one, said he never saw Roe throw a spitter. "If Roe was throwing a spitter, and it was such a good pitch, why did he quit?" Goetz asked writer Karl Lawson. "He was throwing hard as ever last year. He said his spitter came up to the plate and then dropped. I never saw any of his pitches act like that. A spitter is like a knuckler, no rotation and it can break any way, not just down."[8] Larry should have checked the record books. When he retired, Preacher was 39 years old coming off a 3 and 4 season, giving up an average of five runs a game. At his age, what was the point of further tarnishing a great career with that kind of performance?

Some of the Dodgers' comments were interesting. Duke Snider, from whom you would expect condemnation, said, "Anything that pitchers can get away with is all right with me." Erskine would not comment on the pitch but felt that "the Preacher could have won without the spitball. He was a really classy pitcher."

Brooklyn fans finally started becoming aware that the impossible could happen, that they could lose their beloved Dodgers, when on August 16 O'Malley announced a partial move of the team to Jersey City. It wasn't Los Angeles, but it was a move west, across the Hudson. Jersey City wasn't quite a death knell, but the move there came close.

The announcement outlined a plan whereby eight Dodger home games would be played in Roosevelt Stadium the following year, the first time in baseball history a team would split its schedule between two cities, let alone two states. Each of the other seven National League clubs would play one game in Jersey City, plus one exhibition game.

Roosevelt Stadium was, like the future Coliseum, unsuited for major league baseball. Since the Jersey City Giants left, it had been used for stock car racing, so a banked track circling the playing area would have to be eliminated, but none of this mattered to O'Malley. He had two motives in mind: to make believe he wanted to stay in Brooklyn, and to sound out the other National League owners on the Jersey City move. If they would go for such an outlandish proposal, a premier team like the Brooklyn Dodgers playing in a decrepit stadium in a minor league city, he figured they'd go for the final move to California.

Some politicians were frightened, thinking that O'Malley was using the New Jersey move as a threat to make them consider a replacement park for Ebbets Field, which they soon started discussing. It was nothing of the sort. O'Malley, today's revisionists notwithstanding, decided against staying in Brooklyn, or Queens, or wherever, once that California gold started glittering. When they offered him that 300 prime acres in downtown Los Angeles, any thoughts of loyalty to his native city were dismissed, if they ever existed.

There were those who knew the Jersey City move meant goodbye to the Dodgers. It showed the power of Walter O'Malley to do anything he wanted, since not one other National League owner opposed such a drastic move, having their teams play in a stadium that by major league standards was a joke.

Dick Young of the *Daily News*, one of baseball's greatest sports writers, gave the tipoff that he knew O'Malley's true motives when, covering the first Dodger game in Jersey City, he began his overnight lead with the Dodgers, "Inching their way westward...."[9] Today Jersey City, tomorrow Los Angeles.

Young often said he knew earlier than most that O'Malley's goal was California when Walter, in an obviously unguarded moment, told him that Brooklyn and the area was getting "full of blacks and spics and Jews."[10] Dick didn't say whether Walter was drinking at the time, or whether he appeared to be making sense. Jews were a traditional part of Brooklyn, many thousands of them Dodger fans for a good part of the century. The same for the Bronx and its Yankee fans. Ben Chapman, a good-hitting Yankee outfielder, was ridden out of town to Washington for shouting anti–Semitic remarks to the stands from his center field position in the Stadium.

Young was combative, tough, and tenacious, unafraid to confront players who threatened to punch him for something he wrote that they didn't like. Before Young, the Grantland Rices and Bill Slocums lionized the players, throwing the word "hero" around heedlessly, not remembering the true meaning of the word: a man who risks or gives his life for his country or his fellow man. Calling baseball players heroes, as many still do today, is ridiculous. But such was their style as they covered the game on the field only. Anything else was off limits.

Dick Young changed much of that with his wide-ranging reporting. He began his career in 1943 at the age of 25 and soon was fleshing out the ballplayers, not treating them like gods, reporting on things that went on among teammates and in the clubhouse. The ballplayers were no longer a credit to the game just because they put on their uniforms.

Dave Anderson, who worked alongside Young when they covered the Dodgers, explained that Dick was the first morning paper reporter who wrote with an afternoon angle. "He was a terrific reporter and a very hard worker," Anderson said. "I mean, he just dug up stories and was fearless and would write what he thought. And on the *Daily News* you could do that. After a game he would go to the clubhouse while the other writers would write about the game and what they saw. He had an extra early edition and had to come up with stories other than the game itself, so he would go in and talk to the manager, general manager, players, whoever."[11]

Baseball coverage in general would soon include more than just what happened on the field. Young worked hard at his column, "Clubhouse Confidential," and soon others followed his methods. Sports writing was changing for the better.

Dodger fans were furious, of course, at all this Jersey City nonsense. Lunchtime crowds would gather in front of Borough Hall waiting to pounce on President John Cashmore or some other city official for answers as to what was going on. There were no answers because most politicians, even those wise enough, or on the inside enough, to see where O'Malley was heading, didn't want the voters to realize how powerless they were in the face of O'Malley's puzzling clout with the other National League owners. There was no law against moving the Dodgers, to Jersey City or anywhere else.

On the 19th of August, O'Malley finally made the threat that had been in his mind all along. At a meeting with officials at Gracie Mansion he admitted that the Dodgers and Giants might have to leave the city. In his supposed pleading for a city-aided ball park to replace Ebbets Field he told, among others, Mayor Robert Wagner and Robert Moses, the city's Construction Coordinator—one of his many titles—that the problem was bigger than the Dodgers, that the Giants were involved. "It's unlikely that one club or the other would move. You'll find that the two will move. If one team goes, the other will go. It's very serious, Mr. Mayor."

O'Malley knew, from his Jersey City venture, that the other owners would approve of his taking the Dodgers to the Coast, but not alone. There had to be two teams to make the move profitable for all. Flights to California to play just one team would cost too much travel money. Two teams meant profits.

He could be certain of approval because the 50-year configuration of baseball had changed just two years before when Lou Perini was permitted to leave Boston and settle his Braves in Milwaukee. The ice had been broken, making it easier for Philadelphia to move the Athletics to Kansas City later, after the 1954 season. Baseball was on the move and O'Malley reveled in it.

It had been known for some time that the Giants were in deep financial trouble, confirmed by Giants President Horace Stoneham as he told the group that if the Dodgers left, his position would be even more precarious, since "40 percent of the Giants total business" comes from the eleven Dodger games played at the Polo Grounds.

During this meeting O'Malley and Moses started their shadowboxing over the site at Atlantic and Flatbush Avenues, an unused Long Island Railroad terminal. This was O'Malley's smokescreen. He knew he could not have the site, Moses telling him continually during all negotiations that it was slated for redevelopment under Title I of the Federal Housing Act and could not be used for a ball park. Federal agencies, he said, had the area down for slum clearance and would never approve of anything else.

Robert Moses could have cleared that site for O'Malley in an hour if he had wanted to. But he didn't want to and he was adamant about it. "I don't want to see a baseball field in downtown Brooklyn," he said repeatedly. "The streets will never handle the cars. If you build a domed stadium, ballgames will create a China Wall of traffic. No one will be able to pass."[12] He was right and O'Malley knew it.

For reasons sometimes unfathomable, Moses was for years one of the most powerful men in New York state, an imperious, and often cruel man of such family wealth that he at some times held a number of administrative jobs and often worked without salary, such was his mother's fortune. To some, this gave him an air of altruism, but there was none of that. Moses wanted the New York metropolitan area built to his vision: cars and more cars, bridges, expressways, turnpikes. Everything for the automobile, little for mass transit, one reason that the Long Island Expressway, among others, strangles in traffic. He had no time for stadiums. He was also against mass transit to places like Jones Beach on Long Island because as a result the areas would be flooded with "undesirables."

Plus, he didn't like O'Malley, so the phone call to clear the Long Island Railroad site would never be made, which was just fine with O'Malley. To a man of Moses' 15-hour workdays, O'Malley was a fat, cigar-smoking, conniving politico-lawyer. On O'Malley's part, Moses' dislike didn't bother him at all. He wanted the animosity, since it assured him that he would be not be offered a site he didn't want.

At one point, in answer to an O'Malley letter, Moses scared Walter by pointing to a way he could buy the Long Island Railroad site, the last thing he wanted to do. "The natural question everyone will ask about the Atlantic Avenue site," Moses wrote O'Malley, "is if you need only three-and-a-half acres of land, if it is indeed distressed property, if you have a million dollars in the bank, if you have railroad easements, if you really want to stay in New York, why don't you buy the property at a private sale?" Showing some exasperation, Moses continued, "On the other hand, I don't see how you can have the nerve to indicate that you have not received proper support from public officials involved. Every responsible, practical and legal alternative we have suggested has been unsatisfactory to you."[13] O'Malley did not offer to buy, nor did he give Moses a satisfactory answer.

Moses was teasing O'Malley here, knowing there would be no answer, for everyone realized that the downtown site would be an abomination, domed or not. The parking situation would almost as bad as at Ebbets Field, traffic engineers estimating that no more than 2,500 cars could be accommodated. This was the middle 1950s, remember, when people were falling in love with their cars and shunning mass transit, thanks in large part to Robert Moses' love of highways pushing through and encircling the New York metropolitan area.

Brooklyn's city planners dreaded, for example, the prospect of thousands of game-bound cars strung along the Brooklyn-Queens Expressway, one of Moses' worst creations. They would then have to fight through downtown congestion and look for parking spaces where there would be none. The Atlantic and Flatbush Avenues site was therefore truly an O'Malley smokescreen, in the opinion of Dave Anderson, who covered all of the negotiations when he was on the *Journal-American*.

"He kept after it because he knew he could never get it," he said. "Everyone around the Dodgers at that time knew he was on his way to Los Angeles one way or another. In fact he used to say 'Oh, I couldn't take the Brooklyn Dodgers to Queens.' So he takes them to Los Angeles.

"It was very hard for me to warm up to Walter. I always felt that he was always conniving. You ask about the Queens site where the Mets are now. None of us took the city's offer seriously because we knew he wouldn't accept. He was going to California. They annoy me, these people who try to blame Robert Moses for the Dodgers moving. Listen, they could have built a brick wall a mile high around Los Angeles and O'Malley would have broken through it to get his team there."[14]

Retired sportswriter Stan Isaacs feels the same way but expresses himself more strongly about O'Malley. "I despise him for his lying and moving the team from Brooklyn," Isaacs said. "He kept spreading talk that the Borough was filling with blacks who couldn't afford to support the team, that they were urinating in the ramps and other things. I think he would have stayed if Moses had given him the best piece of land in downtown Brooklyn, but in those days cities didn't give things like that to private corporations. Besides, the more he became aware of what Los Angeles was offering the less he was inclined to stay in Brooklyn."[15]

The only concrete development out of the meeting was when Mayor Wagner approved Cashmore's proposal to appropriate $50,000 for an engineering study of the Flatbush and Atlantic site. It seems nobody listened to Robert Moses at the time, but they would soon know better. The man was a highway builder, not a baseball fan.

After the meeting, the vultures started circling around Ebbets Field and the Polo Grounds. On the 23rd the Los Angeles City Council officially announced that the Dodgers or Giants would be welcome if either decided to move. It appointed two of its members as emissaries to discuss any such possibilities. After inviting both O'Malley and Stoneham to visit their city they said their representatives would be in New York in late September to discuss the situation. Los Angeles had tried for some time to lure a major league team to their territory, but was turned down each time for lack of a suitable stadium. But for O'Malley the Coliseum, the worst park in the history of major league baseball, would do.

Duke Snider picked this time of turmoil for his worst moment in the 11 years he played at Ebbets Field. All during those years Duke never seemed to appreciate the Borough or the loyalty of the Brooklyn fans. He never accepted the fact that fans cheer when you're going good and boo when you're not. He had been in a slump during which his average dropped from .331 to .299, and was sulking.

In a childish fit of anger, after another hitless game, he ranted to the sportswriters that Brooklyn fans "are the worst fans anywhere, a lousy bunch of front-runners who don't deserve a pennant." He made it worse by telling the writers that he wanted his remarks printed. After sleeping on it, which often dissipates angry moments, the next day more of the same: "There are some good Brooklyn fans, but maybe there are more bad ones."[16] When you sleep on something like that, it can't be brushed off as a momentary thing. There was a bit of Jackie Robinson in Duke Snider, but at least Jackie had grounds, given all that was done to him. Duke just popped off senselessly. On this latest occasion he said his mother talked some sense into him and he quieted down.

Duke Snider in a characteristic unsmiling pose. Surprisingly, he was sorry to leave for L.A. He loved Ebbets Field, where he became a Hall of Fame slugger, but never formed the relationship he should have with the Brooklyn fans.

Snider was a terrific hitter and a superb outfielder, one of the best centerfielders in history, given the difficulties of playing in a park where he didn't have much room, where the walls out there were confining and dangerous. But there was something missing in the man: it always seemed someone else's fault when things went wrong.

Dick Young got on him often, once calling him a crybaby, and would tell him when he was slumping, "If you want better treatment get some hits." Young was merciless but fair. Of all the beat writers he was the only one unafraid to describe the Golden Boy from California in such terms, unlike Arthur Daley, who defended him consistently. The evening after his rant Snider got three hits, one a blooper and another with eyes, and the fans cheered lustily, not knowing that he was refusing to apologize.

I'm sure I was the victim of Snider's revenge when I sent out questionnaires for this book. My questions to him were sent back unopened, marked "Return" with big black crayon marks over most of the envelope. In my first book on the Dodgers of the '40s I had described the Snider I had watched over 10 years at Ebbets and the man in the clubhouse my *Newark News* sportswriter friends described to me: a 29-year-old man-child who was often sulking or popping off about how tough it was in the major leagues, and who often blamed the fans for his troubles.

From the stands you could tell his moods on the field. If he was prancing around center field, loosening up his legs or throwing arm he gave off an air of eagerness to play. When he walked out there with his shoulders slumping there would be trouble after the game about "the worst fans in baseball" or some other such drivel.

I soon realized I might have violated some rule of the club when other ballplayers would not return my questions. Men I thought I had reached a measure of friendliness with were non-communicative. I still can't figure out what they could be fussing about. I watched the film *Boys of Summer,* based on the Kahn book, and listened as players, including Snider himself, described the Duke's moodiness. Reese, for example: "He'd go 0 for 3 and stand out in center field not thinking about the hitter but that he didn't get a base hit."

Labine: "He pouted. That's the only terminology I can think of. He was a pouter. As great as he was I think he could have risen to even greater heights if he put himself out more at times."

"I think Clem is right," Snider says. "Some guys mature at 30, some at 25. I don't know what turned it around for me from being a worry wart, a moody type person. But you finally realize there's much more to life than a strikeout."

My first experience with Snider was a few years ago when I was writing my first Dodger book. In reply to my questions about Pete Reiser he wrote to tell me he didn't know Pete enough to be able to help me. In my then interviews with Eddie Miksis I brought this up.

"Eddie," I asked, "how could this be? They were outfielders on the same team for two years, and when later Pete was named manager at Triple A Portland he hired Snider as his assistant. Snider took over when Pete got sick. How could he tell me he didn't know Pete?"

"Well," Miksis replied, "he didn't want anyone intruding on his Dukedom," meaning Snider knew that in the mid–'40s he had replaced a Dodger outfielder who once had the potential to be the best of his generation.

Why, I asked, would he write his letter to me printed, even down to his name? "You've got to realize, Rudy, some of these Hall of Famers are weird in ways," he answered. "He didn't want you selling his autograph." I was horrified, but it made sense.

I shouldn't have been surprised at all this. I had been warned years before by Hy Goldberg and others on the *Newark News*. "Rudy, if you come into sports with us never trust a ballplayer, never," he said. "I don't care how close you think you are to any of them, as soon as something you write bounces back on them they holler they were misquoted. Every goddamn one of them does it. I've been burned by guys on the [Newark] Bears and in the majors." I thought of Alex Kampouris.

As for asking Duke Snider's autograph, I thought of Eleanor Roosevelt. In the spring of 1953 she addressed the student body at Columbia High School in Maplewood, New Jersey. Afterwards I identified myself as a *Newark Evening News* reporter and she gave me a lengthy interview as the secret service men looked on somewhat nervously.

I found her gracious, tallish and much better looking than she appeared in photographs. There also was a magnetism there, and I realized what had drawn young Franklin to her before the marriage fell apart. But, true to our newspaper code, I did not ask for her autograph.

When I got back to the *News'* Orange office, one of our deskmen, Leo Tracy, asked to see her signature. He jumped up when I said I hadn't asked for it. "Rudy, what the hell's the matter with you?" he almost shouted. "That wasn't some goddamn movie actor. That was *Eleanor Roosevelt.*" He was right, of course, but I was only 26 and took my press pass seriously. Now, so many years later, I say if I didn't ask The First Lady of the World for an autograph does anyone think I'd bother a Duke Snider?

On the 28th at Ebbets Field, Sandy Koufax was thought to have arrived, as in only his second start at home he struck out 14 in shutting out Cincinnati 7–0. Here was a 19-year-old kid pitching for a $6,000 salary and a $14,000 bonus, the money that was keeping the Dodgers from sending him down to Montreal for some minor league experience.

For Koufax those years were a Catch 22. Alston wasn't using him because he was nervous and wild. But he couldn't overcome the nervousness and wildness unless Alston used him. There were a number of occasions where Alston pulled him too soon and for little reason, because at that stage he didn't have faith in him. On some of those occasions a little more trust would have helped, might even have made Koufax become a star earlier, to the happiness of all of Brooklyn.

Dick Young expressed the feeling of many of the writers, and even of some Dodgers, when he wrote: "A pitching pinch has to develop before Walt uses the kid. Then, it seems, Sandy must pitch a shutout, or the bullpen is working full force and the kid will be yanked at the first foul ball."[17]

The fans were behind Koufax even through all his wild spells because of the occasional brilliance he showed when given the chance and because he was from Brooklyn, a graduate of Lafayette High School. He was born Sanford Braun but later took the name of his mother's second husband.

He had the ideal build for a pitcher, 6-foot-2, 210 pounds and with long arms. But there was something else, something few other pitchers have ever had: his fingers were extraordinarily long. He could therefore wrap his hand around the ball, allowing for a 95-mile-an-hour fastball that flared in to all hitters, and an 85-mile-an-hour curveball, a speed almost unheard of.[18] All that talent, but with an arthritic elbow that eventually forced his retirement at age 32.

His Brooklyn years were difficult in other ways than his manager's lack of faith. As reported in Jane Leavy's book, *Koufax*, he was resented on two grounds: that he was a bonus baby taking another's spot, not an unusual feeling on all teams, and that he was a Jew.

This surprised many, because the Dodgers, being in a Jewish area, had been hungry for another Jewish ballplayer ever since Cal Abrams had been traded to Cincinnati in June of 1952. But this was a front office decision not necessarily popular with the team.

Sandford "Sandy" Koufax was a Brooklyn boy who blossomed in Los Angeles. He was so wild with the Dodgers that no one suspected he would become a Hall of Famer, much less one on the West Coast. Sandy's problems with the Dodgers: he was a "bonus baby" taking a spot on the roster while unproductive, he was a college boy and he was Jewish.

Abrams never had to face what Koufax had to take. He was Jewish, yes, but he wasn't a bonus kid sitting on the bench taking somebody's job who could be more useful to the team. Also, Sandy was tall, handsome, young, and a college kid. There were bound to be jealousies Cal never experienced.

But the vituperation was real, and unexpected on the team that had broken the color line and included so many minority players. Don Newcombe was one of those outspoken in Sandy's defense. "Some of the players didn't like him because he was a Jew, a bonus baby who had to stay on the team. It wasn't his fault. He wanted to go to the minors. I couldn't understand the narrow-mindedness of these players when they would come to us and talk about 'this kike' and this 'Jew sonofabitch' who's gonna take my job."[19]

Six ♦ 1955

We in the stands at Ebbets Field, proud of our liberal reputation for embracing Jackie Robinson while most of the rest of the baseball world jeered, knew nothing of this. Jackie had his Roger Kahn. Koufax had nobody. Not even Dick Young was reporting any of this stuff.

Much of the reason for this was Sandy's reticence. This was a highly intelligent young man, not fearful, but not confrontational either. He was a very private person, even after his world-wide celebrity. And he never changed. As Ms. Leavey points out, there are two kinds of privacy. Joe DiMaggio in his retirement marketed his privacy. Koufax treasured his, never considering becoming a Mr. Coffee or a spokesman for a New York bank.

At August's end another beanball battle overshadowed the ball game with the Cardinals at Ebbets Field. This time Stan Musial was the victim, hit in the hand by a Johnny Podres pitch, after both teams were warned about brushbacks by umpire Jocko Conlon. Stan was taken to the hospital where X-rays proved negative.

The game, won by Brooklyn 10–4, was a signal as to how aggressive the Dodger pitching staff had become. It all started when Campanella came to bat after hitting a homer his previous time up. Tom Poholsky threw one right at Campy's head and at Robinson's head, sending both into the dirt. There is always payback for that sort of thing, but almost never to a star of Musial's magnitude. The one positive aspect was that it showed Podres, just 23, was coming of age as a major league pitcher, doing his job, even against a Stan Musial.

Newcombe, an overpowering pitcher since recovering from his short-lived rebellion, set a record during the Labor Day double-header against the Phillies by hitting his seventh home run of the season, this one with two on off knuckleballer Murray Dickson. Newk, on his way to a 20-game season, was still the best hitting pitcher of his generation. Along with his 20 wins this year, his batting average at season's end was .359, 42 hits in 117 at bats. With his arm, he also would have been a fine outfielder.

The Dodgers clinched their eighth pennant of the modern era in Milwaukee on September 8th, the earliest date in National League history, eclipsing their previous September record. They had little trouble, knocking out Bob Buhl with a four-run first inning on their way to a 10–4 win. Karl Spooner, in his only halfway decent year with Brooklyn, got the win in relief of Roger Craig.

This Dodger team, so used now to winning, took it all calmly, feeling, after all, they had been out front for so long the pennant was long expected. There were the usual poses and faked shouting for the photographers, the usual beer and champagne spilling, but, as in 1953, it's hard to get really excited when you win a pennant by 13½ games.

The champions were given the usual parade ending at Borough Hall on the 16th. As in recent years it wasn't anywhere near the frenzied demonstrations of 1941, with people running under the police horses, jumping on cars and on the roofs of trolleys, but there was a considerable crowd, estimated at about 300,000 cheering the motorcade.

The Yankees clinched their 21st pennant on the 24th in a race that was close until the Indians and White Sox fell off during the final week, with Cleveland ending up three games out and Chicago five. After the game Stengel told reporters: "Don't worry, the Yankees always take care of the Series." For the first time, he was wrong.

For the first two games the Yankees seemed to be rolling again as they beat the Dodgers twice at Yankee Stadium. The opener was a 6–5 Yankee win, Newcombe the loser, Ford the winner. The Dodgers came close on Robinson's steal of home in the eighth, the play that had Berra shouting in protest and jumping up and down, and that to this day he still insists he made the tag for the out. Stop action pictures tend to prove him right.

Game two was Tommy Byrne's as he went all nine for a 4–2 win over Billy Loes. Tommy was the former wild man who once led the league in walks three years in a row, with a high of 179 in 1949. He settled down during this 1955 season with a 16 and 5 record, 3.15 ERA and only 87 walks.

Brooklyn turned it around at home, winning three in a row at Ebbets Field, starting with Johnny Podres going all the way for an 8–3 win over Bob Turley, who was gone by the second inning. Campy started it with a homer with two on and after a homer by Mantle the next inning, Brooklyn came back with two more to knock out Turley, who was followed by Johnny Kucks and Tom Sturdivant. Podres gave up seven hits in this, his first complete game since June 14.

Don Larsen started game four but this was 1955, not 1956, and he lasted five innings, giving up five runs before Kucks came on in the sixth. Labine was the winner in relief of Erskine as the Dodgers won 8–5. Campy and Gil homered but the hitting start was Snider, who accounted for six of the eight Dodger runs, including a three-run homer in the fifth to ensure the victory.

Snider got another home run the next day, helping beat Bob Grim. Alston, hurting for starting pitching, sent Roger Craig to the mound and the rookie responded magnificently, giving up just one run into the seventh inning, when he was relieved by Labine. Roger got the 5–3 win.

Karl Spooner couldn't get out of the first inning on the return to Yankee Stadium the next day. The Yankees scored five runs in that inning, one a disgraceful home run by Bill Skowron. Yes, there can be cheap homers in Ruth's House, this one was one of the worst. Bill hit a low outside pitch to the opposite field where it went into the stands at about the third row, down that 295-foot foul line. Ford went all the way to win 5–1.

For the deciding game, Alston was in a desperate situation. Newcombe and Loes had failed and they and the entire pitching staff were tired, some of them worn out. He took a chance and again started young Podres, the winner four days before. Johnny was ready.

He pitched an eight-hit shutout, obviously very tight in the clutch. Gil Hodges drove in both Dodgers runs in the 2–0 game, saved by what has always been described as a spectacular catch by Sandy Amoros. It was a great catch and came at exactly the right time. With one out and Gil McDougald on first, Berra hit a sharp liner to right. The Dodgers were lucky on two counts: Sandy's great speed and his being left-handed. If he had had to cross his body for the catch it never would have been made, but with his gloved right hand he caught the ball at the stands, almost within reach of the fans. Sandy's throw to Reese for the relay to Hodges was on a line that gave McDougald no chance to get back to first.

John Podres had now come into his own, 23 years old, out of Witherbee, a small town in the Adirondacks in upper New York state. He joined the Dodgers in

Johnny Podres, the pitcher who broke the Brooklyn jinx. Johnny's 2–0 shutout of the Yankees, in the deciding game of the 1955 World Series, gave the Dodgers their first Series win in more than a half century. A mere two years later they were gone.

1953 and went 9 and 4 as a rookie. After the Series he spent 1956 in the Navy, back in '57 in plenty of time to regret, as a New Yorker, the Dodgers' jump to California. Although he spent eight seasons in Los Angeles, he'll always be known as the guy who won the most important game in Brooklyn Dodger history.

As expected, Brooklyn fans went wild, almost as if they knew time was running out. There was the usual motorcade to Borough Hall, where hundreds of thousands greeted the players, followed by a night of noise and revelry with taverns staying open, radios blaring and people banging pots and pans.

The area around Ebbets Field was especially alive, with thousands enjoying, as the *Times* described it, "a night of riotous celebration." Walter O'Malley, his face beaming with victory, kept up his dodge, his pretense of longing to stay in Brooklyn, by telling reporters the team's win was adding "fresh impetus" for building a stadium at Flatbush and Atlantic Avenues, again, a stadium that he knew Robert Moses and the United States Government would not allow to be built.

The following is heresy from a Dodger fan, but since I am writing history here, it has to be said: Mickey Mantle, the heart of the Yankee lineup, limped through the Series with a leg injury, missing the first two games and going 2 for 10, before bowing out after game 4. The Yanks were not the same team without Mantle, who had come off a year during which he led the league in homers (37) and slugging average (611).

Immediately after the Series, Durocher "resigned" as manager of the Giants, saying he wanted to spend more time in California with his wife, the movie star Laraine Day. The resignation seemed amicable but it really wasn't. Seven and a half years of Leo Durocher is a long time.

The Sporting News, looking behind the scenes, noted that Leo's leaving the team was the only option left to him. Although Durocher made statements indicating he'd like to be back, Stoneham "let the string run out" as he planned to hire Bill Rigney at about half Leo's salary. Leo was a hard man to like, but to many it seemed he should have had the job as long as he wanted it, given that magnificent 1951 race.

At year's end O'Malley made it definite about playing in Jersey City, signing the necessary contracts with Mayor Bernard Berry. He also announced that the Dodgers would not play in Ebbets Field after 1957, and added the astounding statement that if a new stadium was not available, Brooklyn's entire home schedule for 1958 would be played in Jersey City.

He also reaffirmed his decision to leave Ebbets Field after the 1957 season, no matter what. "If a new stadium is not ready," he added, "our present arrangement with Jersey City can be viewed as guaranteeing the continuance of the franchise at the nearest point to Brooklyn."[20]

He knew full well where the Dodgers would be playing in 1958. He and California Governor Earl Warren had known it for two years.

As the 1955 season ended, happy as all Dodgers fans were with their first championship, one of the great ones was missing. Billy Cox, he of the great glove and arm, had been traded to the Baltimore Orioles. Doubtless age was a factor, Billy being 35, but also the furor over him being benched as Gilliam and Amoros arrived had never quite subsided.

It didn't really matter much, however. Billy, aging and aching, retired after 53 games with Baltimore. Maybe the change played a part also. Baltimore' Municipal Stadium was no Ebbets Field, as if anywhere else was.

◆ SEVEN ◆

1956
Inching Their Way Westward

By January of 1956 the euphoria of the World Series had died down and many in Brooklyn now faced the dreary prospect of seeing the Dodgers playing in Jersey City, finally realizing that such a ridiculous move could be a prelude to their losing the team to Los Angeles.

By this time just about every sports writer in the metropolitan area knew O'Malley' real intentions, not only those in New York City like Anderson and Young, but also most of those over in New Jersey. We on the *Newark Evening News* had known what was really going on for months, as our sports writers, mainly Paul Horowitz and columnist Hy Goldberg, would come back from the latest O'Malley meeting with resigned looks. "You only have to look at O'Malley's face to know he's lying," Goldberg used to say.

But the charade went on week after week, with most of the people of Brooklyn no longer counting on O'Malley's grandiose plans for a new stadium as his way of keeping the Dodgers in the Borough. In early February the playacting continued as Mayor Wagner and Brooklyn Borough President Cashmore jointly announced sponsorship of a bill to create a Brooklyn Sports Center Authority.

The catch: it called for a $30,000,000 bond issue for a stadium at, again, the Flatbush and Atlantic Avenues site. They repeated, over again, that O'Malley wanted the site for a new Dodger stadium. They were all, including *Times* writer Paul Crowell, dancing around the known fact that the site could not be had, that to surrender it would break federal laws that Robert Moses was determined to uphold. O'Malley, as expected, endorsed the measure, knowing the land was unavailable, and that Robert Moses would make sure it remained so. Looking back now, it's obvious that these politicians knew what was really going on. They had known for more than two years. It is easy to imagine phones in political offices all over the city ringing after the meeting of O'Malley and California's Governor Warren in O'Malley's box at Ebbets Field during that Friday night game in August of '53.

It has often been written that O'Malley's decision to move to Los Angeles was made in 1957, which is ridiculous. The odds are that he made his decision when Governor Warren visited him. It stands to reason: why would the governor of California, one of the busiest men in the world, spend an entire evening watching a game he had no rooting interest in? Three hours was plenty of time to discuss the population explosion in California, its hunger for major league status, the concessions that would be made and the millions of dollars just waiting for the Dodgers. What else would they be talking about? This could not have been just a friendly meeting of old friends. They had never even met before.

New York's politicians knew what was going on but they couldn't admit it. The pretense went on because, though they knew it was hopeless, they had to put up some sort of fight for the benefit of the electorate. They knew they had to submit to O'Malley's leaving because there was no law to prevent it, but they could not do so meekly in public.

It is therefore surprising that some of today's historians have written that O'Malley was thwarted in his plans to stay in Brooklyn by the likes of Robert Moses and short-sighted politicians. Only by taking O'Malley's words at face value can that view be supported.

As the 1956 season opened the Dodgers as a whole were not happy. The team was going, and just about everybody around Ebbets Field knew it. Clem Labine said he felt it in the very atmosphere around the team.

"We knew in 1956," he told me. "It was easy to see. The feeling was there, everybody getting anxious. Especially the people who worked in the offices. You could see it by their expressions. They gave it away more than anyone else did, even Buzzy and Walter. And we could even see how down the fans were. I just think they knew what was going to happen.

"The team was confused about going. We all felt a little lost. We didn't know where we were going to stay, whether our families would be happy. We'd been happy living in Brooklyn. There were mixed feelings by some who lived in California, like Duke, but the general feeling about going was not good at all."[1]

The team, however, was too good to let their inner feelings interfere with their game, their livelihood, as they started toward another pennant, Brooklyn's last. In December they traded for Chicago third baseman Randy Jackson, giving up Russ Meyer, Don Hoak and Walt Moryn. Hoak and Moryn had some decent years left in them, but Meyer was just about through. It looked like a great trade, but Jackson in his two years with the Dodgers never amounted to much.

Alston started the season confident in his team's hitting, but worried about the pitching staff. "If the three who had sore arms last year—Erskine, Spooner and Loes—should be sound for the season we'll have a hell of a staff, with Labine, Craig and Bessent and the others. But with all these sore arms we just don't know." Spooner was finished, so soon, and Loes was traded to Baltimore.

The pitching would come around, but got pounded in the home opener against Philadelphia and Robin Roberts, 8–6. Then, two days later, the Jersey City disgrace started, with the opposition again the Phillies. It was, of course, the first major league game ever played at Roosevelt Stadium, and it wasn't a joy. With chilling winds blowing off Newark Bay the game went 10 innings, drawing all of 12,214 paid, with no telling how many came over from Brooklyn. The Dodgers took it with a two-run rally in the extra inning, 5–4, Labine the winner in relief. The first major league game in New Jersey history and the park was half empty. And not only that, the stadium proved to be in hostile territory as the crowd booed the Dodgers lustily for much of the game. Possible explanations offered by the beat writers: Jersey City people simply like to boo and, more probably, the crowd dated back to the old Jersey City Giants days when it was the New York Giants' Triple A farm team.

A 19-year-old future Hall of Famer, Don Drysdale, made his first start for Brooklyn over the weekend, a 6–1 win in Philadelphia, striking out nine and giving up nine hits, all singles. The writers remarked on the poise shown by one so young, and with fewer than two years minor league experience. At 6-foot-5, he was a dominating presence on the mound and would be for years.

In early May, Duke Snider continued his mysterious ways, turning to a magazine for a number of silly comments bemoaning his life in the major leagues. This time, however, it wasn't during a two-day snit after a prolonged slump. This time it was calculated over some weeks during interviews with *Collier's* magazine writer Roger Kahn, a friend, not an adversary looking for a scoop.

The title alone, coming from a Brooklyn idol, was upsetting to his fans and the club: "I Play Baseball for Money, Not Fun." It may have been true, but why say it, especially in a magazine of national scope? "The truth is," he said, "life in the major leagues is far from a picnic. I feel I'd be just as happy if I never played another baseball game."

"When I was a boy around Los Angeles I used to dream about playing in a World Series," he told Kahn. "Last autumn when I played in my fourth World Series I was still dreaming, only the dream had changed. While we were beating the Yankees I was dreaming about being a farmer.

"From the outside, $50,000 a year to play baseball looks great, and when you're a kid it's your biggest dream, but when you grow up and you're in the major leagues, baseball all of a sudden isn't so great—and sometimes it can be a nightmare."[2]

Red Smith couldn't take it. His words dripping with sarcasm, he pointed out that Snider works "several hours a day with no more than five months" vacation a year and makes $50,000" and can't retire until he's 34. "He buries his tear-stained face against Roger Kahn's lapel and sobs" at the "discovery that ball players have to work for a living, too." Also, that his play is sometimes adversely affected by "sports writers who know just as much baseball as my four-year-old daughter." And during the baseball season he sometimes has to spend as many as 25 nights a year on trains.[3]

This was a 29-year-old man, not a kid, beloved by all in Brooklyn, going out of his way again—possibly for magazine money he didn't need—to turn people against him. He owned a farm, a house on a hill overlooking the Pacific, and earned a salary that the average person couldn't dream of. Plus talent that would someday carry him into the Hall of Fame.

Why, then, this compulsion to alienate himself from Brooklyn fans, probably the most loyal in all of baseball? People in ballparks have short memories and he was soon cheered again for his exploits. But still, what was the reasoning behind these dopey comments, something he never explained? Friends like Clem Labine, Carl Erskine and others say he was always a wonderful guy with a great sense of humor. That makes The Duke of Flatbush even more puzzling.

On Saturday, May 12th, Erskine pitched his second no-hit game, beating the Giants 3–0 at Ebbets Field. Only two walks, to Mays and Dark, prevented a perfect game for the 29-year-old from Indiana. Just two plays during the entire game came close to hits—a liner by Mays that Robinson made a diving catch on and a long fly to right center by Daryl Spencer that Furillo caught at the wall. Carl's first no-hitter had been against the Cubs, 5–0 in June of 1952.

Two days later Billy Loes was gone, traded to Baltimore for $25,000. Billy, hampered by a sore arm for almost a year, was a decent pitcher for the Dodgers. But, given his size and stuff, he should have been much better. He was a high percentage pitcher in Brooklyn at 50 and 26, but his heart and his head were not always in the game, but rather with his boyhood buddies on Long Island. He was only 26 years old but would have only one good year left, 12 and 7 with Baltimore in 1957.

Before the trade Arthur Daley quoted an unnamed Dodger official as saying that he hoped Loes would be a 20-game winner that year "so that we can rid of him. If he can win big we can get big value for him in trade and at the same time get him out of our hair."

To take Loes' place the Brooks bought none other than Sal Maglie from the Indians for an undisclosed amount. Maglie was 39, from Niagara Falls and was 23 and 11 against the Dodgers in six years with the Giants. He had been 0 and 2 with Cleveland, leading many to think he was washed up. But he caught Alston's attention when he pitched four scoreless innings against the Dodgers in an exhibition game in Jersey City.

Alston's hunch paid off, as Sal helped the team toward the pennant with a 13 and 5 record and a 2.89 ERA. Those of us who were there saw him pitch a no-hitter against the Phillies on a misty and sometimes rainy night at Ebbets Field on September 25 as the season was coming to an end. The win was important, since it kept the Dodgers even in the lost column and just one game behind the league-leading Braves.

I experienced O'Malley's contempt for the fans during that game. I had a general admission press pass so I had to sit in the non-reserved area, where it was blowy and wet. The park was half empty so I moved into the reserved area where there were hundreds of empty seats. Soon I was chased by an usher, chased out of an area where almost no one was sitting. I offered the guy a fiver and, unbelievably, he turned it down. Five bucks was five bucks in 1956. As he left, a man gestured to me from a box seat to come over.

"I can't figure out why he wouldn't let you sit there," he said. "It's getting to be like the Gestapo around here. Sit down here. Tonight these are Don's seats and no one will bother you if you stay with us." I looked at him and knew instantly who Don was. There were five people in the box and they all looked like Newcombe, or vice versa. "We're all Don's family. I'm his uncle." We introduced ourselves and I sat enjoying my only no-hitter among congenial Dodger-fan company. I glanced at the usher a couple of times to get his reaction. He didn't bother me, obviously out of respect for the Newcombe family.

That no-hitter was among the 13 games Maglie won that year, important wins that helped toward the pennant. The day he first walked into the Dodger clubhouse, the writers expected fireworks, just as they did when Russ Meyer came over from the Phillies. But it was a quiet welcome for their former Giant nemesis. Even Jackie Robinson and Carl Furillo, for a time sworn enemies of Maglie, greeted him peacefully. These were professionals, remember, knowing that Maglie, if he had much left, could help them toward another pennant.

"I'll tell you this," said Furillo, "he's wearing the same uniform I'm wearing. If trouble starts I'll be out there with him. All that's happened in the past is forgotten." Robinson said, "I'm only sorry he didn't come here sooner—say five or six years ago."[4]

As May was ending, the Giants were in desperate financial straits, with about 25 percent of their schedule completed. The week before they took a double-header from the Cardinals with just 3,938 paid looking on in a stadium that seated more than 55,000. This was on a beautiful Sunday afternoon with Stan Musial out there at first base.

The present downward trend in attendance had started for the Giants in 1952, and by 1955 had dropped to 824,112, as compared to league-leading Milwaukee's more than two million, or even Ebbets Field's more than one million in a park half the size of the Polo Grounds. Stoneham, who had not nearly the financial resources of Walter O'Malley, knew he was facing bankruptcy. City officials, led by Mayor Wagner, kept talking about a stadium at 60th Street and the Hudson River, where the air rights would be purchased from the New York Central Railroad, the site being over its tracks.

Many felt Stoneham, unlike O'Malley, genuinely wanted to stay in New

York, but that was wishful thinking. Horace knew, as everyone else did, that the Hudson River plan was mired in politics and had not even been approved by the New York Central. By the time things were straightened out, if ever, he knew the Giants would be in the hands of receivers. So at private meetings he reached agreement with Walter on the basis of the announcement: if one team goes, both go.

For a time Stoneham negotiated with Dan Topping and Del Webb about sharing Yankee Stadium, but before any decision was reached he realized he'd be no better off there, his team playing an obscure role under the dominant Yankees. In other words, if Giant fans wouldn't come to the Polo Grounds, why would they come to Yankee Stadium?

While city officials were hopelessly dickering around with O'Malley, Horace knew if all else failed him he would be welcome in Minneapolis, home of his farm team Millers. Meanwhile, speaking of the New York Central site, he pretended he was "greatly interested and would like to make a deal when there is something to deal about. So far they do not have much to show." They never did, and before long, as Los Angeles was negotiating with O'Malley, San Franciscans would be calling at the Polo Grounds.

There was, of course, an inevitability about the Giants going to the Coast with the Dodgers, no matter what the city did. For some reason, O'Malley had become a power in the National League, but even with all his influence no other owner would vote for just one team going to California. Again, traveling three thousand miles to play one series would have been insane. As they say in racing, the Dodgers and Giants became stablemates.

The Dodgers were ending May with Don Newcombe, with some luck, stopping one of the great batting streaks of that time. Dale Long, Pittsburgh first baseman, had hit home runs in eight straight games as he faced Newcombe to close out a series at Forbes Field. The game was secondary, a "laugher" in today's sports jargon, with Newcombe going all the way to win 10–0. It was Long's four times up that drew all the interest, but to the crowd's great disappointment, the size of Forbes Field did him in. He struck out and popped up twice, but in his second time at bat he hit one to the deepest part of the Pittsburgh park, 470 feet to left center. Snider, with his great speed, caught it at the last moment, a fly-ball out that would have been a home run in any other park in the league.

The record at that time was an honored one. Three men had previously been stopped at seven, including Lou Gehrig. But in time, shorter fences and livelier balls gave Long some company. Don Mattingly tied him at eight in 1987 and Ken Griffey Jr. did so in 1993.

In mid–June, Dodger fans saw their team drop into third place as the result of a double-header loss to the Milwaukee Braves. But those at the games saw one of the most spectacular home runs ever hit. In the ninth inning of the first game, score tied at four and Ed Roebuck on the mound, Joe Adcock hit the first home run ever over the left field roof at Ebbets Field, winning the game 5–4.*

Joe Adcock was Johnny Schmitz in reverse: he killed the Dodgers with his bat. Not as bad as Stan Musial, but close, homer after homer, year after year. This one, off a Roebuck fast ball, cleared the 83-foot roof near the lights on an arc that went high over the third baseman's head. Unfortunately for Joe, the Dodgers had no Red Patterson to run around to the back of the ball park trailing newsmen behind him as he used his tape measure to announce another "mammoth" home run.

That the Dodger organization took that homer in stride shows one of the great differences between the Yankee and Dodger organizations of those days. The Dodgers were much more low-key, as exemplified by Red Barber, and as opposed to the frenetic, fast-talking and ever-talking Mel Allen. Patterson soon switched over from the Yankees to the Dodgers and was the team's spokesman during the tumultuous days leading up to the move to Los Angeles. As an O'Malley employee he did not carry a tape measure in his pocket.

On the 21st Campanella showed a flash of his former brilliance as he drove in six runs on two homers against the Cardinals in a 9–8 Dodger win. Roy was in the middle of a controversy with Alston over his spot in the batting order, telling writers and whoever would listen, "I'm no eighth-place hitter." They were lucky he was eighth that day, as he came up with one in the ninth, behind 8–5, and tied it, enabling Don Zimmer to drive in the winning run.

Was he, then, an eighth-place hitter? Well, the record book tells the story and, to one who hadn't looked at Campy's stats in a long time, it was surprising. Roy had been in decline for several years, and yes, Alston was right in dropping him to the eighth spot. From 1954 through 1957, the year before the car accident that ended his career, he hit .207, .318, .219 and .242. And his games played dropped to a low 103 in 1957.

Now this was one of the great catchers of all time, but he was getting old. Only 35, true, but he'd been catching professionally since he was 16, and his early years in the Negro Leagues were rough: long bus rides, cheap hotels, and there were those Sundays when he caught a double-header in one city, and another in another maybe 50 or 60 miles away, four games in one day, and that wasn't unusual. And there is a suspicion here that the wrist injury had never fully healed. So he was a worn-down 35, and if he hadn't been paralyzed would probably have had no more than a season or two left. But there was one more pennant down the road.

*It was done this same year, 1955, by Wally Post, but not in a game. During batting practice before a night game with Cincinnati in the spring (I don't remember the date), I was in the upper deck to the right of home plate when Wally hit one over the roof. Even in batting practice it was a hell of a shot.

On June 23rd it happened to Don Zimmer again, another beaning to a man who had almost died from a previous one. This time Zim was wearing a batting helmet but was hit in the face, suffering a broken cheekbone and a concussion. He didn't lose consciousness but scared his teammates by babbling incoherently while lying beside home plate. As Don was being carried off the field there was no trouble, since all realized that Hal Jeffcoat, as upset as anybody else, had not thrown an intentional duster, not being a pitcher of the Maglie or Drysdale stripe.

The guts of this little infielder were amazing. The previous beaning, down in St. Paul in 1953, was partially Zimmer's fault, since he should have been wearing a batting helmet. Severely injured, he was in a coma for 13 days out of 28 days in the hospital, and was operated on twice to remove blood clots from his brain.[5]

As he slumped to the ground after the Jeffcoat pitch, everyone running to his aid was terrified because of the silver plate in his head from the St. Paul beaning. It wasn't true, he revealed later, explaining that they had drilled four holes in his head and plugged them with tantalum buttons, not a silver plate. He would say: "Those players who thought I managed like I had a hole in my head were wrong. I actually have four holes in my head."[6]

Two days later the Brooks traveled to Jersey City again and beat the Cubs 3–2 on two unearned runs in the eighth inning, Erskine the winner, relieved by Labine. The fans, this time more than 20,000, booed the Dodgers throughout the game. "They wouldn't applaud if we gave out free hot dogs," one Dodger official said. And it wasn't just at Roosevelt Stadium. The entire city seemed anti–Brooklyn, even at events like a Little Leaguer's afternoon party attended, as a goodwill gesture, by Irving Rudd, Brooklyn's Jersey City business manager. "When I was introduced," he said, "they booed the be-jabbers out of me." Little Leaguers, yet.

The Dodgers closed out June in spectacular fashion. On the 29th they were down in the ninth inning—again—by 5–2 to the Phillies. Then with a man on, Snider hit a homer, followed by two more in succession by Jackson and Hodges to win the game 6–5. It happened so fast the Phils seemed not to know what hit them: four runs on three homers off just four pitches. The entire Dodger team greeted Hodges as he crossed the plate with the winning run.

The next day, the 30th, they beat Robin Roberts again 10–7 on sixteen hits to keep the Dodgers within one game of Milwaukee and Philadelphia, tied for first place. The crowd was only 12,229 announced paid, the kind of announced attendance that had O'Malley complaining that the fans were no longer turning out as they did in years past.

The problem wasn't with the fans, it was with the things O'Malley was doing to discourage what had been the most loyal fan base in all of baseball: the Jersey City move, the coming abandonment of Ebbets Field, his refusal even to consider the Flushing Meadows site and his consistently negative attitude toward every proposal the city made to keep the Dodgers. As Clem Labine noted, the fans by this time had a discouraged, hangdog look.

The Nationals took the Americans once again, 7–3 at Griffith Stadium in Washington, Bob Friend the winner, Billy Pierce the loser. The Dodgers had three in the lineup, Snider, Robinson and Campanella, but with Roy playing on his reputation, Ed Bailey did the catching. Johnny Antonelli was the pitching star, going four scoreless innings.

A week after the All-Star game, Alston was reported as calling the team "gutless" after losing to Cincinnati, 4–3, in the ninth inning on a Ted Kluszewski single. Although it was leaked to the beat writers by an unidentified player, Alston heatedly denied it, and was backed up by player representative Erskine. The charge had repercussions on the field, however, as Snider got into a fistfight with a fan.

As Duke was walking off the field, the *Times'* story read, a fan approached and said: "What's the matter, Duke? Haven't you any guts?" Snider turned and replied: "I'll show you who's got guts," as he approached the man. The fan, a 33-year-old from nearby Mason, reportedly swung at Snider, bruising his upper lip. Duke hit back and, it was claimed, broke two of the man's false teeth. Snider filed an assault charge, but the outcome was never divulged.

The Sporting News' 1946-to-1955 Player of the Decade award went to Stan Musial, and caused some controversy among newsmen who preferred Joe DiMaggio. Dick Young, who led the dissenters, termed Musial a "near-great hitter" in his column, adding that he was good base runner and a good outfielder, but with only a "fair" arm.

DiMaggio, he wrote, "at his peak was the most perfect ballplayer I've ever seen. There was nothing he could not do, a near-great hitter, a great fielder, a great base-runner" with one of the best arms in the game. Joe, Young pointed out, was handicapped by his personality, cold and reserved, not the type newspapermen love. "He was uncomfortable in crowds and inclined to be abrupt, perhaps snippy, when people tried to make small talk with him." Musial may have won the vote, in Young's opinion, because he's just the opposite: "a warm man with a ready smile who makes friends easily, liked, almost without exception, by newspapermen."

On the last day of July they played a night game in Jersey City, beating Milwaukee. It was great night for Robinson, whose two-run homer in the second and game-winning single in the ninth accounted for all the Dodgers runs in a 3–2 win over Gene Conley. Noticeable at the game were the lights. O'Malley had sworn that all Jersey City equipment was up to major-league standards. But there were those of us who were doubtful, remembering the lights in Newark's old Ruppert Stadium in the late 1930s. We left that park knowing that O'Malley's statement that the team might play its entire schedule there in 1958 was crazy, something not even Walter would subject his franchise to.

The Brooks played their last New Jersey game, another night under the so-called lights, two weeks later as Newcombe and Antonelli pitched one of those classic 1–0 duels that bores people who like nine and ten homers a game. McGowen wrote that a lefty hadn't shut out the Dodgers in well over a year, forgetting that this minor league park and its lights were in Jersey City, not Brooklyn, and in some ways was bigger. The team announced after the game that the total attendance for the Jersey City games was 148,371, more than 21,000 a game and 6,000 over the announced average Ebbets Field attendance.

The following week Brooklyn's pennant chances took a jolt as they beat the Cardinals but lost Clem Labine for at least two weeks. Labine, in saving the game for Roger Craig, suffered a chipped bone in his right wrist when he was hit by a high inside pitch from Larry Jackson. Newcombe was having a great year and Maglie and Labine were carrying their share, but on the whole this was not a distinguished pitching staff, not one that could suffer the loss of a Clem Labine.

At year's end Erskine was 13 and 11, Craig 12 and 11, Drysdale 5 and 5, Roebuck 5 and 4, and Bessent 4 and 3. Newcombe carried the staff at 27 and 7, his best year, and Maglie in his four months with the club was 13 and 5. Alston said he would depend on Koufax and Lehman to fill in, but neither worked out. Losing Labine going into September hurt, but the team proved resilient.

On September 11, Maglie beat the Braves 4–2 to pull into a tie with them for first place. Sal drove in two runs and Joe Adcock hit his usual homer against the Dodgers. Maglie, recently one of the most hated of the Giants by Brooklyn fans, received a standing ovation by most of the 33,384 paid, Ebbets Field's largest crowd of the season, one that had the park bursting. With the park that filled there was no way O'Malley could juggle the attendance figures.

On the following Sunday, Brooklyn took the league lead for the first time since April 28 as Newcombe shut out the Cubs 3–0 at Ebbets Field, putting the Brooks two percentage points in front of Milwaukee. The hitting of Robinson and Gilliam gave Newcombe the runs he needed on the way to his 24th win. Don was by now one of the class pitchers in baseball, having conquered his rebelliousness but, sadly, not his drinking. This was to be his greatest season before the plunge to 11–12 in '57, the year the drinking started to get out of control, as he has often admitted in the years since.

On September 18, Brooklyn held a "Night" for Jake Pitler, long-time minor league manager and since 1948 first base coach for the Dodgers. By now Pitler was an institution in Flatbush, liked and respected by many of the Dodgers he had shepherded through the minors, such as Snider, Hodges, Branca and Labine, who played for him in such outposts as Olean, New York, and Newport News, Virginia.

Thus he was a great coach for that team, having known many of them since they were teenagers. But in all the write-ups on his "Night," none pointed out his great value as liaison man with the large Jewish community of Brooklyn, who thought so much of him they dedicated a room to him at Beth El Hospital. Accordingly, a Jewish holiday never went by without either Red Barber or Connie Desmond having a camera cover the first base coaching box while they reminded their audience that "Jake's not coaching today because it's a Jewish holiday."

The Yankees clinched their 22nd pennant in Chicago on the 18th when Mantle hit his 50th home run of the year in the 11th inning to break up a 3–2 duel, with pitching aces Whitey Ford and Billy Pierce going all the way. Mantle would hit two more home runs in this, his Triple Crown year: 52 homers, 130 RBI and a .353 average.

The Triple Crown is baseball's most elusive hitting feat, since all three components must come together in the same season. It has been won but 13 times in the modern era and only two men, Rogers Hornsby and Ted Williams, have won it twice. Usually those who achieve it are automatically Most Valuable Players, except for Williams in 1941, the year of DiMaggio's 56-game hitting streak, when the Yanks took the pennant by 17 games with Boston in second place.

September 25, 1956, was the date of Maglie's no-hitter, a 5–0 win over the Phillies in the mist and rain of a miserable night at Ebbets Field. He was with the club from May 15, 1956, to September 1, 1957, a little more than 10 months' playing time. In going to the Yanks for a reported $37,500 he became one of the few men to play for all three New York teams, an impossibility after 1957.

Maglie was one of the National League's most storied pitchers, one of the few who jumped to the Mexican League, as he did in 1945, and later achieved stardom back in the majors. After Commissioner Chandler forgave all, the pitcher seemed to come out of nowhere to go 18–4, the highest pitching percentage in the league in 1950. There were rumors that with the Dodgers moving after 1957, he didn't want to play on the West Coast, so far away from his Niagara Falls home. But as he went to the Yankees later that year, he was 40 years old, almost finished as Sal the Barber.

The last five days of the pennant race were typical of this Dodger team's history of going right down to the last day. On the 26th Roberts beat Newcombe 7–3, dropping the Brooks one game behind the Braves, who were off that day. Robin gave up two homers to Snider, making him the "Gopher King" of the league for the second straight year, 41 last season and 43 this year.

Roberts was having a so-so 19 and 18 year after winning 20 or more for six straight seasons. Of all the Hall of Fame pitchers, he was one of the oddities: he consistently refused to throw at hitters, and thus gave up many home runs but, like Preacher Roe, few with men on base. He had the most early-innings problems of any great pitcher in memory. It was known throughout the league that if he got through the first couple of innings, especially the first, he had you. But get to him early on and you had a chance. He played on some good Philadelphia teams but too often on those of the later 1950s that finished in the second division or last place, leading to many of his 245 losses.

On the 28th the Braves lost to the Cardinals, 5–4, in Sportsman's Park, cutting their lead to one-half game over idle Brooklyn, rained out that night at Ebbets Field. It is understandable that the Cardinals, though true to the code of playing hard, were not happy with their win, Robinson and the Dodgers not popular around the league. Besides, many people, Yankee fans excepted, simply do not like a consistent winner.

Most of the Cards admitted they wanted to see the Braves win the pennant. "Everybody would," said third baseman Ken Boyer. The attitude of the St. Louis papers reflected this sentiment, editorializing that the Dodgers had won enough for the time being.[7]

The Dodgers were glad of the night's rainout as they gathered in the clubhouse for a daytime double-header. Night lights, even at that time, were excellent, bathing the field in brightness. But no matter the claims, day ball is better on the player's eyes, unless you're playing a sun field, as in left at Yankee Stadium. The team was confident, even though the Pirates had beaten them three of four the previous week.

After Maglie had walked in to tell the team the game was cancelled, Snider was there in the locker room, expressing the team's relief that they wouldn't have to face Bob Friend, who had beaten them three out of four times that season, in a night game. Although he hit right-handers consistently, Friend, he said, had a rotation on his pitches that was hard to see in the glare of the klieg lights. "That's right," Reese agreed. "I know I can see his pitches better in the daytime, anyway."[8] To face Pittsburgh, Alston would open with Brooklyn's one-year wonder, the 13 and 5 Salvatore Anthony Maglie.

Friend at the time was the workhorse of the Pittsburgh staff, having pitched 314 innings that year to lead the league in durability. His record of 17 and 17 for a seventh-place club made various general managers look his way, but the Pirates hung on to him through lean years until they traded him in 1965 to the Yankees for Pete Mikkelsen and cash. If Bing Crosby had not forced Rickey out years before, Pittsburgh would have traded him back in the '50s for a few quality players and a bundle of money.

It was a beautiful fall day as Maglie warmed up for the first game. It started out badly for him, a Dale Long single and Frank Thomas homer with two out in the first inning. In their half, Brooklyn came back with three scored on Robinson's single with Gilliam on second, and then Amoros' home run to right, scoring behind Robinson.

For the years he was with Brooklyn, Sandy had a knack for the big play and the big hit at the right time, even though he was just a .255 career hitter. At 5-feet-7½ he had flashes of power and, though he spoke no English and had no interpreters on the team, he seemed to always know what was going on, seldom missing a sign.

From that first inning Sal gave up only four singles and went on to win 6–2, backed by homers by Furillo and Hodges. As he left the mound the crowd again gave a standing ovation to a man they had hated just a few months before.

Alston pulled a surprise between games. He had announced Craig as the starter but switched to his premier relief pitcher, Clem Labine, his wrist now healed. Walter knew, as did the team, that if Labine hadn't had that mixture of confidence, cockiness and guts that make for a great reliever he would have been one of the league's best starters. He had a history of great starts under tremendous pressure: the four down the stretch in '51, and his shutout of the Giants in the subsequent playoff.*

Clem was magnificent, a 3 to 1, 10-strikeout complete game under the greatest pressure imaginable. Campy homered in the third for Brooklyn's first run off Ron Kline. In the fifth, umpire Vic Delmore made one of the worst calls ever seen at Ebbets Field, or at least it appeared so on television. Campanella had singled and Labine bunted him to second. On TV the throw to Pirate shortstop Dick Groat looked so high that Campy was on the base before Groat came down with the ball. But Campanella was called out as the TV boomed the crowd's roar of protest. Pennants often swing on calls like that, but Labine remained unflustered, even though he knew his bunt had been successful.

The fans were still protesting during the next inning, having suffered through what they considered one of the worst calls in memory. It got so that television cameras panning the stands showed the field being showered with beer cans and other debris until the umpires threatened a forfeit if it continued. It stopped immediately, the crowd knowing what was at stake.

Pittsburgh got a few hits late in the game and broke the shutout in the ninth but Labine hung on, tired as he must have been. At the end he got the ovation treatment as he left the mound after pitching his only complete game of the year. He knew he had just pitched the Dodgers into first place, at least for the rest of the afternoon.

That kind of game would be impossible for any of today's relief pitchers. Men like Labine and Goose Gossage are from the Stone Age of relievers. Today, Mariano Rivera of the Yankees and Tom Gordon typify the current breed: "set up men" and "closers" who go one or two innings late in the game. For such pitchers, never having gone through the long grinds of yesterday, nine innings are unheard of. Without denigrating today's relievers, Gossage has been saying this for years, to deaf ears.

That night Warren Spahn went all the way against the Cardinals in a 2–1 loss, literally in tears as he left the mound knowing his team was now one full game behind, and that if the Dodgers won the next day it was all over, no matter what his team did.

As we'll get to later, he had another magnificent start, shutting out the Yankees 1 to 0, beating Bob Turley in the sixth game of the upcoming World Series.

Warren wasn't the nicest guy in baseball, but as a pitcher he was one of the top four or five in the game's history, his 363 wins the highest total ever for a left-hander, a total that will probably never be equaled, given the handicaps placed on today's pitchers. Bobby Del Greco cost him the game, and Milwaukee the pennant, with his speed. Bobby never could hit much, but he could run, so fast that the Yankees tried him in centerfield for a while, but traded him away soon after.

With the score tied in the ninth, Mathews drove a Herm Wehmeier pitch toward the wall in deep center, Bobby making the catch at the last moment. Jack Ditmer, after a Joe Adcock single, drove another to the wall where, again with his speed, Del Greco caught it, taking the game into extra innings.

Things that break a pitcher's heart: the game was lost, after twelve grueling innings, on a bad hop. In the last of the twelfth Musial doubled, followed by a deliberate walk to Ken Boyer, setting up for a double play. Rip Ripulski hit a hard grounder to third, where Mathews was poised to step on third and throw to first for the two outs. But the ball hit a pebble, or something, then bounced off Mathews' leg into left field while Musial crossed the plate to end the game.

Spahn was so distraught in the clubhouse that when a photographer got in front of him to take a picture, the pitcher threw his glove in the guy's face. As he tried again Spahn's teammates dragged him away. Again, Warren wasn't the nicest guy in baseball.[9] He and all the rest knew the outcome was now out of their hands, that if the Dodgers won the next day it was over.

They did win, thus sweeping the series as Newcombe won his 27th game, 8–6, with relief help from Don Bessent. Vern Law started, a good pitcher on a bad team. It looked easy for a while after Snider hit his 42nd homer in the first inning with Gilliam and Reese on base. Brooklyn got two more in the fifth with Newcombe, always a formidable hitter, doubling, advancing to third on an out and then scoring on Reese's sacrifice fly. Snider followed with his 43rd home run, becoming the first Dodger since Dolph Camilli in 1941 to take the home run crown.

The Pirates were teeing off as Newcombe was weakening in the seventh. Bill Virdon drove in three runs with a base-clearing double and then in the eighth Lee Walls made it 7–6 with a homer into the left field upper stands. Now it was a ball game, with Don Bessent coming on to save it. After Bessent struck out Dale Long with two on in the eighth he pitched a scoreless ninth for the pennant. Amoros had finished the scoring with a home run in the eighth to make it 8–6.

As the game ended at exactly 4:30 P.M. on the scoreboard clock, the crowd did its usual run onto the field, jumping up and down and pummeling the players and themselves, many of them no doubt not realizing that this would be Brooklyn's last pennant, that O'Malley's plans were now firm.

Roscoe McGowen described the clubhouse scene as bedlam, but there were those who felt otherwise. The *Newark Evening News'* sportswriters often came into the city room, or held forth back in the sports department, telling us on the nightside of the day's developments.*

Paul Horowitz, our Dodger beat writer at the time, said the crowd on the field was crazy, as usual, but the clubhouse scene seemed forced, even though they had just squeaked in for the pennant. "It was eerie sometimes," Paul said. "There's always some forced gayety in a winning clubhouse, players jumping around for the photographers. But this time it was different. A lot of the faces on the sidelines were sad. Everybody in the room knew they were going west, leaving Brooklyn and uprooting their families. They talked about the money, but let me tell you, most of that team would rather stay."

There were sad faces on our sports writers, too, as they walked through the *Newark News* city room. I remember thinking that my decision not to join our sports staff was a right one, given the grimness of that evening. These men, after all, were thinking of their livelihood, covering baseball. There were 17 to 20 newspapers in the metropolitan area, including New Jersey, Long Island and Connecticut. All those sports writers couldn't cover just the Yankees. Many knew they would have to relocate, and many did.

Meanwhile over in Brooklyn, the *Times'* Murray Schumach, one of many reporters roaming around looking for feature material, wrote of a fairly calm Borough, nothing like the riotous celebrations of the past. The people seemed calm, he wrote, and those who were carrying Dodgers banners put on no displays, some of them even acting "sheepishly."

Even on Bedford Avenue, right there near Ebbets Field, people's "feet were on the ground," Schumach reported, adding that the only dancing in the streets, as in former days, was done near a few bars and for the benefit of photographers.

The people of Brooklyn were never stupid.

O'Malley, of course, continued his deception by issuing a statement after the game saying that "real progress" was being made toward building a new Dodger stadium in Brooklyn.

Out in St. Louis the scoreboard flashed the word that it was over, as the Braves battled the Cardinals in the sixth inning. Milwaukee went on to win it 4–2 for second-place money. Their clubhouse was especially tomblike, nobody talking, players sitting dejectedly smoking cigarettes or drinking beer. It was especially crushing for them, a team that had been in first place for 124 days, more than four months.

The crowd was waiting, though, when they landed at Milwaukee's Mitchell

---

*I worked the Newark News nightside, 4 P.M. to whenever, for two years from September of 1955, the crucial two years during which the Dodgers and Giants planned their 1957 westward moves. Thus I was there as our sportswriters arrived after Dodger, Giant and Yankee games. They filled us on the nightdesk in on the games as we filled them in on the night's events in Newark.

Field that evening, thousands cheering their losers. The euphoria was still there for a team that had transferred to their city just four years before, and would continue for a few years as the Braves became winners. But attendance started dwindling in the early 1960s and by 1966, with attendance fewer than 600,000 the year before, the Braves were on the move again, this time to Atlanta. Big league musical chairs again: Seattle to be the Milwaukee Brewers, the Braves the Atlanta Braves.

Back in Brooklyn, it was Maglie versus Ford in the Series opener, with Sal the winner, 6–3, giving up nine hits and striking out 10, with President Eisenhower there to throw out the first ball. Maglie started out shakily, a two-run homer by Mantle in the first and a solo shot by Martin in the third. After that it was all Brooklyn, with Sal in complete charge with his sinker and various curve balls.

Brooklyn went ahead in their half of the third, scoring a total of five runs on six hits, one a three-run homer by Hodges, to finish Ford. From the sixth inning on only two Yankees reached second base, Bauer and Carey. Maglie was particularly rough on Bill Skowron, up four times, leaving a total of six men on base.

In his story on the game, *Los Angeles Times* writer Frank Finch reported that the Dodgers got Maglie for only $1,000 from Cleveland after every team waived on him, thinking that at 39 his career was over.[10] *The Baseball Encyclopedia* gives no specific figure on the Maglie trade, listing it as "cash." Whatever the amount, Maglie's value to Brooklyn in his short stay was worth many thousands.

In a reversal of the last Series, the Dodgers went up by two games the next day, not giving up after the Yankees scored six runs in the first two innings, four on a Berra grand slam off Newcombe. Behind 6–0 after Newcombe had been knocked out in the Yankees' five-run second, the Dodgers came back with six to tie in the bottom of the inning, mainly on a three-run homer by Snider. The Yanks threw a whole crew of pitchers at the Dodgers: Larsen, Kucks, Byrne, Sturdivant, Morgan (the loser), Turley and McDermott, but the Brooks came up with 13 runs to win it 13–8. Brooklyn sent in Roebuck in the second, and in the third Bessent, who went the rest of the way for the win.

It was Whitey Ford again the next day, this time against Roger Craig. The Yankees won their first game, 5–3, with 40-year-old Enos Slaughter driving in the winning runs on a three-run homer in the sixth inning. It must have occurred to many of the politicians attending that the size of the crowd underlined the need for a new stadium in Brooklyn. The almost 74,000 paid was a good 3,000 more than those at both games in Ebbets Field. But few of the politicians and civic leaders paid much attention. They knew it was too late, that the western moves were inevitable.

Snider, in a reversal of his at bat against Tommy Byrne the day before, struck out three times against the lefty Ford. In the previous game Stengel had brought in Byrne, also a lefty, specifically to pitch to Snider, but the Duke crossed him up with the three-run homer. Craig took the loss and Ford got the win, but Slaughter was the Yankee star of the day, proving, as he predicted when the Cardinals traded him, that he was not through, but had a lot of baseball left in him.

Erskine took the loss the following day, 6–2, evening up the Series. Tom Sturdivant went all the way for the Yankees, with Mantle and Bauer homering. The game was tougher for a struggling Sturdivant than the score would indicate. The leading Dodger got on base seven times, as the team had base runners on in every inning but the eighth and had the bases loaded in the ninth when it ended as Gilliam flied to Mantle for the final out. Erskine didn't have much going, pitching just four innings before Eddie Roebuck took over.

October 8th, 1956, the day of a game never seen before and probably will never be seen again: Don Larsen's perfect game, 27 men up, 27 men down. The unheard of feat was a shock to the entire baseball world, for Larsen, 27 and 6-feet-4, never gave any sign of greatness, even though Stengel used to say Don could be one of the best pitchers of his day if he ever decided to put his mind to it, that is, stop partying. Just that spring in St. Petersburg he was driving in the early morning and wrapped his car around a telephone pole, saying later that he fell asleep behind the wheel.

Whatever. This mediocre 81–91 right-hander pitched the game of the 20th century, one, however, that was always in doubt. Larsen was up against Sal Maglie, who gave up just two runs on five hits in going the route. He was beaten by a Mantle home run and a Bauer single with two on.

All the press reports agreed that only four balls hit by the Dodgers might have caused trouble, and one was a long drive by Amoros that would have been a home run if it had not gone foul by inches. In the second, Robinson banged a vicious grounder off Andy Carey's leg but it caromed to Gil McDougald for the throw to first. Then Hodges was the victim twice, first by a long drive that only a centerfielder with Mantle's speed could have caught. Then again, in the eighth, Gil hit a smash to Carey's left, a hard-hit certain single. But the third baseman lunged and caught it, or scooped it. To make certain he threw to first for the out.

Larsen's pitching was unusual in that he was throwing with a motion he had adopted just a few weeks before. All of his 97 pitches were from the stop position, not one from the stretch. The Stadium was deathly quiet as he needed only three outs for the perfect game. Furillo was first up and lifted a fly to Bauer in right as a roar went up. Campanella slapped a grounder to Martin for number two. Then it was only Dale

Mitchell, who came to Brooklyn that year after a decade with Cleveland. Mitchell, hitting for Maglie, was no patsy, a .312 career hitter who had been one of the American League's best pinch hitters.

Mitchell fouled off a pitch and then after a swinging strike, took one on the outside corner for a called third strike by umpire Babe Pinelli. As the crowd was up and cheering, Mitchell whirled on Pinelli, protesting the call. He said later it was a fastball outside the strike zone. The thousands of Brooklyn fans who even today swear that pitch was bad are probably wrong.

Today it is possible to view the pitch in slow motion on ESPN Sports' "The 1956 Dodgers," a videotape that includes much of that historic no-hitter by Don Larsen. Although Berra's crouching body blocks the outside corner, it is obvious after watching the pitch a dozen or so times that it was on the corner by inches or off it by inches, probably a good called strike. In any event, Mitchell should never have taken that pitch. His claim that it was a foot outside was ludicrous. It was on or very near the corner.

Maglie, who gave up only five hits, was philosophical, knowing that he had pitched a fine game in losing. Every Yankee hit, he told the press, was off a breaking ball. "That home run pitch to Mantle," he said, "was a curve that broke, I'd say, right over the middle of the plate. In the sixth inning when they got their three hits and second run—well, that's what happens when the control goes a little off."

Sal was speaking of Andy Carey's single, but even more of the perfect sacrifice bunt laid down by Larsen, a fairly decent-hitting pitcher. With Carey on second, Hank Bauer hit a single to center, sending him home with the insurance run. Maglie, remember, was now 39 years old, without the fastball he had years before. He depended on guile, his curves and control, and these momentarily left him, costing him the game.

Another masterful game followed the next day in Ebbets Field, Labine against Turley, both having one of their finest hours. Clem again came through magnificently as a starter, shutting out the Yankees in 10 innings 1–0 on seven hits. Turley pitched a game he would have won almost any other time: one run, four hits, eleven strikeouts. But, as John Drebinger pointed out, he faced Jackie Robinson once too often.

In the eighth inning he got away clear as Robinson popped up with two on to end the inning. But in the tenth Robby ended it with a line drive over Slaughter's head in left field that scored Gilliam from second. It started when Gilliam walked and was sacrificed to second, followed by an intentional walk to Snider. Jackie fouled off a pitch, took another and then hit one with a low trajectory out toward Slaughter. Enos, having trouble with the sun, started forward for an instant and then streaked back as the ball went over his outstretched arms and crashed against the wall. All agreed the ball was uncatchable, even given the start forward. Slaughter, now called "Old Forty," had earlier lost a Gilliam fly ball in the sun, but after it dropped in front of him for a single he quickly grabbed the ball and threw to second to get Junior trying to stretch it. "Old Forty was never one to give up in any situation," Drebinger wrote.

Drebby, as his fellow writers called him, covered all three New York teams during his 41-year career on the *Times*. He was the son of a Metropolitan Opera orchestra violinist and was a boyhood pianist and high school sprinter on Staten Island. During his newspaper career he was one of most prolific and stylish writers on the New York scene, and from 1929 through 1963 wrote the *Times'* lead World Series story 203 consecutive times.

Yankee power and a career game from Johnny Kucks ended the Series the next day, 9–0, Johnny shutting the Dodgers down on just three hits.* The word anticlimax fits this disappointment for Dodger fans who had to watch Newcombe routed early and then Bessent, Craig, Roebuck and Erskine parade to the mound, none able to stop the battering. Berra hit two homers and Howard and Skowron one each, Skowron's a grand slam off Craig in the seventh that just about ended the competition.

The game was probably the most frustrating of Newcombe's career, thanks to Yogi Berra. Don, like many another pitcher, found there was no way to pitch to Berra. Yogi hit two two-run homers off him, the second one driving him out of the game. If memory serves, the first was hit off a high inside pitch and the other just the opposite, a high outside pitch. Don was fuming as he left the field and later fuming as he left the park, so much so that he got into an argument with a parking lot attendant that led to a fight. Poor Don had to take it out on somebody.

At Series' end, the most successful franchise in the game's history found a way to win another, just as it had 17 previous times, starting back in 1923 when the team took their first from John McGraw's Giants. The Dodgers, on the other hand, had lost eight of nine, six to those same Yankees. But soon their fans would suffer no longer, since they would not have a team to suffer over.

This became starkly evident as they opened their newspapers on October 31 to the announcement that Ebbets Field had been sold. Ebbets Field, the home of the celebrated Brooklyn Dodgers, was to be razed to make way for a $25 million middle-income housing and commercial complex. O'Malley signed the contract with the stipulation that the park would be available under lease to the Dodgers until the end of the 1959 season.

O'Malley's threats were now becoming reality. The sale of the ballpark, on top of his moves to Jersey City, made it clear that he was going, that he had no intention of playing in Ebbets Field through 1959, despite Dodgers spokesman Arthur (Red) Patterson ending the sale announcement by saying that "no serious offer" from another city was being entertained. He should have said there was no concrete offer, knowing that negotiations with Los Angeles officials had been going on since their mayor invited both O'Malley and Stoneham out to LA on August 23rd to inspect possible playing sites.

---

*Johnny celebrated the Series win by getting married soon afterward. Being on the nightside, I covered his reception in Newark's Essex House down below City Hall on Broad Street. I was surprised that there were no other Yankee players there.

Don Newcombe (right) during his finest hour, with no one suspecting that the end of his magnificent career was approaching. Here, with rookie Don Drysdale, he displays his 1956 Cy Young and Most Valuable Player awards.

O'Malley had been stating repeatedly that Ebbets Field was dirty, run-down and had inadequate parking facilities. That's how you get fans to come to your ballpark: tell them how decrepit it is.

Amid this gloomy time for Brooklyn, Don Newcombe was named Most Valuable Player and winner of the Cy Young Award as the league's best pitcher, the first pitcher to ever win those two in the same year, and the only pitcher to win them plus Rookie of the Year.

Those who watched him through the years knew that Don had only one serious weakness: he would sometimes lose concentration and his control and pitching sense would vanish. Robinson was always on him at those times, telling him to turn in his uniform because he didn't belong in the big leagues, didn't want to pitch. At one crucial point, in the 1951 playoff, Jackie misunderstood the situation when Newk asked to be relieved at the end of the seventh inning. "Goddamn it," Jackie was reported as saying to him, "cut out this horseshit and get in there and pitch. We're all counting on you." Don did and got through the eighth, but in the ninth everyone knew, including Robinson, that he couldn't go on, that he was just worn out. Fact is, it's a wonder he went so far after the previous week of the intense, grueling pitching he had done.

On December 14, the people of Brooklyn woke up to another shocker, the unbelievable trade of Jackie Robinson to the New York Giants. Word swept around that it was just a rumor, that not even O'Malley would dare trade such an icon. But it was true. For $35,000 and pitcher Dick Littlefield, Horace Stoneham purchased his new first baseman, the man who broke the color line in the major leagues.

"The deal was closed by Stoneham and O'Malley at the Chicago meetings," Giant spokesman Gary Schumacher said. "The announcement was withheld until the players concerned could be advised." O'Malley was finally getting rid of a ballplayer he despised, and for good bit of money, or so he thought. If it was to humiliate Robinson, he didn't know his man. Jackie was no Durocher, switching to a team and some players that he had hated for years.

Jackie, in fact, would not give O'Malley the satisfaction. He followed his conscience and rejected the deal, deciding to retire instead, even though he was offered $60,000 by Stoneham, almost $20,000 more than he had ever made with the Dodgers in his 10-year career.* There was word that Stoneham wanted him for a drawing card, plus the fact that he had a decent season the year before: 117 games and a .275 average. In any event, Robinson was going on 38 and had been talking about retiring for some time.

He delayed his decision while both the Dodgers and Giants, Bavasi especially, accused him publicly of playing them along for more money. The fact is he had a $50,000 deal with *Look* magazine for an article on his retirement and didn't want to announce until that issue came out. "There was so much pressure from fans and youngsters for me to remain in the game that I did have some vague second thoughts," he said. Instead, however, he accepted an offer to be a vice president of Chock Full O' Nuts.[11]

Amid the controversy over the trade and his withholding his announcement until the *Look* publication, Jackie made things worse by saying the Milwaukee Braves lost the pennant that fall because of their "playboy" lifestyle and nightlife. The Braves, naturally, erupted, calling him a "meddler" and "headline hunter" while daring him to prove the charges.

He couldn't, of course, leading Johnny Logan to accuse Robinson of "popping off to keep his name in the headlines." Instead, Johnny should have asked why Robinson time after time was saying things that created controversy. This wasn't about race, a legitimate Robinson concern. This was maligning a ballclub that his team had beaten, but had put up a gallant fight right up to the last day. We Brooklyn fans admired Robinson, but few of us could figure him out.

Before his announcement, all of Brooklyn was "rocked" by the trade, the *Times* reported the next day. Numbers of callers telephoned the Dodgers offices at 215 Montague Street, expressing disbelief and shock, but also to verify the truth of the story. The Giant office at 100 West 42nd Street was overburdened by calls throughout the day, some skeptical and some in favor of the trade.

Bavasi and his fellow team officers were bitter, saying that Jackie led everyone along, delaying his retirement to boost his story in *Look*. Stoneham had counted on Robinson being a draw, especially with him on the Giants and Maglie on the Dodgers.

"That's typical of Jackie," Bavasi said. "Now he'll write a letter of apology to Stoneham. He has been writing letters of apology all his life."[12]

Whether Robinson played or not eventually made no difference. Within a few short months all of Brooklyn, the thousands of fans who had followed the team all their lives, and all those who were furious at the Robinson trade, would find out that nothing made a difference. For soon, there wouldn't be much baseball at the Polo Grounds, or at Ebbets Field. A few college games, a few high school games and then, apartment houses.

◆ Eight ◆

1957
Over the Sierras to La-La Land

The Dodgers' last year, 1957, started with O'Malley heading out to Los Angeles, reportedly to confer with Edward Pauley and his Dodgers-for-California movement. As he was leaving he made the usual threatening announcement that his organization "may be forced to commit the Dodgers elsewhere."

The dance with the politicians continued, the charade about a new stadium constantly trumpeted in the press, but only the diehards were still listening, hoping it was all an O'Malley bluff. The rest of us knew it wasn't and never had been. One of the most storied franchises in the history of sports was leaving, and not even the powerful Robert Moses could stop it if he had wanted to.

He had done his best, Mr. Moses, with his offer of a site out near Flushing Meadows, an offer many teams would jump at, a site that has been home to the New York Mets some 45 years now. Everything O'Malley said he wanted would have been available out there: ample parking, a new stadium, and good public transportation and highways that would, as they do now, give access to the entire metropolitan area. But there wasn't the quick buck, the easy millions that beckoned from the Coast.

While he was playing the politicians along, O'Malley had a solution to the gloom Clem Labine saw spreading around Ebbets Field. He hired Emmet Kelly, the world-famous clown, to make the fans laugh. Were sack races and dish nights just around the corner? Taking the team away from Ebbets Field wasn't enough. Degrade the place first.

On his way to California, O'Malley stopped off at his Vero Beach training camp to drop one of his final bombshells: the Dodgers had traded their Texas League Fort Worth franchise to Cub owner Phil Wrigley in exchange for the Los Angles club of the Pacific Coast League. He now had a foothold on the Coast, in the city he'd been planning on all along. The California predators were overjoyed, knowing what the franchise trade meant.

After his announcement, O'Malley told the press conference, "We are not at a point now where we are considering shifting the franchise to Los Angeles." He added, however, that the 20,000-seat Wrigley Field in Los Angeles "could easily be expanded to a 60,000 capacity." Then, ominously, measuring every word, he added: "It is my considered opinion that they will have major league baseball on the Pacific Coast by 1960."

In closing, he repeated his by now tiresome litany that no one in the room believed any longer: he still wanted the Atlantic and Flatbush Avenues site in downtown Brooklyn, and he would accept no other. Yeah.

The Brooks opened the season in Philadelphia, beating Robin Roberts again, this time by 7–6, with rookie left fielder Gino Cimoli's home run in the 12th inning the winner.* Don Newcombe got knocked around but was rescued by winner Labine's scoreless five innings after Gil Hodges' homer tied it in the eighth.

After being the enemy for so many years Sal Maglie helped the Dodgers win the 1956 pennant with a 13 and 5 record, including a no-hitter on a rainy September evening. One of his finest efforts was his 2–0 loss to the Yankees, overshadowed by Don Larsen's perfect game. Unlike many others who jumped to Mexico, Sal became a star in 1950.

Then they all went home to Ebbets Field where Sal Maglie, one week from his 40th birthday, again pitched brilliantly, beating the Pirates 6–1 on a four hitter. Paid attendance was announced as 11,202, adding weight to O'Malley's campaign to denigrate the stadium and keep fans away, thus bolstering his argument that he must leave.

Next stop, Jersey City, Station West in O'Malley's plan. Attendance there was a mite better than the Brooklyn opener, 11,629. But the Jersey fans already knew they had a lousy ballpark, and didn't need Walter's gloom and doom to keep them away. The game was a 5–1 win for Roger Craig over Jim Hearn, recently traded by the Giants to the Phillies. Jim had some good years, especially his 17 and 9 that helped the Giants pull off their miracle,

*To many Dodger fans Cimoli symbolizes those final bleak Dodger months through no fault of his own. He just came along at the wrong time. He played in all those ridiculous Jersey City games and was gone with the rest of the team in 1958. Gino lasted 10 years, playing for six teams.

but was almost through, a 10 and 6 total over the next three years before retiring.

After beating the Giants 4–3 at home, the Dodgers went on their first western swing and started with a 16-inning, 3–2 loss to the Cardinals. Eddie Miksis, now with St. Louis, dribbled one down the third base line for a hit to start the 16th, was sacrificed to second and scored on Don Blasingame's line shot to right, defeating Don Bessent.

Three days later the career of Cleveland's Herb Score, one of the best lefties to come along in a generation, was virtually ended in Municipal Stadium when a Gil McDougald line drive struck him in the right eye, breaking his nose and later arousing fears that he would never see out of that eye again. He was only 24, a well-liked fastballer who had won 20 games the year before.

The game was only three minutes old when McDougal's liner, hit so hard that Herb couldn't get his glove up in time, sent him sprawling on the mound, with players rushing to his aid. He said later that as he hit the ground he kept saying, "Hey, St. Jude, stay with me," thinking that he was blinded. At Lakeland Hospital, doctors found hemorrhaging so severe that they wouldn't be able to tell the extent of the injury for several days.

McDougald was devastated, hanging around the hospital all day so he could visit Score with his apologies and good wishes. Finally, with Herb asleep in intensive care, he was unable to see him and had to rejoin the Yankees on their road trip.

Score was never the same again, with no one certain whether the injury or psychological problems ruined his career. His eye cleared up, leaving his sight intact, enabling him to pitch a few more years. He hung on for a while, drifting to the White Sox in 1960, but the hope that he could make a real comeback was gone by the time he retired in 1962.

That weekend, San Francisco stepped up its pursuit of the Giants, sending Mayor George Christopher to New York to meet with Stoneham, O'Malley and then Commissioner Ford Frick. The purpose of the meeting was obvious, but Frick looked foolish by ordering all parties to tell the press that "no comment is permitted."

But Stoneham didn't listen, telling the press the meeting "was the first discussion of any kind we've had concerning a possible move of the Giants from New York." Mayor Christopher left, saying that San Francisco had raised $5 million for a new park and "can get more."

Whatever was really said during the discussions left Christopher feeling supremely confident. Back home he announced that the decision would be made by July and revealed by August 30th. He added a prediction that baseball on the Coast would start the very next year, 1958. Later on he enlarged on his statement, saying both teams would commit as soon as stadium plans in both cities were completed.

The following week *The Sporting News* ran a story citing the most serious letdown in Dodger attendance in the history of Ebbets Field. For the first 15 home dates, Flatbush attendance was 182,077, or about 12,000 per game, an unheard of average at Ebbets Field of that day. Unheard of before O'Malley's deal with the Coast people, that is.

Writer Dan Daniel put the blame where it belonged, on O'Malley for the Jersey City moves, for the constant publicity about Los Angeles, for his almost daily bitching about the condition of Ebbets Field, and for his hedging on attendance figures. In an interview, O'Malley denied there was a fan rebellion, and kept up his downtown Brooklyn smokescreen, adding that "we cannot accept the Robert Moses plan for a stadium on Flushing Meadows, outside of Brooklyn, in the County of Queens." As Dave Anderson has said, he couldn't move to Queens, but Los Angeles was no problem.

In mid–May Sandy Koufax took one step closer to stardom. On the day of his second anniversary with the Dodgers he was taken off the bonus restriction list and could be sent to Montreal. Alston decided against it, saying Sandy had arrived as a major league pitcher. That same day he beat the Cubs 3–2, striking out 13. His path from then on was Los Angeles and the Hall of Fame.

On May 18th Bob Cooke reported in his *Herald-Tribune* column that Los Angeles was so sure of the Dodgers that officials there turned down an offer from the Washington Senators to move to LA. The offer was no doubt genuine, since Washington, like the Giants, was facing eventual bankruptcy. The problem there was that Washington was never a baseball town. Every year the president would throw the first ball out and then he, like most other citizens, stayed away. In all its history the team never drew a million paid, or even close. Even in 1933, their last pennant year, they drew a miserable 437,533. After the Los Angeles refusal Calvin Griffith braved it out for another couple of years and then moved his team to Minneapolis in 1961, naming it the Minnesota Twins.

So, with a team virtually in their hands, LA officials refused the Washington offer. "We don't want Washington," came the reply. "It's a second-division team. We'll only settle for Brooklyn."[1] That's how sure they were of O'Malley's intentions. These were the same people who just a few years before came east trolling for a team, trying for the St. Louis Browns, among others.

At May's end the National League owners, meeting in Chicago, approved the shifts of the Dodgers to Los Angeles and the Giants to San Francisco. O'Malley was thus proved right in his Jersey City strategy, knowing that if that move was approved they'd let him do anything. As if to prod the teams to move quickly, the approval had two provisos: that both teams request the moves before October 1st and that both teams move together.

In their approval, the owners, like O'Malley, were thinking of money, not the good of the game. They were aware that they had never been allowed to share in the lucrative television and radio money in New York, the $900,000 or so O'Malley, for example, received at the start of each season but seldom mentioned. So, with New York attendance declining, they knew they'd all make a lot of money on the Coast, where the novelty of the game would draw for years.

At this point Roscoe McGowen went around among the Dodger players to see how they felt about the "proposed" move to Los Angeles. (As Clem Labine said, by this time everyone connected with the club knew the move was coming.) Most of the older players, especially those who lived in Brooklyn or nearby eastern states, were reluctant about the move. The young men looked upon it as an adventure. Campy, who lived on Long Island, was one of the diehards, refusing to believe what was all around him. "Up to now I never thought it could happen. But now, I dunno. It could."

The older Dodgers knew the move was coming and many had regrets. "The adjustment was tough for us who had out best years behind us in Brooklyn," Erskine said. "We had lived there for 10 years and were part of the community."[2 The] feelings were even deeper for those like Labine and Maglie, whose roots were in the east. Even Snider, a Los Angeles native, wasn't happy with the move. Years later he said on the ESPN program *The 1956 Dodgers* that he and his wife cried at the news. "None of us wanted to leave," he said. "As far as baseball was concerned we were born and raised in Brooklyn."

On June 6th a game was called at Ebbets because of fog, the first time it ever happened in the major leagues. Over in Newark, fog and smog from the meadowlands would blanket Ruppert Stadium every once in a while, but it was unheard of in Brooklyn or the Bronx.

On every fly ball the outfielders groped around, hoping not to get hit in the head and, as a result, almost everything hit out of the infield went for a double while the fielders circled around for the ball. Umpire Tom Gorman, trying to get the game in because of the Dodgers fighting for first place, called time in the second inning. But after waiting well over an hour he called the game, fearing that an outfielder could suffer a serious injury.

A week later the Braves came in for a game that included one of the worst brawls ever seen at Ebbets Field. It started in the second inning when Drysdale hit Johnny Logan in the back after Billy Bruton had homered. On reaching first, Logan shouted to Drysdale, "I'll get you when you come into second base." Drysdale, who had a temper, replied, "If you've got a beef come on and get it over with now." Johnny did and got hit with the only punch that landed, a straight right by Big Don that opened a cut above his eye.

By that time both teams were involved: Hodges, trying to intervene, was tackled from behind amid a swirl of bodies. Then Mathews ran from the batting circle and jumped on Drysdale, knocking him on his face and pummeling him until Hodges shook loose and got to the mound. Gil, one of the strongest men in the game, got Eddie by one foot and dragged him off the field, kicking and inflicting some spike cuts on Gil's legs.

With Mathews off, catcher Carl Sawatski jumped on Drysdale, punching him as he was still on the ground. Finally, Newcombe got Sawatski off and Drysdale up, getting the now-disheveled Don in a bear hug and, with help, pulled him off the field. Drysdale was still struggling as he disappeared, obviously wanting to get back and get even. When order was restored, Milwaukee went on to win, 8–5, and take over first place.

Later that week, Bobby Thomson went back to the Giants in a swap with Milwaukee for Red Schoendienst. Bobby was traded away by Stoneham on February 1, 1954, for Johnny Antonelli, in one of the best deals the Giants ever made. There are many who think trading Thomson away, the man who hit the most famous home run in history, was hardhearted, but Antonelli, in that multiple trade, was the prize. Out of mediocrity with the Braves he sprang into stardom at the Polo Grounds, pitching the Giants to a pennant that year with a 21 and 7 record and a 2.30 ERA, both best in the league. For some reason Bobby couldn't stick with the Giants, traded away to the Cubs the following year. Maybe he had lost a step or two after breaking his ankle in the spring of '54. Memories of 1951 were fading already.

Just one week after being in first place the Dodgers were down in fifth after coming off a 6 and 8 home stand and ready to go on a 15-game road trip in 14 days. One of few bright spots was Labine, rolling along as one of the best relievers in the big leagues. One of the big factors in his success, he told Drebinger, was a crooked right index finger he suffered in an accident. As first he feared his career was over until he noticed the break caused a certain pitch to drop suddenly and at a baffling angle, adding another killer pitch to his dazzling curve, fast ball and control.

Why not be a starter, Drebinger asked, knowing of Clem's clutch wins against the Giants and Yankees as a starter, a far more glamorous role than relief? He replied that he'd thought of it in his younger days, but decided against it. "I came to the conclusion that I'd do best for myself concentrating on relieving," he said, adding that "it pays pretty well." Enough so that Labine, at $32,000, was the highest paid pitcher on the staff.

But Clem couldn't pitch every day and as it happened the mound staff was pretty well shot up: Podres' elbow, Koufax out two weeks with arm trouble, Erskine with recurrent shoulder trouble and Maglie out with a sprained thumb. Danny McDevitt had come up from Montreal to help and did with a couple of wins. What no one could make up for was that Don Newcombe had become an 11 and 12 pitcher. The Dodgers managed a half-hearted run toward the end but couldn't overcome the fact that Don's career was winding down.

At June's end Commissioner Frick took positive action in the "Great Ballot Box-Stuffing" scandal. Because of last-minute urging by the *Cincinnati Times-Star*, a flood of 550,000 ballots came out of Ohio that would have placed eight of the Reds on the All-Star team, substituting Wally Post, Gus Bell and George Crowe in place of Musial, Mays and Aaron.

Frick countered the move, saying an over-balance of pro–Cincinnati votes would result in a team not representative of the league and unpopular with fans all over the country. As it turned out, the Ohio voters still placed five on the team: Johnny Temple, Roy McMillan, Don Hoak, Ed Bailey and Frank Robinson. All for nothing when the Americans beat the Nationals 6–2, Jim Bunning over Curt Simmons.

On July 3rd O'Malley was called down to Washington to testify before Emanuel Celler's House Judiciary Subcommittee on Anti-Trust Matters. As O'Malley took the stand, Celler's first question was, "Will the Dodgers play in Los Angeles next year?" Walter said he did not know the answer because there were too many variables. In his two hours of testimony Walter again blamed city officials for "sabotaging" his efforts to stay in Brooklyn, a statement in tandem with his whining about the deterioration of Ebbets Field and the resultant drop in attendance.

What drop in attendance? If attendance drops, shouldn't that be reflected in a team's earnings? It would unless the figures were inaccurate. Back in 1951 O'Malley announced that the year before the Dodgers had a year-end deficit of $129,313, claiming the farm teams put the organization in the red.

Representative Celler released figures the next day that showed the deficit was the result of O'Malley writing off a $167,000 loss in promoting a football team, a loss that should not have been charged to the Dodgers. Celler also released figures showing the Dodgers to be one of the most profitable teams in baseball: earnings of $2,364,500 for the years 1945 through 1949.

In its coverage of O'Malley's testimony *The Sporting News* ran financial tables that cast doubt on O'Malley's attendance figures. The lists of major league team earnings for the years 1952 to 1956 showed that the Dodgers were the most profitable team in all of baseball, earning more money than even the Yankees with their big stadium.

The big three were Brooklyn, $1,860,744; the Yankees, $1,444,369; and the Red Sox, $1,113,309. Even in 1955 and 1956, the years of Walter's constant criticism of Ebbets Field, his Jersey City maneuver and obvious eyeing of Los Angeles, the team cleared $427,195 and $487,462 respectively. This above all expenses such as taxes, salaries, bonuses, etc.[3]

As an example of how well the Dodgers were situated as compared to the rest of the National League was their television/radio income. For 1956, the year before they left, Brooklyn was paid $880,270, with only the Giants close at $730,583. The other six teams were nowhere near, with Pittsburgh lowest at $158,580. Figures like that show the Dodgers' market as excellent, its income at the top.[4] O'Malley, therefore, could have waited years in Ebbets Field for a new stadium, if he had wanted to.

Looking at the missing figures, Brooklyn's paid attendance in 1950 was 1,185,896 and in 1951 it was 1,282,268. Therefore, for all the post-war years, 1945 through 1956, the Dodgers were the most profitable team in all of baseball, O'Malley's claims notwithstanding. O'Malley could release any attendance figures he wanted, but the earnings figures were something else. With them he was dealing with the Internal Revenue Service, an organization that could put you in jail. Not even O'Malley, brazen as he was, would mess with the IRS.

O'Malley's old mentor, the banker George McLaughlin, still a power in New York, got into the stadium picture when he appeared at the National League Owners Annual Meeting in St. Louis to urge that a new franchise be granted and a stadium built out in Flushing Meadows, Queens, in the event the Dodgers leave.

Such was O'Malley's power at the time, the owners turned down his plea flat, with not even a minute's discussion. Dick Young used to say that no group in the world was as dumb as baseball owners. Imagine them letting their league abandon New York City. Years before McLaughlin had made him politically and had allowed him to purchase 25 percent of the Dodgers, but O'Malley no longer listened to him.

Looking back, McLaughlin was years ahead of his time, his ignored proposal made years before New York lawyer William Shea succeeded in obtaining the Mets franchise. The stadium named after Shea was completed in 1964 at a cost of $29.5 million. If O'Malley hadn't been in such a hurry that kind of money could have been easily raised for the Dodgers.

The Dodgers seemed to be always fighting during their last days in Brooklyn. The latest brawl took place against Cincinnati on July 11th, started by a Raul Sanchez pitch that sent Junior Gilliam sprawling. Junior then bunted a popup down the first base line and barreled Sanchez over as he tried to field it. They came up punching, soon joined by all. The highlight was a straight sucker punch right by Charlie Neal that bowled Don Hoak over. Don came up looking for revenge but by that time Hodges, ever the peacemaker, grabbed him around the waist and carried him off the field.

Because of Gilliam, Zimmer, Neal and others thrown out of the game, a weird lineup went the rest of the way to win 5–4, thanks to two Snider homers. Gil Hodges played second, John Roseboro first and Bob Kennedy third. Hodges at second, his first time, seemed really strange. Gil was back at first the next day, hitting his 13th grand slam, then a National League record.

Stoneham, much less cagey than O'Malley, came right out and announced that the Giants were definitely leaving, probably for San Francisco, and that his decision was irrevocable, no matter what plans New York officials came up with. On July 24th *The Sporting News* carried a story that expanded on Stoneham's testimony earlier before Congress when he raised the possibility of a new Giant stadium in the East Bronx, near Eastchester Bay.

In an apparent change of mind, Horace called a news conference back in New York to announce that he was recommending to his Board of Directors that San Francisco can have the franchise, since "we have no chance to survive here. I will show them the money they can make by moving." He pointedly made no further mention of a New York site. "I want a percentage deal from them [San Francisco]," he added, "and if they are willing to extend it, I will recommend that it be accepted." Although the other owners had barred any move by only one team, he said the Giants would move no matter what the Dodgers did.[5] He must have been thinking of Minneapolis, practical since it is so much nearer to Chicago than any Coast city. Several days later he got a letter from San Francisco an offer that Stoneham called "a good proposition."

On August 19th it was all settled. Stoneham got the anticipated approval from his board, starting a period of rejoicing on the Coast and hand-wringing in New York. Celler led the mourners, saying the move proves the owners' "only motive is the money motive."

Of all the officials involved in the negotiations, Representative Celler is the most puzzling because he was the most powerful. It was strange that as the head of the House Subcommittee on Anti-Trust matters he never once used the power of his office to threaten the owners by holding the reserve clause over their heads. With Marvin Miller far in the future, it might have worked. Congress was reluctant to even discuss the reserve clause at this time because some thought chaos would result without it. They were right, as the situation today shows, but they were facing an unprecedented situation. The league was abandoning New York City. Besides, the owners knew their precious clause was shaky, having already bribed their way out of one anti-trust suit. Whatever; it would have been worth a try, but all Celler did was conduct a few toothless hearings during which he treated O'Malley and Stoneham like royalty.

Mayor Christopher was, of course, jubilant in his moment of triumph after months of hard work. Other city officials said their next move would be to start work on their planned $10 million home for the Giants, a park seating 45,000, with enough surrounding area for parking 10,000 cars.

Stoneham had some crocodile tears to spill. "It's a tough wrench," he said. "We're very sorry we're leaving. I'm very sentimental about the Giants and New York City." Yeah. He did get himself a nice deal, though, mentioning a 35-year lease, with a rental of five percent of receipts after taxes, with a minimum rental guarantee of $135,000.[6]

By now the officials of Los Angeles were so sure of the Dodgers that they were getting feisty. No longer hat in hand, they demanded of O'Malley a showdown on his plans by the end of September. Obviously encouraged by Stoneham's declaration, they wanted a decision so they could start discussions on a stadium. Their major concern was clearing title to the 300 acres of downtown Los Angeles that was part of their offer to O'Malley. Walter, cagey as ever and as sure of them as they were of him, did not respond. Nonetheless, the Los Angeles City Council the following week voted 11–3 to make a firm offer to the Dodger president.

On September 8th, Tommy Holmes of the *Herald-Tribune* covered the final game of the 58-year-old modern-era rivalry between the Dodgers and Giants. The game, at the Polo Grounds, ended at 4:05 on a Sunday afternoon, the Giants winners by a 3–2 score. Paid attendance: 22,376, bringing the yearly total to 639,529, the final year of a once-great team.

For history buffs: the series, dating back to 1900, ended at 650 wins for the Giants, 606 for Brooklyn. There were home runs by Gilliam and Hank Sauer and, fittingly, the last hit in the historic old park was by Willy Mays, a triple off Duke Snider's glove. For trivia buffs: Don Drysdale was the last pitcher to lose a Dodger game at the Polo Grounds.

Two weeks later, on September 24th, the Dodgers played their last game in Ebbets Field, beating Pittsburgh 2–0 behind Danny McDevitt. In a funeral-like atmosphere, with only 6,702 in the stands, Danny pitched a five-hitter and was almost matched by Pirate rookie Bennie Daniels. It was the start of a nine-year career for Daniels, but McDevitt, with a world of stuff, admittedly partied himself out of what should have been a great career.

Gladys Gooding, the Dodger organist since the Larry MacPhail days, played appropriate tunes throughout the game. After the Brooks scored their run in the first inning, she played "After You've Gone" and "Am I Blue." The run came on a walk, an error and a double by Elmer Valo, with Brooklyn that one year out of his 20 in the majors. After the second run, Cimoli driven in by Hodges, she played "Don't Ask Me Why I'm Leaving," finally at game's end, "Thanks For the Memories" and "Auld Lang Syne."

The crowd, contrary to years of mythology, was orderly, no ripping up of seats or railings or any of that sort of thing. When Tex Rickard asked them to take the exits without going on the field, they complied, filing out quietly to the sounds of Gladys Gooding's nostalgic tunes. The park was silent within minutes. McDevitt won his seventh game that day, recalling years later the workaday atmosphere during the game and at its end. "I don't remember anyone making a big deal after the game," he said. Danny, like Campanella, was one of the diehards, not yet believing, like Roy, that the team would leave. Although the veterans on the team discussed it, he said "I never thought it was gonna be."[7]

Dave Anderson agrees that no one, particularly the Dodger management, made anything of the game, held no ceremony or had Rickard wish the crowd farewell. "There was nothing of that sort," he said. "The Dodgers certainly didn't want anything like that. They treated it as just another game because, remember, the Los Angeles deal hadn't been closed yet."

Anderson is a footnote in Dodger history as the last sportswriter to leave Ebbets Field. Of the hundreds who covered the team since 1913, he was the last, as he let Bill Roeder of the *World Telegram* go out the door into the rotunda ahead of him.

"There were other people there, like a cleanup crew and the Western Union man, but Bill and I were the last writers," he said. "We were always last because we both worked for afternoon papers. As we were leaving it occurred to me, we were side by side, that if he left first I'd be the last baseball writer to leave Ebbets Field. So I just stepped back and let Bill go first. It wasn't a big thing. I didn't do it for posterity. I just did it for my own amusement. Nobody cared then, but 50 years later it's different.

"When the Brooklyn Cyclones came to Brooklyn my office asked me to write about them. At the end of the piece I wrote about me being last out of Ebbets Field, the first time I ever wrote about it. Now every two months or so somebody mentions it."

The wonder of such things, he said, is that 50 years later there is all this Dodgers nostalgia and none at all about the Giants. "Nobody cared that they were leaving, and that's one of the reasons they had to leave. There's still a lot of resentment, even today, about the Dodgers leaving, but you never hear any of that about the Giants."[8]

The last game at the Polo Grounds, unlike Ebbets Field, was a riotous affair after closing ceremonies by such as Mrs. John McGraw and a number of Giants old-times including Carl Hubbell, Rube Marquard, Hal Schumacher and the like. The crowd then went wild. Souvenir hunters not only ripped up the field, but removed home plate, the bases, and the pitching rubber, demolished the shelter over the bullpen and tore loose much of the protective foam rubber off the outfield walls, and even ripped up a number of seats.

The game was viewed by 11,606 paid as the Giants lost the last game in their historic park, 9–1, to the Pirates' Bob Friend. Some fans carried signs reading Polo Grounds: 1905–1957, giving the scene a funereal touch. For the record, Johnny Antonelli took the loss, his 18th win against 12 wins during that lackluster season. Bobby Thomson, back with the Giants for a while, played third base "for old times' sake," and Dusty Rhodes not only drove in the final run, but made the final out, fittingly, a broken-bat grounder to short.

Meanwhile, wherever he was, Charlie Dressen could finally say "The New York Giants is dead," and he'd be right, at least according to officials at the Brooklyn Board of Education.

On that same day in Philadelphia the Brooklyn Dodgers played the last game of their storied team's life. They lost 2–1, Seth Morehead over Roger Craig, the very last Brooklyn Dodger run driven in by Gil Hodges. But it didn't really matter to anyone. They were leaving Brooklyn, they were 11 games out, and as W.C. Fields would moan, they had to end it all in Philadelphia.

On October 7th the Los Angeles City Council decided to make Brooklyn a solid offer. By a vote of 10 to 4 they moved to send Walter O'Malley a binding contract with all the provisions necessary to persuade him to accept. When word reached O'Malley the next day it was all over. The stockholders and directors of the ball club unanimously voted for the move, ending 68 years of the Dodgers representing Brooklyn.

Among the team's office people, vice presidents and all the rest, the feeling was anything but unanimous. Well before accepting the Los Angeles offer, O'Malley met with his office staff in Brooklyn's Hotel Bossert to find out how they felt about the move. According to Buzzy Bavasi, O'Malley went around the table to ask each person's opinion. All talked of mortgages, children in school and their overall desire to stay in the New York area.

"O'Malley first counted the votes," Bavasi said years later, "and then said: 'Everyone wants to stay except me, so we're going.'" Bavasi was not at all surprised, recalling how many times O'Malley said to him that if he were going to move to Queens he might as well move three thousand miles away.[9]

There were many who through those agonizing months thought O'Malley sincerely wanted to stay in Brooklyn but, as Arthur Daley put in his October 14th *Times* column, "Once Los Angeles began the Siren Song, O'Malley was so beguiled that he was lost." Daley went on: "A bitter end it was for those faithful Brooklyn fans who enabled the Dodgers to amass a profit of $1.8 million over a five-year span. That's the one ugly and inescapable fact that sets this deal apart from all other franchise transfers. Other teams were forced to move by apathy or incompetence. The only word that fits the Dodgers is greed."

The next day Red Smith did a column saying that some of the other National League owners, unidentified, were regretting their votes to allow the franchise shifts. He quotes Lou Perini, of the then Milwaukee Braves, as telling anyone who would listen, "We must have a team in New York, even if it means a nine-team league." Since there wasn't one dissenting vote, Red asked, "Where was he three months ago when the deed was done?" Where was anybody?

Later when they realized what they had allowed—the abandonment of New York, the long plane rides to the Coast and back, the hatred aroused among millions of fans—some of them tried to defend their votes by saying they never thought O'Malley would really go, that they were helping him pressure New York into a new stadium. The Lords of Baseball, dumb as ever.

On October 24th, TV station WOR entered the picture, reaching an agreement allowing them to broadcast the 77 home games of the Philadelphia Phillies to the New York area, among them all 11 Dodger games. Hilda Chester, the legendary Dodger fan with her ever-present cowbell, spoke for millions of us when she was asked during an interview if she would watch any of them.

"I wouldn't be caught dead watching the Dodgers in Philadelphia," she answered.[10] A woman scorned, an entire Borough scorned.

Aftermath

Before the last game was played, plans for the enormous apartment complex that would replace Ebbets Field were underway. In Brooklyn it took three years before all plans were final and demolition started on April 23, 1960. For some crazy reason Carl Erskine posed with the wrecking ball as photographers took pictures before the first smash. Carl is smiling as though at a celebration instead of a funeral. For one of the brightest stars at Ebbets Field, it was a strange farewell.

Before that wrecking ball struck, the park had been empty for many months, its grass green as ever, seemingly waiting for an opening day game that would never be played. Instead there were 13 college baseball games and 33 soccer matches, mostly international, played before sparse crowds during the park's final months. Typical of the end was an April 1958 game between host team St. John's of Brooklyn and Rutgers of New Brunswick, New Jersey, with Rutgers the winner, 4–3. Although his team won, coach George Case, the old Washington Senator, was unhappy with his team's performance. Both he and the ballpark had seen better days.

The Polo Grounds was taken over by the city, so there were years of red tape before its destruction. It finally began coming down on April 10, 1964, with no Giant callous enough to pose as a pallbearer. Like Ebbets Field, it is the site of one of those massive housing developments that blight the city's landscape.

With both parks finally gone, there were only memories for Dodgers fans: MacPhail and Rickey, who between them made the Dodgers the powerhouse they became; the excellence of Wyatt, Higbe, Newcombe and Erskine; Reese with his arm around Jackie Robinson; Dixie Walker playing those right-field caroms; the Thomson home run and Branca's agony; Lavagetto breaking up Bill Bevens' World Series no-hitter as Henrich scrambles to the wall; the curve ball of Clem Labine; Pete Reiser being carried off the field; Billy Cox killing another double; Robinson, Campanella, Newcombe and Bankhead making the game interracial;

Furillo's arm; Hodges' strength and power; Snider hitting one into Bedford Avenue; Shotgun Shuba's line drives; the clutch relieving of Casey and Labine; Joe Medwick lying stretched out at home plate seriously hurt; Erskine's two no-hitters; Robinson tormenting pitchers; Campy in a wrecked car, paralyzed in Glen Cove; Owen scrambling back for that spitball wild pitch; Wyatt and Higbe in that '41 pennant drive; Reese, the best two-strike hitter in baseball; Dick Sisler's home run; Durocher snarling at umpires; Abe Stark and his "Hit Sign, Win Suit" advertisement at the base of the right field wall, a sign never hit; the tantalizing pitches of Preacher Roe. Then there is always the memory of Tex Rickard and his scrambled syntax as he did the Ebbets Field public announcing. One of his best efforts was at a night game with Roe against the Cardinals. In the fifth inning with a shutout going, Preacher didn't appear. Rickard came on with: "Preacher Roe can't finish the game because he don't feel good." Vintage Rickard.

And the names: Frenchy Bordagaray, Boom Boom Beck, The Preacher, The Duke, The Reading Rifle, Whit Wyatt, Pistol Pete, Shotgun Shuba, Babe Herman, Dazzy Vance, Mad Monk Meyer, Zim, Cookie Lavagetto, Dixie Walker, Hot Potato Hamlin, Goody Rosen, Pee Wee, Uncle Robbie. Those were good, but best of all think of Van Lingle Mungo and Heinie Manush. Mungo reminds one of the old Flash Gordon serials with Emperor Ming of the planet Mongo. Manush is strange enough, but Heinie?

In a poignant interview after he retired, Walter (Red) Barber, the Dodger broadcaster for many years, was asked how he felt about Ebbets Field being demolished. "I wasn't there," he said. "I didn't see it come down. In my mind's eye it is still there."[1]

A nice sentiment, Red, but there's a family living right on home plate, another where the Hit Sign, Win Suit sign used to be, and another out in center field where Hilda first started ringing her cowbell. There aren't many of us left who knew the old park and when we're gone even the memories will fade away. One consolation: Walter O'Malley went before us.

The official abandonment of Ebbets Field began on October 29th, 1957, as O'Malley flew 29 of his staff to Los Angeles where, as expected, they were greeted at the airport by a cheering throng that crowded around the plane in a welcoming bedlam. Within a month of their arrival Bavasi announced advance ticket sales of some $1,000,000, amazing since no one even knew where the team would open the season.

That abandonment left the Borough without a team just two years after losing the *Brooklyn Eagle*, its only daily voice. If independent, Brooklyn would be the fourth largest city in the country. It was left huge but impotent, relying for all these years on Manhattan for news and sports.

In a strange twist, however, some Los Angeles officials immediately started giving O'Malley a bad time about the stadium he was planning, and his interim move into the Coliseum. This situation somehow got lost in translation back on the East Coast. The impression throughout Brooklyn was that the entire city of Los Angeles was waiting for the team with open arms. Or perhaps many of us were so disgusted we simply ignored any news out of LA.

Almost from the time he arrived on the Coast, O'Malley was harried by various citizen groups who declared the Chavez Ravine deal a giveaway, which it was, as they were circulating petitions demanding a referendum on the issue. Walter was now being called "harried" in the Los Angeles press as things got so bad for a while that he started his old Brooklyn routine: threatening to move the team—this time before the team had even played a game.

During the December major league meeting in Colorado Springs he went so far as to announce that the Dodgers might well go back to Brooklyn for the 1958 season. "If anything should happen to make it impossible for us to open in Los Angeles we could still return to Brooklyn," he said during a press conference.[2]

The things he had counted on for attendance were proving elusive, as both the Rose Bowl and the Coliseum were presenting O'Malley with unforeseen difficulties. The Coliseum issue was rental money for the two years it would take to build Dodger Stadium in Chavez Ravine. Therefore, on December 20th the Coliseum Commission voted down the proposal to lease the field.[3] In Pasadena the City Council favored baseball in the Rose Bowl but various citizen groups were threatening lawsuits if it came about.[4]

Even given that Los Angeles was known for its nut fringes, many were surprised that a city would in effect steal a baseball club and then haggle over where it could play. As the *Times* pointed out during this period, the more trouble O'Malley was being given, the happier the people of Brooklyn became.

As negotiations dragged on, the thing O'Malley feared most was what the Giants were facing in San Francisco—playing in a minor league park. Walter's dream of immediate riches were threatened by the possibility that he would have to settle for the 23,000-seat Wrigley Field, as the Giants had to make do with Seals Stadium.

Finally, after four months during which O'Malley worked his way through threatened lawsuits and municipal objections, he offered the Coliseum people a $600,000 rental fee for the two seasons, up from $400,000, and after it was accepted signed a two-year lease for 1958 and 1959.

Even today so many years later, it seems incredible that the other owners would allow their teams to play in that disgraceful stadium even on a temporary basis. A graphic published in the *Los Angeles Times* on lease-signing day highlighted the unbelievable dimensions of that football field. Screen or not, the left field foul line was 250 feet, and the right field line 300. Center field had a six-foot fence 440 feet from home plate. The worst park in major league history, but such was the mysterious power of Walter O'Malley.

Players thought the whole stadium was ridiculous, and some comments sparked a war in the press with a defensive Red Patterson. The Giants' Johnny Antonelli, for example, called the left field fence "the biggest farce I ever saw."

"Look who's talking," Patterson responded, "I can't understand why a guy who has pitched in the Polo Grounds would enter into a controversy like this. He'll recall the Dusty Rhodes homer to beat Bob Lemon. That was the granddaddy of all Chinese homers (258 feet)."[5] When Spahn, Friend and others started echoing Antonelli, O'Malley stepped in with the lame argument that the Coliseum "isn't perfect, but it's the best that can be done as a stopgap measure."

Opening day at the Coliseum, April 18, 1958, was the beginning of the kind of attendance O'Malley sold out Brooklyn for. The largest opening day crowd in National League history, 78,682, saw the Dodgers beat the Giants 6–5. It was the start of many such crowds as the money started rolling in. It didn't matter to any of the league owners what kind of baseball was being played. Blinded by gold, they glossed over the 250-foot left field foul line, shorter even than the Polo Grounds, and the 300-foot line in right. What was the difference? The Los Angeles fans didn't care. They didn't know enough baseball to realize that Wally Moon's pop up home runs over the left field screen—called Moonshots by the press—were an insult to people who knew and loved the game.

The inevitable Hollywood touch brought glamour to the Dodger games, with movieland types like Edward G. Robinson, Doris Day and Dinah Shore running around getting photographed. But it was like one of those fake Hollywood sets, those make-believe storefronts. Look behind all that glamour and you find an aging team playing in a travesty of a ballpark. Dinah in her perky way made light of what was going on at a welcoming party by singing the ditty:

> All the Bums are older
> So we used our common sense
> Livened up the baseball
> And shortened up the fence.[6]

Obviously she didn't realize that what she was singing was a mockery of baseball.

The field was a nightmare for left-handed hitters like Duke Snider, since the oval stand in right field dropped back to 441 feet, not that far from the foul pole. From 40 homers the year before he dipped to 15 for all of 1958. And this was a legitimate long-ball hitter, Ebbets Field or not. Remember all those World Series home runs into the upper deck of Yankee Stadium.

Tommy Holmes, the old *Brooklyn Eagle* traditionalist, railed against all this in his *Herald-Tribune* stories. In one he analyzed the effect the left field screen was having on the scoring. During the first nine games at the Coliseum he noted that of 90 balls hit to left, 82 percent were hits—82 percent. Of that 82 percent, 29 were home runs and 46 either hit the 42-foot fence or bounced safely. The hitters named left field "Chinatown" and right and center "Outer Mongolia."[7]

The Dodger pitching staff was going crazy over all this, made the worse for them by the opposition hitting twice as many "Moonshots" as their hitters. The eight principal pitchers on the staff went 64–67 as the team finished in seventh place, 12 games below .500. Worse, as the season wore on some of them changed their style because of the left field screen and came up with sore arms.

We in the East were gloating, of course, but it was short-lived. The very next year, after only two years on the Coast, aging as they were, they won the pennant and the World Series. All those years the Brooklyn Faithful suffered, and then to see their transplanted team win a Series within two seasons.

The Giants weren't so lucky out there because they didn't have the leadership O'Malley gave the new franchise. O'Malley always knew what he was doing, was never distracted by a drinking problem, as Stoneham was.

Baseball had been part of Brooklyn culture for 100 years, the subject most talked about in bars, team doings vital to the metropolitan newspapers. A good part of a way of life had been taken away.

What was probably the first of the teams that would popularize baseball in the Borough were the Atlantics, established in 1855 in the Bedford section of Brooklyn, where Ebbets field was eventually built in 1913. Given its location, the team was probably the ancestor of the Dodger club, and like its descendant, was avidly supported by its largely Irish immigrant population, with its working class mores and Democratic political ties.[8] The O'Malley clan was never part of that Irish mix, never part of Brooklyn until Walter's time.

While not realizing it, Jack Newfield and Pete Hamill were in tune with millions of us regarding Walter O'Malley. Once, over dinner, Newfield and Hamill began to joke about writing an article on the 10 worst human beings that ever lived, and each agreed to write down the very worst three. Both listed and then compared, having in the same order: Hitler, Stalin and Walter O'Malley.[9]

Strangely, there has never been that sort of hatred for Stoneham. After neglecting his New York team for two decades and then bailing out, he seemed no wiser in San Francisco. They were wildly welcomed, of course, but then Horace approved construction of the worst of all the new stadiums. Didn't anyone think of testing the wind velocity at Candlestick Point? The Giants out there seemed always second fiddle to the Dodgers, one reason being everyone hated that cold and very windy Candlestick Park, particularly the ballplayers, who kept comparing it to the beautiful park O'Malley had built in Chavez Ravine. Remember Stu Miller being blown off the mound at Candlestick before a national television audience during an All-Star game? The announcers tried to cover baseball's embarrassment by repeating what a small, slight man Miller was. He was 6 feet, 165 pounds, not exactly small. The park became a national joke.

Personally things didn't start too well for some of San Francisco's black players, particularly Willie Mays. Willie was sharp-tongued and often impolite, but it was his color that was the problem. While house hunting, he made an offer on a home near the exclusive St. Francis Wood section, but looked elsewhere when the owner took it off the market, "suspiciously," as realtors agreed. Willie bought a house in the same area and then had trouble closing on the deal because of white objections on racial grounds. The seller at first gave in to pressure from the area but Willie's money talked and the neighborhood finally gave in to the inevitable.[10]

Of course most objections ceased when the permanent parks were completed and attendance continued soaring. Money even quieted the opponents who had to play in Candlestick Park with its winds. Then followed the golden years of LaSorda, Koufax, Drysdale, Parker, the Davises, Tommy and Willie, Wills, Sutton, Osteen, Mays, McCovey, Cepeda, Antonelli and the rest. Winners far more often than not. But during the 1990s, after all those years, things turned sour in Los Angeles.

After they won their last pennant in 1995, the Dodgers started an erratic pattern, two games out one year, 23 another, 11 another as the front office disintegrated. Many blamed it on the fact that Peter O'Malley, after taking over from his father, was shunned in major baseball matters by Commissioner Bud Selig and other leaders.

Peter finally gave up and sold out, but the front office chaos continued. In his analysis of that Dodger organization, Murray Chass in his *Times* column said the word was *dysfunctional*, as in the Dysfunctional Dodgers: officials hired on five-year contracts and dismissed after two, ownership changes within a couple of years and the latest owner firing a dozen executives within 21 months. The organization that began crumbling at the core under Peter O'Malley has recovered slowly.[11]

The Los Angeles Dodgers franchise in chaos? The Dysfunctional Dodgers? How sweet it was, how very sweet.

Chapter Notes

Introduction

1. Brooklynese, a way of making fun: Cohen, *Dodgers, The First 100 Years*, p. 1.
2. Mullins' world-famous Bum: *New York Times*, 9/22/78, p. B6.
3. They have to make a living, too: Holmes, *Brooklyn's Babe*, p. ix.
4. Babe had to pay the price: *Ibid*, p. 221.
5. The wealthy Babe Herman: *Baseball Magazine*, 9/45, p. 331.
6. Drink gin, no worms: Parrott, *The Lords of Baseball*, p. 91.
7. Drink likker, no worms: Allen/Fitzgerald, *You Can't Beat the Hours*, p. 124.
8. Pete's pinch-hit grand slam: W.C. Heinz, *The Rocky Road of Pistol Pete*, p. 392.
9. Didn't face Bowman for a month: *New York Times, Herald-Tribune, Brooklyn Eagle*, 4/23/41 and 5/26/41.
10. Some big writers avoided Ebbets Field: Kahn, *The Era*, p. 24.
11. Brooklyn a provincial outpost: Ibid, p. 112.
12. Brooklyn farther than Philadelphia: Parrott, *Op. cit.*, p. 97.
13. Woodward on the Dodgers: Kahn, *Beyond the Boys of Summer*, p. 120.

Chapter One

1. O'Malley's financial panic: *The Sporting News*, 10/4/50, p. 2.
2. Why was Governor Earl Warren at Ebbets Field: *Ibid*, 8/29/53, p. 11.
3. Why LA correspondence kept secret: Shapiro, *The Last Good Season*, p. 323.
4. Walter lied about baseball background: Kahn, *The Era*, p. 264.
5. Drysdale's uncles: Kahn, *The Head Game*, p. 229.
6. I got along with all the writers except Dick Young: *Labine interview.*
7. He should have said nice catch: Kahn, *Boys of Summer*, p. 236.
8. We tried everything for Barney: *New York Herald-Tribune,* 4/10/50, p. 20.
9. Allow blacks into Atlanta stands first time: *The Sporting News*, 5/19/50, p. 5.
10. The shooting of Eddie Waitkus: *New York Herald-Tribune*, 6/16/50, p. 1.
11. Wakefield's mistake was $51,000 bonus: *The Sporting News*, 1/4/50, p. 14.
12. Gionfriddo's catch better than Mays': Kahn, *The Era*, p. 128.
13. Baseball immune from antitrust laws: *New York Times*, 10/10/22, p. 17.
14. Reserve clause would have to go: *Ibid*, 2/10/49, p. 39.
15. Gardella's $300,000 bribe: *Ibid*, 6/16/50, p. 32.
16. Furillo's leukemia: Kahn, *Beyond the Boys of Summer*, p. 339.
17. Mazzone on anti-pitcher moves: Kahn, *The Head Game*, pp. 280–281.
18. Furillo's feud with Durocher starts: *Brooklyn Eagle*, 6/29/50, p. 21.
19. Furillo the outsider: *Labine interview.*
20. The drinking Horace Stoneham: Durocher, *Nice Guys Finish Last*, p. 288.
21. Spaulding Company denies ball juiced: *The Sporting News*, 7/5/50, p. 29.
22. A killing at the Polo Grounds: *New York Times*, 7/8/50, p. 1.
23. DiMaggio's post-war decline: *Ibid*, 8/16/50, p. 35.
24. Rickey a professor in Greek, German and Shakespeare: *American National Biography*, pp. 480–481.

25. Dodgers of the '40s much closer to the fans: *Howie Schultz interview.*
26. The phony Robinson contract: *George Shuba interview.*
27. O'Malley/Rickey cursing match: Barber, *The Broadcasters*, pp. 169–170.
28. O'Malley stays with fiancée: *New York Times* obit, 8/10/79, p. A13.
29. Rickey, O'Malley get share of team: Helyer, *Lords of the Realm*, p. 40.
30. Squeezing O'Malley: Barber, *Rhubarb in the Catbird Seat*, pp. 280–281.
31. Abrams was really slow: *Eddie Miksis interview.*
32. Dick Sisler's stutter: Erskine, *Tales From the Dodger Dugout*, p. 60.
33. Dick conquered his demon: Allen, *Brooklyn Remembered*, p. 35.
34. Old Pete with the standees: *New York Times*, 10/7/50, p. 12.
35. A historian's mistaken assumption: Rader, Baseball, *A History of America's Game*, p. 131.
36. Walter terribly sorry to accept Rickey resignation: Kahn, *The Era*, p. 267.

Chapter Two

1. Dressen: I'll think of something: *Labine interview.*
2. Joe DiMaggio: I intend to stay alive: Kahn, *Memories of Summer*, pp. 74–75.
3. Bowman denied bad blood with Medwick: *New York Herald-Tribune*, p. 27.
4. Medwick beaned because of crossed signal: Frommer, *American Book of Baseball*, p. 180.
5. MacPhail's batting cap ready: *New York Times*, 3/8/41, p. S1.
6. Helmets give both pitchers and hitters confidence: *Bragan interview.*
7. Zim not wearing helmet, almost dies: *St. Paul Pioneer Press*, 7/8/53, p. 15.
8. Dressen overused and overworked his pitchers: King, *A King's Legacy*, p. 77.
9. Dressen gets Reynolds drunk: Halberstam, *Summer of '49*, p. 74.
10. O'Malley purges Rickey men: *The Sporting News*, 12/13/50, p. 2.
11. To O'Malley I was an uppity nigger: Robinson, *I Never Had It Made*, pp. 93, 96 and 100–101.
12. Wanted vacancy, so they named Frick: *Time*, 3/12/84, p. 58.
13. Robinson: Bunt and run up their backs: *Brooklyn Eagle*, 5/2/51, p. 21.
14. Many black players did not side with Robinson: Frommer, *Rickey & Robinson*, pp. 113 and 178.
15. Hermanski plan to protect Robinson: *Hermanski interview.*
16. Chandler's parting shots: *The Sporting News*, 8/15/51, p. 7.
17. Hugh Casey's wife tries to prevent suicide: *Ibid*, 7/11/51, p. 40.
18. Stengel tells Sain he'll never be a starter: Kahn, *The Head Game*, p. 180.
19. Johnny Sain's pitching philosophy: *Ibid*, p. 195.
20. Ominous statistics for New York City: *The Sporting News*, 9/5/51, p. 1.
21. (Dressen) just sat me down. *Clem Labine interview.*
22. They got Clem through luck: *Baseball Biographical Encyclopedia*, p. 631.
23. Dressen didn't use pitching coaches: *National Pastime*, SABR, 5/05, p. 70.
24. The curve ball I bounced: Erskine, *Op. cit.*, p. 87.
25. Stealing signs by telegraph wire: *Sal Yvars interview.*
26. Branca blames Dressen for lost pennant: *New York Times*, 2/1/01, p. D1.
27. Some Giants didn't want to know: *Wall Street Journal*, 1/31/01, p. 29.
28. Similar scheme in 1898: *Ibid.*
29. Don Newcombe becomes an alcohol/drug counselor: *Baseball, The Biographical Encyclopedia*, pp. 828–829.
30. The dismal scouting report on Joe D: Kahn, *Life*, 10/22/51, p. 134.
31. Mantle blames DiMaggio for knee injury: Kahn, *The Era*, p. 289.
32. Yankee arrogance: Kahn, *Memories of Summer*, p. 65.

Chapter Three

1. No two fastballs in a row: *The Woonsocket Call*, 10/22/05, p. 8.
2. Henrich and Walters: Baseball strategy no mystery, since game not that complicated: Allen, *You Can't Beat the Hours*, pp. 120–121.
3. Cobb's view of baseball: *Life*, 3/17/52, p. 137.
4. Hornsby answers: *Look*, 7/17/52, p. 55.
5. Why Chandler suspended Durocher: *Brooklyn Eagle*, 4/30/52, p. 24.
6. Congress reports: reserve clause needed, *New York Times*, 5/3/52, p. 21.

7. Johnny Rutherford's troubles with arm and Dressen. *Rutherford interview.*
8. Johnny had it all: *Labine interview.*
9. George Blaeholder, father of the slider: *The Sporting News,* 9/24/52, p. 4.
10. Gomez on the curve ball: Kahn, *The Head Game,* p. 4.
11. Erskine's 12-year sore arm: *Erskine interview.*
12. He hid it from the coaching staffs and managers: *National Pastime* (SABR), 5/05, pp. 68–69.
13. Hodges, half price: *The Sporting News,* 10/15/52, p. 9.
14. Robinson: Yankee management prejudiced: *Ibid,* 12/10/52, p. 3.
15. Weiss defends Yankees: *Ibid.*
16. Casey: Howard can't run: Light, *Op. Cit.,* p. 178.
17. First all-black lineup: Appel, *Armchair Book of Baseball,* p. 26.

Chapter Four

1. Pafko puzzled by trade: Kahn, *Boys of Summer,* p. 268.
2. Write baseball, not race relations: *Ibid,* pp. 135–136.
3. Problem of Negroes in baseball unresolved: *New York Herald-Tribune,* 3/21/53, p. 12.
4. Billy Cox on Guadalcanal: McNeil, *The Dodgers Encyclopedia,* p. 39.
5. The differences between Jackie and Roy: Robinson, *Op. cit.,* p. 98.
6. Campy changed as he got older: *Ibid,* pp. 262–263.
7. Roy has "a little Tom" in him: Kahn, *The Boys of Summer,* p. 390.
8. Robinson's problems in the Army: Robinson, *Op. cit.,* pp. 16 and 22.
9. Reese befriends Robinson: Robinson, *Ibid,* p. 65.
10. Cronin says Reese will never make it: Durocher, *Op. cit.,* p. 133.
11. Joe Black on the downhill: Kahn, *Boys of Summer,* p. 179.
12. Jackie replaces Cox at third: *New York Times,* 3/22/53, p. S3.
13. Robby: I can't carry his (Cox') glove: *The Sporting News,* 5/6/53, p. 7.
14. Hodges always gives up outside of plate: Anderson, *Pennant Races,* p. 239.
15. We can finish last without you: Kiner, *Baseball Forever,* p. 106.
16. Shoeshine boy, porter: *Brooklyn Eagle,* 8/6/53, p. 15.
17. The Giants is dead: Kahn, *Boys of Summer,* p. 181.
18. Brooklyn Board of Education to the rescue: Allen, *Op. cit.,* p. 154.
19. Gov. Warren and O'Malley at Ebbets Field: *New York Herald-Tribune,* 8/29/53, p. 10.
20. Stanky doing an ape act?: Prince, *Brooklyn's Dodgers,* p. 14.
21. Furillo attacks Durocher: *New York Times,* 9/7/53, p. 1.
22. A lot of the Giants hate him too: Kahn, *The Era,* p. 314.

Chapter Five

1. On Alston if a player rebelled: Carl Erskine interview.
2. The first open break between Alston/Robinson: *Bill James Guide to Baseball Managers,* p. 224.
3. A humiliating moment for Jackie: Robinson, *Op. cit.,* pp. 117–118.
4. How the Orioles became the Yankees: Thorn, *Total Baseball,* p. 43.
5. Joe D dumps Joe Page: Cramer, *The Hero's Life,* pp. 230–231 and 251.
6. Monte Irvin versus Russ Meyer: *The Sporting News,* 7/21/54, p. 14.
7. Negroes outnumber whites as starters: *New York Times,* 7/16/54, p. 25.
8. Why isn't he a Dodger? He's black enough: Golenbock, *Bums,* p. 333.
9. Smith fed up with Robinson antics: Kahn, *Memories of Summer,* p. 208.
10. Smith compares Dodger Fans to cockroaches: *New York Herald-Tribune,* 10/21/47, p. 29.
11. Robinson the cause of beanball fights: *Ibid,* 8/29/54, p. S3.
12. Roe to Robinson's defense: *The Sporting News,* 3/15/55, p. 14.
13. Dick Young calls Robinson a man of moral purity: Robinson, *Op. cit.,* p. 143.
14. Bing Crosby gets Rickey demoted: *The Sporting News,* 8/15/54, p. 23.
15. *The Sporting News,* 9/24/54, pp. 21 and 26.

Chapter Six

1. Brooklyn was too far: Golenbock, *Op. cit.,* p. 333.

2. Jackie had to win to eat: *Look*, 1/25/55, pp. 26–27.
3. Alvin Dark on minority ballplayers: *Stan Isaacs interview.*
4. Jackie was after Maglie, not Williams: *The Sporting News*, 22/1/56, p. 10.
5. Newcombe thinks it over: *Ibid*, 6/22/55, p. 3.
6. Roe and his spitter: Kahn, *Sports Illustrated*, 7/4/55, p. 19.
7. Roe outstanding Harding University alumnus: *Harding University Program Honoring Elwin Charles Roe*, 10/25/2002.
8. Umpire Larry Goetz denies Roe spitter story: *The Sporting News*, 7/13/55, p. 1.
9. Inching their way westward: *New York Times* (Young obit), 9/1/87, p. B7.
10. O'Malley: Brooklyn filled with blacks, spics and Jews: Kahn, *The Era*, p. 327.
11. Dick Young came up with stories other than game: *Anderson interview.*
12. Moses against downtown Brooklyn stadium: Kahn, *The Era*, pp. 335–336.
13. O'Malley couldn't be satisfied: Sullivan: *The Dodgers Move West*, p. 48.
14. Walter would've gone through a brick wall to get to LA: *Anderson interview.*
15. O'Malley kept spreading lies: *Stan Isaacs interview.*
16. Snider: Brooklyn fans the worst: *New York Times*, 8/27/55, p. 10.
17. Alston lacks faith in Sandy: Leavy, *Koufax*, pp. 118–119.
18. Koufax could hold baseball almost like a golf ball: *Ibid*, p. 7.
19. Koufax resented as bonus baby and Jew: *Ibid*, p. 72.
20. If no new stadium, Jersey City for 1958: *The Sporting News*, 10/5/55, p. 5.

Chapter Seven

1. We all knew we were going: *Labine interview.*
2. Snider: I play for money: *Colliers*, 5/25/56, pp. 42–46.
3. Red Smith: Poor Duke Snider: *New York Herald-Tribune*, 5/10/56, p. S1.
4. The welcome mat for Maglie: *The Sporting News*, 5/23/56 p. 6.
5. Zimmer: coma, two brain operations: *St. Paul Dispatch*, 8/3/53, p. 15.
6. I had four holes in my head: *Zim*, p. 9.
7. Everybody wanted Brooklyn to lose: Shapiro, *Op. cit.*, pp. 278–279.

8. A player admits seeing ball better in daytime: *Ibid*, p. 277.
9. Spahn: No Mr. Nice Guy: *Ibid*, p. 282.
10. Brooklyn got Maglie for $1,000: *Los Angeles Times*, 10/4/56, p. 1.
11. Jackie decided he had to retire: Robinson, *Op. cit.*, pp. 121–122.
12. Bavasi: Jackie's been writing apology letters all his life: *The Sporting News*, 1/16/57, p. 3.

Chapter Eight

1. Los Angeles officials: We'll only settle for Brooklyn: *New York Herald-Tribune*, 5/18/57, p. S1.
2. The move to LA was tough on the older established players. *Erskine interview.*
3. Dodgers one of baseball's most profitable teams: *New York Times*, 11/7/51, p. 42 and 11/8/51, p. 39.
4. Dodgers TV and radio income at the top: *The Sporting News*, 7/3/57, p. 15.
5. Stoneham announces San Francisco commitment: *Ibid*, 7/24/57, p. 1.
6. Stoneham's crocodile tears: *New York Times*, 8/20/57, p. 1.
7. McDevitt: Last game at Ebbets field no big deal: *National Pastime* (SABR), Number 24, 2004.
8. The last writer to leave Ebbets Field: *Anderson interview.*
9. O'Malley: Everyone wants to stay except me, so we're going: Shapiro, *Op. cit.*, pp. 314 and 321.
10. Hilda Chester: I wouldn't be caught dead watching the Dodgers in Philadelphia: *New York Times*, 5/18/58, p. S3.

Aftermath

1. Ebbets Field is still there: Barber, *Rhubarb in the Catbird Seat*, p. 291.
2. O'Malley hints return to Brooklyn: *New York Times*, 12/7/57, p. 33.
3. Coliseum Commission votes no: *Los Angeles Times*, 12.21.57, p. A1.
4. Citizens objections to Rose Bowl: *Ibid*, 12/25/57.
5. Feud over Coliseum left field: *Ibid*, 1/22/58, p. C1.
6. Dinah's ditty: *New York Times*, 4/20/58, p. S2.
7. Hits off left field screen: *New York Herald-Tribune*, 5/4/58.

8. The Dodger ancestor: Terry, *Long Before the Dodgers*, pp. 15–16.
9. Hitler, Stalin and O'Malley: Goldenbock: *Op. cit.*, p. 448.
10. Mays' house troubles: *New York Herald-Tribune*, p. 1.
11. Dodger organization crumbling: *New York Times*, 11/8/05, p. D3.

Bibliography

Books

Allen, Maury. *Brooklyn Remembered*. Champaign, IL: Sports Publishing, 2005.
Allen, Mel, and Ed Fitzgerald. *You Can't Beat the Hours*. New York: Harper & Rowe, 1964.
American National Biography. New York: Oxford University Press, 1999.
Anderson, Dave. *Pennant Races*. New York: Doubleday, 1994.
Anderson, David W. *More Than Merkle*. Lincoln: University of Nebraska Press, 2000.
Barber, Red. *Rhubarb in the Catbird Seat*. Lincoln: University of Nebraska Press, 1968.
_____. *The Broadcasters*. New York: Dial Press, 1970.
Bildner, Phil. *The Shot Heard 'Round the World*. New York: Simon & Schuster, 2005.
Campanella, Roy. *It's Good to be Alive*. Boston: Little, Brown, 1959.
Caro, Robert. *The Power Broker*. New York: Alfred A. Knopf, 1974.
Chalberg, John C. *Rickey & Robinson*. Wheeling, IL: Harlan Davidson, 2000.
Cohen, Stanley. *Dodgers!: The First 100 Years*. New York: Birch Lane Press, 1990.
Cramer, Richard. *Joe DiMaggio: The Hero's Life*. New York: Simon & Schuster, 2000.
Durocher, Leo. *Nice Guys Finish Last*. New York: Simon & Schuster, 1975.
Erskine, Carl. *Tales From the Dodgers Dugout*. Champaign, IL: Sports Publishing, 2000.
Fetter, Henry D. *Taking on the Yankees*. New York,: W.W. Norton, 2003.
Frommer, Harvey. *Rickey & Robinson*. New York: Collier Macmillan, 1982.
_____. *American Book of Baseball*. New York: Macmillan, 1985.
Golenbock, Peter. *Bums*. New York: Putnam's, 1984.
Halberstam, David. *Summer of '49*. New York: William Morrow, 1989.
Heinz, W.C. "The Rocky Road of Pistol Pete." In *The Best American Sports Writing of the Century*, edited by David Halberstam and Glenn Stout. New York: Houghton Mifflin, 1999.
Helyer, John. *Lords of the Realm*. New York: Villon Books, 1994.
Historical Briefs: Them Wonderful Bums. New York: Verplanck, 1993.
Holmes, Tot. *Brooklyn's Babe*. Gothenburg, NE: Holmes Publishing, 1990.
_____. *Brooklyn's Best*. Gothenburg, NE: Holmes Publishing, 1988.
James, Bill. *Guide to Baseball Managers*. New York: Scribner's, 1997.

_____. *Historical Baseball Abstract*. New York: The Free Press, 2001.
Kahn, Roger. *Beyond the Boys of Summer*. New York: McGraw-Hill, 2005.
_____. *The Era*. New York: Ticknor & Fields, 1993.
_____. *The Head Game*. New York: Harcourt, 2000.
_____. *Memories of Summer*. New York: Hyperion, 1997.
Kiner, Ralph, and Danny Peary. *Baseball Forever*. Chicago: Triumph Books, 2004.
King, Clyde, with Burton Rocks. *A King's Legacy*. Chicago: Masters Press, 1999.
Leavy, Jane. *Koufax*. New York: HarperCollins, 2002.
Light, Jonathan. *The Cultural Encyclopedia of Baseball*. Jefferson, NC: McFarland, 1997.
Marshall, William. *Baseball's Pivotal Era, 1945–1951*. Lexington: University Press of Kentucky, 1999.
McNeil, Bill. *The Dodgers Encyclopedia*. Champaign, IL: Sports Publishing, 1997.
McGee, Bob. *The Best Ballpark Ever*. New Brunswick, NJ: Rutgers University Press, 2005.
Parrott, Harold. *The Lords of Baseball*. New York: Praeger, 1976.
Pietrusza, David, Matthew Silverman, and Michael Gershman. *Baseball: The Biographical Encyclopedia*. Kingston, NY: Sports Illustrated, 2000.
Prince, Carl. *Brooklyn's Dodgers: The Bums, The Borough and the Best of Baseball, 1947–1957*. New York: Oxford University Press, 1996.
Rader, Benjamin. *Baseball: A History of America's Game*. Urbana and Chicago: University of Illinois Press, 1992.
Robinson, Jackie. *I Never Had It Made*. Hopewell, NJ: The Ecco Press, 1995.
Shapiro, Michael. *The Last Good Season*. New York: Doubleday, 2003.
Smith, Red. *Red Smith on Baseball*. Chicago: Ivan R. Dee, 2000.
_____. *The Red Smith Reader*. New York: Random House, 1982.
_____. *To Absent Friends*. New York: Athenium Publishers, 1982.
Snider, Duke, and Bill Gilbert. *The Duke of Flatbush*. New York: Zebra Books, 1998.
Stout, Glenn, and Richard Johnson. *120 Years of Dodgers Baseball*. New York: Houghton Mifflin, 2004.
Sullivan, Neil. *The Dodgers Move West*. New York: Oxford University Press, 1987.
Terry, James. *Long Before the Dodgers*. Jefferson, NC: McFarland, 2002.
Thorn, John. *The Armchair Book of Baseball*. New York: Scribner's, 1987.
Thorn, John, Pete Palmer, Michael Gershman, and Matthew Silverman. *Total Baseball*. Kingston, NY: Total Sports Publishing, 2001.
Warfield, Don. *The Roaring Redhead*. South Bend, IN: Diamond Communications, 1987.
Young, Dick. "Obit on the Dodgers." In *The Best American Sports Writing of the Century*, edited by David Halberstam and Glenn Stout. New York: Houghton Mifflin, 1999.
Zimmer, Don, with Bill Madden. *Zim*. Kingston, NY: Total Sports Illustrated, 2001.

Interviews

Dave Anderson
Bobby Bragan
Carl Erskine
Gene Hermanski
Stan Isaacs
Clem Labine

Eddie Miksis
Johnny Rutherford
Howie Schultz

George Shuba
Sal Yvars

Newspapers

Brooklyn Eagle
Los Angeles Times
Newark Evening News
Newark Star-Ledger
New York Herald-Tribune

New York Times
St. Paul Dispatch
Wall Street Journal
Woonsocket (RI) Call

Magazines

Baseball Magazine
Colliers
Life

Look
Time
Sports Illustrated

Other

National Pastime: SABR Publication.
Program, *Harding University Tribute to Preacher Roe.*
The film: *Boys of Summer,* 1983, based on the Kahn book, VCA Programs, Inc.
The film: *The 1956 Brooklyn Dodgers,* ESPN S.

Index

Abrams, Cal 41, 150
Alston, Walter 21, 117, 118, 119, 124, 136
Amoros, Edmundo (Sandy) 84, 156, 126
Anderson, Dave 74, 146, 186–187
At bats 39

Barber, Red 17, 37, 38–39, 190
Barney, Rex 16, 17
Batting helmet 45
Bauer, Hank 74
Bessent, Don 168, 223
Black, Joe 87, 89, 103, 122
Black players, arrival of 31
Blaeholder, George 87–88
Boom Boom Beck 6–7
Bragan, Bobby 61
Branca, Ralph 28, 67–68, 109
Brooklyn 140, 141
Brown, Tommy 14–15, 16

Campanella. Roy 101, 131, 132
Carey, Max 3
Cepeda, Orlando 51, 139
Chandler, Albert 54, 55, 80
Chester, Hilda 188
Cobb, Ty 79
Cooke, Bob 19, 180
Cox, Billy 27, 99, 123, 154
Craig, Roger 152
Crosby, Bing 130

Daniel, Dan (sportswriter) 180
Dark, Alvin 138, 139
DiMaggio, Joe 25, 33, 73
Drysdale, Don 21, 174, 204, 214, 236–237
Durocher, Leo 27, 28, 45, 48, 50, 71, 48, 154

Ebbets Field 1, 6, 11, 21, 84, 90, 127, 144, 146, 151, 154, 173, 183, 186, 189
Erskine, Carl 90, 91, 114, 119, 120, 140, 150, 185, 223, 235, 247

Furillo, Carl 32, 36, 54, 81, 119, 137, 142, 148, 150, 169, 170, 181, 183, 206

Gaedel, Eddie 58, 59
Gardella, Danny 22, 23, 24, 25
Gilliam, Jim 98, 99, 117, 123, 128, 184
Goldberg, Hy 98, 149, 155

Hermanski, Gene 20, 33, 53, 54
Hoak, Don 97, 106, 123, 156
Hodges, Gil 2, 29, 35, 54, 65, 66, 93, 106, 108, 153, 183, 186
Hornsby, Rogers 78–79
Horowitz, Paul 169

Irvin, Monte 31, 51, 59, 71, 79, 114, 119

Jackson, Randy 156, 162

Kahn, Roger 13, 25 73 97, 99, 112, 124
Kampouris Alex 32
Kansas City 62
Kiner, Ralph 108, 180
King, Clyde 46–47
Koufax, Sandy 149, 150, 151, 180
Kuzava, Bob 93

Labine, Clem 14, 15, 27, 44, 60, 63, 65, 76, 87, 103
Larsen, Don 152, 171
LaSorda, Tom 127
Loes, Billy 91–92, 116, 131, 152, 158

MacPhail, Larry 1, 5, 45, 46

Maglie, Sal 18, 49, 50, 61, 64, 66, 67, 158, 159, 165, 170, 172, 178, 206
Mantle, Mickey 29, 73, 74, 75, 92, 105, 116, 154, 165, 171, 215
Martin, Billy 66, 74, 87, 88, 92, 115
Mazzone Leo 26
McCarthy, Joe 16, 26
McGowen, Roscoe 11, 45–46
McLaughlin, George 38
Medwick, Joe 45
Meyer, Russ 53, 104, 107, 124
Miksis, Eddie 15, 20
Milwaukee 104
Morgan, Bobby 15, 125
Moryn, Walt 156
Moses Robert 144, 145, 146, 177
Mullin, Willard 2
Mungo, Van Lingle 3, 5

Newcombe, Don 41–42, 72, 120, 124, 140, 150, 151, 168, 174

O'Malley, Peter 11, 194
O'Malley, Walter 2, 7, 11, 13–14, 39, 47, 57, 97, 104, 111, 112, 140, 142, 144, 154, 155, 156, 173, 177, 184, 187, 188

Pafko, Andy 54, 65, 68, 97
Palica, Erv 30, 46, 56
Parrott, Harold 4, 5–6
Podres, Johnny 109, 116, 131, 151, 152–153, 182
Polo Grounds 73

Reese, Pee Wee 89, 102, 103, 123, 125–126, 130, 148, 153, 166
Reiser, Pete 1, 4, 6, 13, 16, 46, 84, 148

Rickey, Branch 1 2, 6, 10–11, 12, 14, 17, 19, 28, 34, 36, 37, 39, 43, 108
Robinson, Jackie 1, 6, 12, 24, 36, 47, 50, 51, 53, 64, 81, 95, 96, 98, 101, 112–113, 118, 119, 129, 139, 175, 192
Roe, Preacher 89, 116, 123, 129, 132, 141, 142
Roebuck, Eddie 161
Roosevelt, Eleanor 146
Roth, Alan 6
Rutherford, John 86, 87

Schmitz, Johnny 20
Schultz, Howie 37
Shotton, Barney 35, 41, 47, 77
Shuba George 15, 16, 37, 93, 94, 100, 128
Sisler, Dick 42
Skowron, Bill 29
Snider, Duke 5, 21, 22, 39, 41, 89, 116, 120, 125, 130, 142, 147, 148, 157, 163, 181
Sternhagen, Ruth 18
Stoneham, Horace 2, 28, 59, 72, 73, 144, 154, 159, 160, 173, 180

Thomson, Bobby 60, 61, 65, 67–68, 71

Waitkus, Eddie 18
Walker, Rube 65
Warren, Earl 112
Williams, Ted 10, 21, 27, 30, 79, 165

Young, Dick 7, 14, 129, 149
Yvars, Sal 68, 69

Zeckendorf, William 11
Zimmer, Don 123, 162

www.ingramcontent.com/pod-product-compliance
Ingram Content Group UK Ltd.
Pitfield, Milton Keynes, MK11 3LW, UK
UKHW042001140426
5217IPUK00015B/919